Voices:

Mental health survivors, carers, therapist, family and friends

D1795144

Steve Walter

True-life stories in conversation

with **Jenny Bloomer**
(MA(Lond) DipCouns MBACP(Accred)
UKRC RMN)

chipmunkapublishing
the mental health publisher

Published by
Chipmunkapublishing
PO Box 6872
Brentwood
Essex CM13 1ZT
United Kingdom

http://www.chipmunkapublishing.com

Edited by Faith Mmadubuike

ISBN   978-1-84991-793-3

Cover images: original artwork © Hannah Worsley (including chapter headings)

Reversed composite design and graphic placement © Ellen Montelius

Chipmunkapublishing gratefully acknowledge the support of Arts Council England.

Steve Walter

For Dad

Voices

I love how wine continues to evolve, how every time I open a bottle it's going to taste different than if I'd opened it any other day...

Maya on Wine, from the screenplay to Sideways

Much Madness is divinest Sense -

To a discerning Eye -

Much Sense --the starkest Madness -

Emily Dickinson, Much Madness

Tread softly because you tread on my dreams.

W.B.Yeats, He Wishes for the Cloths of Heaven

Voices

A work of art: not necessarily a measure of quality,

but a measure of conviction…

Voices

ACKNOWLEDGEMENTS

A Big thank you to Liz, for being there, not least for creating the title, and also especially for Liz, Kyla and Sarah, for taking the time to help edit many pages of revisions. And to Jenny Bloomer for being prepared so diligently to draw out the links, the connections between the different stories, and for sharing her story. Also to Emma, Padraic, Steve Anthony and the Pineapple Writers for their thoughts and comments.

And to all who've raised their voices here and shared their stories: Ted and Hazel (Mum and Dad), Amisha, Jenny Parkes, Cara, 'Abacus', Janet Hart, Jane, Jonathan Naess, 'Matthew,' Peter and Ross Wilson, Steve Anthony, Susan Kerr, Michael Kerr, Joyce, Amy, David, Tim and Jenny Bloomer.

Thanks especially to Ellen Montelius for the photography and design and to Hannah for her original artwork, her magic with Indian ink, creating the symbols which represents each tai chi stance. I'd also like to acknowledge the welcoming staff of the Lava Bar (now St John's Yard) who kindly helped things along.

And to Steve, the Big Issue seller, who always greeted me cheerfully on the Strand, near Charing Cross station, as I wound my weary way to work. In spite of sleeping in a doorway, he'd be consistently more cheerful than me in the mornings and, when I lost my job, he'd say positively 'you'll be ok', and he'd lighten my day. Steve, you are a true hero!

To Mum for always being there. And finally to Dad, who died unexpectedly as this book neared completion and for who we grieve and are left memory and spirit hopefully for generations.

Voices

CONTENTS

- **Transition: Something in the water**

6 - REPULSE MONKEY

- **The Cockroach Saga**
- **Transition: Broken shells**

7 - STROKING THE PEACOCK'S TAIL - Left

- **Jenny Parkes**
- **Transition: The Testing Pool**

8 - STROKING THE PEACOCK'S TAIL - Right

- **Cara**
- **Transition: Event horizon**

9 - SINGLE WHIP

- **Abacus**
- **Transition: So many lives**

10 - HANDS IN CLOUDS

- **Brighton 2008**
- **Transition: Caroline**

11 - SINGLE WHIP

- **Janet Hart**
- **Transition: Edinburgh, approaching day zero**

12 - HIGH PAT ON THE HORSE

- **Jane**
- **Transition: Edinburgh Day One**

13 - KICK WITH RIGHT HEEL

- **Jonathan Naess**
- **Transition: Edinburgh Day Two**

14 - BOXING EARS

- **Matthew**
- **Transition: Edinburgh Day Four**

15 - KICK WITH LEFT HEEL

- **Peter & Ross Wilson**
- **Transition: Edinburgh Day Seven**

16 - GOING DOWN - Left

- **Steve Anthony**
- **Transition: Edinburgh Day Nine**

17 - PUSH DOWN – Right

- **Joyce**
- **Transition: Edinburgh: more from the Fringe**

18 - LADY'S SHUTTLE

- **Susan Kerr**
- **Transition: 2010-2011**

PREFACE

After my first book, *Fast Train Approaching*...I am writing this to embrace other people's experience of mental ill-health, not only my own. These original voices - true-life stories from the edge - share differing perspectives from friends, relations, and strangers becoming friends, on surviving fractures of the mind both first hand (or as care givers), and range from mild depression to schizophrenia, from the younger woman to the older man.

This book is for those who may identify with these stories, whether directly or through caring for friends and relations who have had, or may yet have, similar experiences. One in four of us will have a common mental health problem at some time in our lives and about 1% of us will live with a severe mental illness, such as schizophrenia, bipolar disorder or severe depression, which may require continuing, treatment and care. However, remember this...

...a person with an anxiety disorder can be housebound and require intensive support from a carer, whereas a person with schizophrenia can lead a normal life in all respects other than the subjective experience of their symptoms.

Mental Health and Work, Royal College of Psychiatrists, 2008

Describing our state of mental health goes to the root of our being. As we attempt to define or express a sense of who and what we really are, we can be led deep into creativity and even into the realm of spirit. And when we are shaken, when we lose that connection with the real and stumble into illness, we become strangers to those close to us, those who care for us.

Before each of these stories, heading every chapter, are a series of movements from the yang 24 style of Tai Chi[1]. I have chosen this meditation of spirit in movement since Tai Chi has played a major part in my growth and healing following my experience of breakdown. The body dancing in slow motion, realizing moments of reflection, of focus and reaching different states of being.

All must stay connected; if one part of the body moves all parts must move. If one part of the body is still all parts must be still...

Cheng Man Ching (1947)

These stories, which have been gathered since 2007 (after publishing *Fast Train Approaching...*) follow both the clarity and natural imperfections of each individual's voice and flow of narrative in their own words. They include the experiences of:

Ted and Hazel *(Mum and Dad)*, and how they were with me through a night of the bizarre, of torment and more.

Amisha and the early loss of her father

Cara and her experience of hospital and sectioning

Jenny, my aunt, saving herself from being close to the edge, through her creativity and working with psychotherapy

---

[1] The graphics are Hannah's delightful representations of the Tai Chi moves

Jane, the profound effect of her hemiplegia, her depression, and the split with her boyfriend

Jonathan, founder of Stand to Reason and his experience of bipolar disorder

Matthew, wrestling with the urge to thump the living daylights out of his manager

Peter and Ross, father and son coping with Ross's schizophrenia and his experience, down and out saving the world in New York

Steve, poet and musician with his own depression and the shocking discovery of his brother in law, as he lay dying; plus the untimely death of his friend Paul; and the depressive episodes of another friend, Ryk.

Susan's transport to other worlds and **Michael** her husband, helping her to heal. And from beyond the grave, an insight into the life of musician John Ogdon

Janet's plunge into a disturbing, disoriented space

Abacus's wild journey and recovery

Joyce, my former wife, and her concern for those labeled 'carers'

Amy, my daughter and how things were with her at the time of my breakdown

David, my son, and his refreshing perspective on the mind and what is normal

Tim, my brother, and his insight into *his* brother's madness, and finally

Jenny Bloomer, my former psychotherapist, sharing the tragic loss of her sister and mother at an early age. She also shares her thoughts, on each of these stories (as a psychotherapist), in a moment's reflection and conversation immediately after each of the individuals has spoken.

Some might say 'why bother with psychotherapy, why not just talk with your friends?' Or 'you can't have any friends if you need to see a psychotherapist'. Of course it is important to talk with friends, but friends are rarely objective and not everyone wants to laden their friends with heavy problems in their lives.

Psychotherapists have the training and experience in working with people to help create self-awareness and understanding about themselves, being non-judgmental, unshockable and always completely confidential. The psychotherapist helps you to see outside of the box you've put your life in.

Interwoven with these stories are threads describing how I came to share my own experience of mental ill health and recovery live on stage at the Brighton and Edinburgh Festival Fringes.

Between each chapter, each Tai Chi stance, is a connecting move - a link, a transition, continuing the flow. Ideally, in a true meditative state, these movements would be clear, free from extraneous thoughts. But the mind often wanders into memories, dreams, reflections. And so, in the flow of these transitions you will find assorted experiences from the humorous to the tragic.

It is in these transitions that you will learn how I took An Acute Psychotic Episode as a stigma busting show to perform live on stage, with Steve Antoni's music, at the Brighton and Edinburgh Festival Fringes in 2008, 2009 and with Hugging Barbed Wire in 2011.

Towards the end, the transitions also tell of my partner Liz and her sister Susan's story through the tragic loss of Susan's daughter, Caroline.

Living human documents

As Jenny says: the universal thread running through these stories is surely the process of life that can have intense effects on most of us, as *living human documents*. Life is unpredictable and we are thinking, feeling creatures. We experience joy, sadness, pain, distress, hurt, confusion, anger, and injustice. That's the way it is.

She has adopted the phrase 'The Living Human Document' from Michael Jacobs, who is well known in the world of counselling and psychotherapy. Her own, very strong, feelings about the uniqueness of individuals and the fact that each has, as reflected here, a different story to tell, she feels are encompassed in this phrase.

For her, **Living** means not only to be alive with the natural instinct for survival, but possibly in many cases, just existing. To be **Human** separates us from other living organisms, with our capacity for highly developed thinking that begins from the moment of birth and is rare in most other animals. Human means not only acting from instinct, but having: the capacity for thought, feelings and reactions; the capacity to care/not care about others and/or ourselves; the ability to suffer mentally as well as physically, and to recognise that we are fallible and don't always 'get it right'. And the **Document** is something for reading and understanding; it can vary in size and content; it is sometimes damaged with words, paragraphs or even whole chapters missing; or even in fragments for various reasons.

By putting 'living' and 'human' in front of the word 'document', it ceases to be just paper or another material object, it becomes a 'someone' – a subject rather than an object.

If, as Jenny believes, the uniqueness of each person is to be accepted, then each living human document is going to be different and not necessarily straightforward. Neither can it be put into a convenient box. This emphasises the need for that Document and all it holds to be treated with respect and care in order to read and understand it.

Jenny also says that "occasionally, the Document is easily read. Its story may unfold without difficulty. However, with some, there may be scattered, buried or missing fragments. These need collecting and assembling often over long periods in order to complete the Document before real understanding can take place.

"It goes without saying, that in order to understand other Living Human Documents, one has to develop self-awareness and personal insight. This can be painful! Self-awareness can cause much heartache. To recognise our failings as well as our strengths, to admit these rather than conveniently bury them and to perhaps work at changing those we can change, is difficult enough. To understand why we react to people and situations in the way we do – in fact our own document with all its chapters – can help considerably with that challenge."

Jenny Bloomer

In the streets and the bars, everybody has scars…

Fran Landesman (21st October, 1927 – 23rd July, 2011)

Rethink Mental Illness had a story in their magazine[2] about human libraries (part of Time to Change), where people can select real life stories and actually meet the person and hear their story first hand and learn of their experience and survival of mental ill health - truly Living Human Documents.

I hope that you may enjoy the Living Human Documents you find here and may discover something in the connections between them of interest, and even of some help in caring for those close to you. You may well have shared similar experiences. It can mean so much to realize that we are not alone, and to know that there are profound connections between us. The stories highlight the power of healing and recovery and I hope your journey is all the better for coming to know these true-to-life companions.

...

NB There are a few references to my first book **Fast Train Approaching...** *which describes my experience of breakdown and recovery, and these links are annotated by the superscript [fta]*

---

[2] *Your Voice* (September 2011)

Voices

PROLOGUE

Nothing is the answer to everything...

A restaurant table overlooking a skinny brown sea: three windows. In the first, straight ahead of where I'm sitting, two wind surfers, one surfing, one standing waist deep in the water. Through the second window, slightly to the right, in the angled flank of the building, families, couples, walking along the sea wall. Then immediately to my right, only a few feet away on the other side of the glass, embossed on brickwork the original, ornate, freshly painted sign for the Royal Native Oyster Stores with the royal coat of arms; lion and unicorn either side of the shield.

Throughout these pages, three windows: the story of the narrator; the experiences of individuals known to him and, probably from the right side of the brain, surprising, unexpected, almost poetic phrases and memories bubbling up from the sub-conscious, the way seemingly endless connections can coincide with a psychotic episode.

A bottle of red wine with a screw top for easy access - like a skirt...

The waitress talks of motorbike rides in South America. She twists open a fresh bottle of wine, pours me a glass - Shiraz. Then she places a glass jug of water in front of me, embossed with the name St. Germain, and it awakens memories of Café de Flore, Paris and its famous writers. Here, at the farmhouse- style tables, sit church chairs with little racks, empty spaces for hymnals and prayer books. Mosaic strips of mirror run the length of the dado round the room, reflecting tabletops set with wine glasses. The sound of footsteps, of heels on the wooden floor; a floor made of wide oak floorboards, distressed wood (or original?). Spikes of rosemary grow in window boxes, beneath elements of blue, set against the dull, brown sea.

From this point at the edge of the sea, the edge of the land, all journeys begin. Moments which are normal, special but normal, and moments which escalate into a very real, unreality. Views of life through glass: fragments which piece together the origins of depression, breakdown, psychosis.

Visions of angels…

The personal stories contribute to breaking down the stigma attached to problems of the mind. And there are so many more who choose not to speak, who fear the consequences. People have come up to me since my first book, thanking me for raising my voice and being open about mental health. Yet even now there are situations, when I choose to hide and, like Peter (the so called 'Rock'), deny my truth.

And, at both the beginning and the end…

Prayer on Ward 10

Our father who art in hospital, hallowed be thy persona, thy spirit come, thy section be done on ward 1 as it is in ward 2, give us this day our medication and forgive us our episodes as we forgive those who are deluded against us, lead us not into mania, but deliver us from psychosis, for thine is the mood stabilizer, the brain and the anti-psychotic, for ever and ever. Sane again.

The shadow of the double-decker bus lingers after the bus has passed and turns my wine a deeper shade of red…

1. HOLDING BALL

The first chapter of 24 moves: be present. From the moment you stand feet together, arms by your side, palms resting against the front of your thighs, breathing gently from your diaphragm, in through your nose, out through your mouth, you are raising chi.

When you are ready (and at the appropriate point, if you are moving to the traditional Chinese music) place your left leg so that your feet are shoulder width apart. Half-bending your knees, lower yourself slightly, then slowly, as you stand straight, raise your arms out in front of you to chin height, then gently lower them again, as if making a wave in one fluid movement, as you also lower your body.

Chi: the life force - the natural energy inside all of us.

Now shift your weight to your right leg, your left foot pointing down, touching your right and the ground. Bring your right arm up to chest height, your left at waist height, both hands relaxed, curved as if holding a ball in front of you, a large one, like a beach ball. Be sensitive to the very slight resistance, the elasticity of the ball - your ball of energy, of chi focused in front of you. As if a protective force were centred before your solar plexus, protecting a vulnerable part of you.

Your mind should be clear from the moment you stand still and are present, and by the time you are Holding Ball it should be completely so. All too often though the mind raises a seemingly random collection of thoughts, memories and reflections, and these are hinted at here through these moves and the transitions between them. The thread of continuity through these 24 moves, is the fine line of existence, what it is, what it means, how it ends.

Tai Chi has been with me since I began the path to recovery. It was practiced in China for centuries as a martial art, as exercise, and as a means of improving the flow of internal energy within the body. It is conducted very slowly and gently, focusing on consistent form and feeling each movement. It is completely non-impact, involves the entire body, promotes strength, stamina, and flexibility. Because the whole body moves as one, Tai Chi nurtures the link between mind and body, enhancing balance and coordination, and developing confident ease of movement.

The Taoists felt that stagnation was the cause of disease and aging. Nature moves and evolves unceasingly, and movement prevents stagnation. Tai Chi was developed as a martial art/movement and breathing system that, while exercising all the joints and major muscle groups circulates chi, the internal energy. It's this circulation of the chi that prevents or mitigates disease and debility. (The Tai Chi Academy).

She arrives clutching a small, black and purple bag from La SenZa…

Yang & Yin

I first took up Tai Chi in the summer after my breakdown in 1997. I learnt the Yang style, 24 form described here, which is perhaps the most commonly practiced, and was handed down as the official form from the Chinese communist regime in 1956. The pace is smooth, uniform and slow, with no variation in speed during transitions. The hands are mostly relaxed and open; the fists are not clenched during punches. Continuity, without break or pause, is the key. Some of the moves repeat (not all the repetitions are described here).

By the time I returned to hospital in 1999 the form had fused with my earlier experience of Kyokushinkai karate at college during the 80s, and for me the stylized moves had become powerful weapons for fighting off malevolent spirits.

All flesh is grass...

(Isaiah 40:60, but remembering a classic science fiction, pale blue hardback of the same title from the glass fronted mahogany bookcase in my parents' living room, by Clifford D Simak)

Poems were my first written attempts at expressing experience, but they rarely got close to the root of what I was feeling. I guess, as I said in my first poem after my breakdown - In Place of Silence[fta] - that I was looking for something or someone which was always out of reach: 'the indefinite beauty that defines a craving heart'. It seemed then that some of the drugs I ended up on, such as olanzapine, actually helped me write, to think and create more clearly, and make better poems.

Go on, let me watch you knock one out - the speed, the wrist, the straining and the gasp...

Marie

As we begin our journey through, in and around these stories, I remember Marie- her spirit - an elderly, blind lady who held a great enthusiasm for life, in spite of her difficulties getting around and looking after her older husband, Tom. How I used to help with simple DIY and read to her...

Tree of Paradise

It grows tall in your wide bay window, the

succulent leaves spilling over the window sill

among the spider webs, clouded glass.

The room with the baby grand and the huge

armchairs with their red, stretch covers, wood-chip

wallpaper, which I painted Sunshine Yellow -

a colour you would never see. You sit facing

the heat of the electric fire, its warmth

penetrating the thick jumper you'd knitted.

How we explore books together, as I read

aloud - Lyall Watson: Supernature, Lifetide

and more, and you anticipate the cup of tea

and slice of your own lemon cake I bring you,

as we share our excitement of the wonderful

the universal, the mysterious; happy for now.

Bingo

Not the game but another kind of love to hold at this moment
– love for a pet - my greyhound, Bingo. She was saved from
the Last Chance rescue centre, chosen by my son and lived
with us for some ten years through my separation and
impending divorce. I had to decide on New Year's Eve 2007
to put her down through old age. Being there, agreeing to
the needle, holding her as she drifted away and, muscles
relaxing, entered the sleep of no return.   For Bingo and all
who loved her.

Not warm like a baby

less than half the weight

a plastic bag, full of fine white sand, dust.

We walked through the daffodils of the grove

to the edge of the field

where I ran in a wide circle, not half as fast as she

but now, look, watch her fly once more

catching the breeze, settling

among ten thousand blades of grass.

Susan

And I would also like to think especially of Liz's sister, Susan, who had jumped off a bridge onto a motorway in 1998. She'd survived but was left paralysed in both legs. Paraplegic. Confined to a wheelchair. Some of her story runs invisibly through the writing of this book.

I'd intended to interview her, for her to share her story of mental ill-health, but I wanted to wait until I was closer to finishing. Sadly she deteriorated psychologically into what seemed to us at first as psychosis, but has been labelled cognitive dementia. Her more recent story and the tragic death of her daughter, Caroline, are told nearer the close.

In the garden the plastic garden chairs tipped forward, as if kneeling at prayer, in a huddle around the oiled teak table...

TRANSITION: Review

The first of a series of transitions flowing between the Tai Chi moves, incidental moments, imagery, aspects of life, bubbling through consciousness and scattered throughout: fragments, twitterings.

What follows is a review of our Edinburgh show - An Acute Psychotic Episode II - by Colin Hambrook from Disability Arts Online. Edinburgh formed a backbone to my experience over several years and (excuse the pun) the yarn weaves a weft, a pattern of continuity throughout the true-life stories of this book.

Colin Hambrook drops in on the Edinburgh Fringe
16 August 2009

I've been away for the past week, staying in Dunbar with friends. I thought I'd pop in on the Edinburgh Festival to see what disability-related arts I could find in the theatre section. From looking through the brochure it seems there is some mental health-related work amongst the enormous panoply of shows, exhibitions etc, happening this year. So I made it into town to see Steve Walter's An Acute Psychotic Episode (II) – billed as "a good-humoured, confessional, raw, honest, sometimes shocking account of breakdown, setting out to challenge common perceptions." It did everything they said it would do on the tin – although from personal experience, I wouldn't have called it 'shocking.' In fact, if anything, it impressed on me that maybe there is some hope that we are moving away from the punishment model of psychiatric care, that I grew up to fear and loathe. Accompanied by singer/

song writer Steve Antoni, *An Acute Psychotic Episode (II)* was a moving and powerful piece of dramatic storytelling. It was deliberately paced to take you on what felt like an urban train ride through the writer / performers' life-story. It began appropriately with *Brain Damage* and *Wish You Were Here* – two songs written by Pink Floyds' Roger Waters for and about Syd Barrett who died last year after 40 years of being labelled insane.

Steve Walter's prose was filled with the pacing of hospital corridors and questioning of what happens when you become psychotic; how scary that sense is, of not daring to believe what your own mind is telling you. It is very hard to put into words what that fear is like – when everything your mind and senses are telling you is true, you know rationally cannot be true. Where do you turn? How do you gauge reality? And if you are unfortunate enough to get locked up for having ideas others don't agree with, how do you contain the frustration? I felt not a little admiration for Steve Walter as I have personally been trying to write my own life story, in an attempt to make sense of it, for some years. It is not just that the writing down is incredibly painful, if you are totally honest. But there is also the fear of making yourself even more vulnerable, by opening up to others. Even those you think you can trust, cannot be trusted not to use your honesty against you. Such is the stigma of mental health. I feel passionately that this kind of clear, concise storytelling, breaking through the silence – is needed more in theatre, and in the arts in general. I bought a copy of Steve Walter's book *Fast Train Approaching…,* which contains a lot of the poetry and prose from the theatre piece.

I'd recommend the website www.makingconnectionsmatter.org. Here Steve explains a lot of his search, research, poetry and ramblings on all things from spiritual awakening to a *request to hear from others who have had experience of mental illness for a new book in the pipeline.*

Colin Hambrook - http://www.disabilityartsonline.org

The Diving Bell and the Butterfly

I first discovered this real-life story while browsing in a small, independent bookshop in Ambleside in 2006, well before the film was made. I was attracted by the title which held for me echoes of Sylvia Plath's The Bell Jar. When I began to read the Diving Bell...I was stunned and amazed that this man, Jean-Dominique Bauby, survived a massive stroke, was able to describe his experience of locked-in syndrome, and 'wrote' his story when the only movement he could make was to blink his left eyelid.

After the stroke he'd lapsed into a coma on the 8th December 1995, then 'woke up' 20 days later mentally aware of his surroundings but completely physically paralysed (apart from his eyelid). The book took ten months to write, at four hours a day. With a transcriber he used a French language frequency-ordered alphabet, blinking to choose the next letter. Over and over. An average word took about two minutes.

The book was first published in France in March 1997 and became a bestseller across Europe. Bauby died two days after it was published...

So why the Edinburgh Festival Fringe?

Do you ever have that feeling when you're so moved by an event, a happening, or even somebody else's comment, that you desperately want to say something, but don't know quite what to say? Or how to say it? Or you may be in a group of people, part of a committee, or a member of an audience and you have thought of a question or a comment but you can't form the words. Why? Perhaps you're simply too shy, too afraid that you'll be made to look like a fool, that what you say will seem stupid, ridiculous even?

I have often felt this. Almost as if 'locked in,' a little like Bauby. And yet, where I have been given permission to speak, invited to speak, I can usually find the right words, make a comment, a contribution. In the extreme, when I have been given someone else's words, or my own written words, a script even, I have played a role, created a character, made a success of the part and performed on stage.

And I wanted to create something more out of the experience of breakdown, other than a book - to raise *my* voice. A voice; to have a voice and to raise that voice, not in shouting or argument but clear, firmly, precisely, assured of some inner truth. I aspire to such a voice. Bauby raised his voice in complete silence. I have tried to find some truth through performance, through sharing experience, poetry, and other peoples' song.

My first encounter with drama was as a child in primary school. I was eight or nine years old. We'd been given a choice of activities we'd like to do. I liked the sound of drama but then, as a young child, I thought it meant playing the drums! Imagine my disappointment. I was terrified of the stage. I remember walking in pairs across the playground in the dark after school to perform in the nativity play. I was a shepherd, drowning in fear. Somehow I uttered the right lines, a wave of empathy welled up from the audience (affirmed by my parents afterwards). The mixture of fear and praise stayed with me, even 'til this day...

And yet, in 1995, I was planning an event for the millennium at the Royal Albert Hall[fta] which would have meant presenting centre stage for some of the time. Fear and praise: the child seeking recognition, acceptance and understanding.

Light up your life! Plug into someone on lithium today!

2 - PARTING HORSE MANE

This is the first move with direction. From Holding Ball, slowly step out to your left, and as you do so brush your left hand forwards as if the back of your hand is gently parting a horse's mane. As your left hand does this forward stroke, let your right hand come down to rest beside your thigh, the arm still slightly curved, palm towards the ground, notice the resistance, the energy of the earth.

Sit back slightly, turn your front (left) foot outwards then step forward for a second time, Holding Ball, left hand on top right hand underneath, then slowly into Parting Horse Mane again, this time with your right hand parting the mane. Repeat this once more, stepping forward again, going back from your right to your left leg forwards, Holding Ball to Parting Horse Mane.

This book is about other people's voices and yet there is the thread running through of my voice and my experience. And here it all begins, naturally enough, with my parents and their reflection on my experience of breakdown and recovery. Stepping forward, into the unknown, we begin our journey with other voices as if with the spirits of wild horses as our companions.

Look Mummy, look Daddy, I caught a leaf, I caught a falling leaf...!

Ted & Hazel's (Dad & Mum's) **story**

Interviewing Dad…

I thought it would be an easy conversation, and it was, except for the pain I took him through, reliving his guilt, his regrets, everything that he couldn't really help, because that's the way things are. Mum preferred to add her contributions after the interview was written - her comments shine extra light on the events.

(I was not to know then that I would never have this conversation with my father again)

Dad, how do you feel now looking back on my breakdown?

How did you feel at the time?

What have you learnt from this experience?

What comment would you like to make?

I was very conscious that I didn't want to drag you through a lot of stuff today, but I'm hoping to weave in other people's accounts of mental ill health or close to it…

So it's really an open book for you, whatever you might like to record about the experience, having gone through it – it's so long ago now I feel like I'm trawling a lot of stuff up that's almost unnecessary but I guess I'm trying to find a few clear thoughts or reflections – things that you may take out of it that may be of value or things that were particularly difficult at the time – your

reflection on that stuff that happened, well, twelve years ago now...

It's amazing isn't it, so long ago, since you started with making connections matter and the Albert Hall. What I think I found was that we took that suggestion of yours as being quite an ordinary thing for you to do because you were enthusiastic and you wanted to really make something big...so the Albert Hall was a marvellous decision and whether you were going to do it or not was another matter, but it had a sense of a grand gesture, which I really liked. It was only in retrospect that it may have felt to be a bit over the top. But the thing was you were actually going ahead and getting people interested...that was one thread at the time, and then the next one is...

I'm standing in your bedroom at Tunbridge Wells and looking round the picture rail with all the bottles and how you were telling me that all the bottles had got quite serious connections to make...I could see where you were...that it was interesting to be...eh...collecting bottles but it felt just fractionally obsessive, but nevertheless ok if that's what you wanted to do. In with this I've got memories of your visits to the church that you went to, which was it? **Westminster Abbey...**and you had a sense of desperately searching for peace ... the cockroach event had happened hadn't it*fta*? Well before the poetry slam...**was that the day before I went in?** Yes I think so because it was you and your black cloak, and almost nothing else, quite disturbing, a fantastic performance but by heavens a sense of not being in our world ...and of course in that environment all the more, not macabre, but Gothic because...what was the name of the place...**The Forum...** yes, it was all a little bit scruffy and dark and you picked up the kind of atmosphere there.

I don't remember the timing of that, the Forum[3], because I remember it in relation to work, being told to go to the doctors the next morning, so was I doing the slam that evening?...

Yes you were doing the slam...I really think that in the slam you were in your own world, not in our world. I believe you won the slam, there weren't many people there but a good number who were seriously concerned about you...that image of you on stage was the last one before we had a call from Joyce the next morning...

Then when we came to see you at Ticehurst[4], I came over first, & found how you were...I think underlying it all there was a sense of you being highly amused by the whole situation thing; every now and again that what you were telling me about everything, there was a sense of amusement which for me, to a degree, made it easier, because there was the feeling that if part of you could see it like that then that was fine, because, as it were, the central you was still operating...

And of course then, I can't remember how long you were there, but I know that Mum and I came down several times & walked round the garden with you while you told us the story of the cars and the police, and I mean it was disturbing, but it was hilarious! I found that I was almost doubtful about the idea of imagining you being dealt with by policemen who were in fear of what you might do...it was something that in a way I ought to have been worried about, but having been a police officer and thinking what I would've felt like if someone tapped on the windscreen of the car that I'd driven

---

[3] The Forum, Tunbridge Wells

[4] Ticehurst hospital, Ticehurst

there, with a wrench wasn't it...**yes a monkey wrench...**I could see it from their point of view...[fta]

The long, yellow sun coaxing tall and taller shadows from the figures striding across the blazing lawns.

Throughout the whole thing there was this sense of understanding that what had happened was an imbalance of whatever helps the mind to work, and I was also sorry, in a way, that our idea of normality tends to predispose us to stopping the wild fancies if they get out of hand. There were some of your wild fancies that, I thought, ought to have been given their freedom.

And, of course, that is in fact that what has gone on to be proven; that making connections matter was so important a concept, that it has fundamentally driven what you have been doing since, and you may not have got there without the experience...

So it was good to come down to you and gradually find you recovering and that's what made the next one all the more traumatic really...**it didn't make it easier?...**No, well no, not in the impact, because we hadn't had, I don't remember having, a warning that things were getting bad again...I **came up to see you didn't I before I went to Sheffield...**Ah that's right, yes you did. Yes, that's true...**but it wasn't a warning...**no but you were...as if you were hovering, you weren't totally sure of who you were...and then of course we learnt that coming back from Sheffield things had been pretty strange. You'd phoned from the train, or whatever, I think so. There was something odd about the journey back...

That's where I had the image of the different scenery going on either side as if it were back projection, as if the train weren't really moving at all, that it was all a set up...

...but it still meant that your arrival up the side of the house, here, that morning was almost out of the blue....I'm trying to remember, I don't think we'd had a call, were Amy and David at home?

Mum: I had both David & Amy on the phone I think, crying. Amy took David to school and explained to his teacher. She had said, "Steve is coming up to you."

...I thought it was just David, I said to him not to worry but think about mummy and I'll be back later and he phoned up Joyce in Italy, he got the number off the fridge and rang her up... I'm sure that you didn't give us notice, at least not that I remember...(Mum)

So then the initial strongest memories are of you out in the garden and doing your Tai Chi which at the time - I'm pretty certain that one of the BBC introductory logos that they were doing then was of these people in red and they had a group that were on an island somewhere doing Tai Chi - I found watching you was *so* disturbing. It sent a tremor from then on with that logo...

I knew that you did Tai Chi and I'd seen you do some of the movements but not enough to have thought about it, and they are very strong attitudes of the body, and not positions or postures that you normally expect to find. But then of course you had a fixation on the drain cover, and what might have lain beneath, and you wanted that up, please, and it was difficult to persuade you that it wasn't necessary...**did**

you take it up?...I can't remember whether I did or not...**I think I said I was going to break through it...**

At some point we were in touch with Ticehurst to find that they couldn't take you in...I mean this was all going on, and we realised, well we were told that they weren't going to be able to admit you until the next day...and they must have advised - we were able to get a couple of pills, for you, I must have gone to get them, but you'd come in by that time and were quieter...although you had a concern in the front room about ...I think that was where the water idea began...I think you ate something, we were trying to keep things as normal as possible.

And then the fractured memories are there because when we were able to talk to you, you were in here quite a while (Ed: Dining Room) and I can remember getting you to talk about what you were thinking or what you felt was going on just to keep you feeling, as it were, that there was somebody listening. And then I think we went upstairs, you must have had medication at some stage maybe with the meal (<u>Mum: the first pill was at bedtime</u>). And I think it must have been before we thought about going to bed that you decided to swim along the top landing. I found I was in two minds about this; I was seriously concerned about you obviously, and wondering whether there was anything that actually could be said to help, but also there was a degree of fascination with what your mind was actually telling you...I kept a tight grip on being shit scared because that wouldn't have helped at all! But your moving along the landing, really almost as though you'd got a snorkel on, and your breathing was absolutely right, and your arms: I could have sworn myself that the house was under water, it was extraordinary...It was real for you...

The whole experience left me totally aware that the filter within our brains of the alleged real world, and the world that we might create for ourselves, is unbelievably fragile, that if we find that the filter begins to let through strong aspects of our imagined reality then there's nothing to stop it becoming more real than the so called real world that we inhabit ...and that to me was a truly illuminating sense of understanding just how easy it is...and more than that how lucky for all those who never find that the filter breaks down... how lucky they are...

And yet even then I'd want to be closer to the divide to allow access to the imaginative world into my own reality, rather than to feel that I could block the entire thing off...there is a place where you need an ability to access the visionary, the extreme other reality... It's just that we haven't got there yet...Our development is only childlike to what we're actually going to be able to do...eventually.

But then it came to getting you to bed. (Mum: the first pill) You must have quietened down enough. We must have gone to sleep. And then there was the crash and the scream of ...it wasn't pain, it was a kind of anguish.

Mum: I was frightened by a shout and a crash with the noise of breaking glass. We both shot out of bed. I was terrified that you might be trying to get out of the window, but thank goodness, no.

I think I came to realise what the word anguish holds, and what it means. And the crash, I didn't know what that was. And I came in and of course I had to wrestle you, because you were convinced that I was about to attack you. And I thought I've got no chance here - I just had to sort of virtually grab you and hold on... and you quietened ...but you were so hot. At one point I was convinced that you'd probably pissed yourself, because there was this sense of the heat and I could've sworn that I was going to find that we were going to have to change the bed. But I think what might have happened was that you spilled a bit of water in the glass before you threw it and it hit the window, but the curtains were drawn so that there was just a slight scratch on the window glass, and I'm pretty certain the glass must have smashed – it would have done I'm sure because the incredible energy that you released in that cry...

Mum: Dad had told me to stay out and I stood on the landing wondering what was happening for some time, then as things became quieter I went in.

So yes, then you settled down and there was a sense of you actually being comforted, almost like having you as a boy again, because that quietening was a recognition, it felt as though it were a recognition, that you were safe after all and that was again the unbelievably positive side of the seemingly negative and threatening situation, because I felt that at last I'd been there for you...

It throws up a sense of one's regrets which is always present in parenting - the living through and caring for young children - you've never got the wisdom when you need it, and so a lot of reactions to children are a product of other frustrations and things, and under circumstances like this of course you tend to find that all the negative memories tend to surface and you forget the storytelling at bedtime and all the good things. And it was because I'd been able to do that that I was subsequently able to write the poem the Burren...

The Burren [bhoireann – a stony place]

for Steve.

The road from Shannon to Ennis

Put us at ease, the inside lane

Marked for slow traffic and, strangers,
We took our time. In silences,
The mortar of marriage, we knew
Our thoughts were homing to you,
Sedated now, calm. Guilt easing
Under the miles to Mullaghmore
We were unprepared for the bare
Limestone, the alien uprising,
The scouring of land back to bone.

Only now, your scream in the night,
Explained - the agony of minds
Throughout time, in torment,
Searing through you - can the Burren
Be seen to have held your long howl.
That week it was right to walk out
From the cottage, breathe the release,
Putting aside the fear, the hurt
We felt for you, to step where glaciers
Had once scored rock, to study flowers.

That pavement, abundant with orchids,
Gentians, wood-sage, cat's foot, told
Of healing, of how the most barren
Of places recovers. Low cloud
Mimicked escarpments, softening

Harshness. Wells filled as we spoke

On the phone: you, yourself almost,

Echoes of cries in the dark

Diminishing, and we with a host

Of futures held in the Burren's past.

*By **Ted Walter***

Because that was the other thing that we were concerned about, in a way, that we were going to be going on holiday the day after we got you into Ticehurst. It was all booked but, we thought we'd got to think about cancelling but once you were there, there was no point in not going. But getting you there was 'fun'...

Do you remember not wanting to get into your car. <u>Mum: We were trying to get the second pill down you and eventually did</u>. And there again I'd always been friendly with B, and trusted him, but that was an extraordinary offer of his...I don't quite know why I rang him, perhaps knowing that he might be at home, but it was an answer to what might otherwise have been a dodgy situation really... **with me in the car**... Yes, you'd then become fairly adamant that you didn't want to know any more about any interference...

Because we had got the car on the drive but you had to get in it...you didn't want to put the safety belt on...**I was concerned there was going to be a bomb or a trigger device or something...**this is what's so illuminating, in a way, that we who are in, what we like to consider our normal world, see your decisions as coming from being bloody minded – it's all very well thinking there might be bombs but for goodness sake... But that is where the experience of sharing with you has meant that I have had no difficulty in finding enormous sympathy with anyone I've come across who's had anything like the same experience in one way or another ...you can't live through that and not take on board how delicate the whole business it is...and the one bit of the drive down to Ticehurst that I can remember is on the hill down from Badgers Mount onto the motorway, just actually getting onto the motorway and then... it was on the hill going down towards Riverhead that you appeared to accept the fact that this was your car and I was driving it...and you were ready to trust me to drive it without hitting anything... because I have no memory at all of the rest of the journey, whether we were talking or whether you were quiet, just the fact that B was behind and keeping an eye on him and then driving into the drive at Ticehurst.

And then when we arrived, and B came in and sat in with us. You were as far as I was concerned, pretty lucid with your understandings when Dr M came in, but it was quite obvious to B - where were you, what sort of world were you in? But compared to the time we'd had, I was almost relieved that you were there and talking to Dr M who understood.

And I was still doing my Tai Chi stuff?... Yes I think you did that in the reception room...**I think I was quite relieved to be there**...yes I think so, we only had two tablets for you, I know getting to take them was a bit of a problem, especially for the first one but it meant that there was a part of you that was working on an understanding of the need then, I think that's probably why you quietened down in the car...although you had had the second pill.

Having got you there, Mum and I carried on with our preparations and went to Ireland. The next day that telephone call from a telephone box in the evening in the middle of nowhere, at a junction of a couple of fairly minor roads from the cottage. Driving to the box, there was a place - one of the many, many wells in Ireland with healing powers, we passed that and learned that ...I think we probably talked with you, did we? Anyway we learned that you were ok & calm and that enabled me to later use the Burren, and create the poem. And creating the poem virtually put the trauma to rest...not only did it feel like being a statement of all that mattered, and understanding and healing but then, I was just later so reassured about the poem because Michael Donaghy, himself an Irishman, gave it a second prize in a competition, and that tended to really ground it as being a healing process...**what competition was that?...** it was WEA London Voices....one of my students got first prize...**it worked well on stage...**

I've felt that what you've done since has been built on a kind of recognition. You've been doing the sort of thing that I would've wanted to do, if I was your age and had that experience - I could feel, if circumstances had been different and I was younger, and had the opportunity to operate where people listened, I would want to make them aware of the dynamics of the situation. Even going through it as an onlooker, and being that totally involved because I learned it was almost not a *learning* experience it was...an illumination which continued when you'd recovered, and were able to confirm to me that you'd been aware of, in a sense, the two worlds that you were in ...Because from the outside it looks as though you can't possibly know the outer world when you're so totally caught up in your inner world; that somehow you won't have a memory of the outer world reality, and that didn't seem to happen when you were here with us because you could virtually recall just what was going ...**what was going on outside**...Yes, for instance when you were swimming along the landing, you knew that's what you were doing, it was the landing you were swimming along, but there was the water there, the impact of that process was so powerful that I could've sworn that you would've not known where you were, and that the swimming would've had to have taken place in a place where you would normally find yourself swimming, like a swimming pool or the sea or... and you couldn't carry the juxtaposition of this deep water and the landing...

I was interested as well in this question about your Dad and what he'd been labelled with, neurasthenia....yes, whatever that is...**which was quite often used to describe a breakdown or a psychotic episode**

Well, all that was very under wraps, it's only what I've gleaned from my mother, she must have said something. I don't think Dad ever said anything at all, no it would've been Mum. Dad was an only child and, as far as I can tell, his mother was pretty possessive. He was brilliant, he had an extraordinary brain he won the all-Kent essay competition when he was 14. He'd got a pedantic turn of mind, he was reading Plato and Socrates in his late teens and he won a scholarship to Sevenoaks school. But he wasn't allowed to go, because he was the son of the servants of St Julian's whose son was going to go to Sevenoaks school at the same time and they would not allow the son of a servant to go to a school their son was going to ...

That robbed Dad of the opportunities that he'd been coached for. His headmaster, Mr Knuckey, subsequently became my headmaster, at Swanley, and Mr Knuckey told me just how fantastic Dad was and how much he admired him and his potential but it was knocked on the head. And at that time Mum knew him soon after that, because I think then Dad went into printing at Salmons in Sevenoaks and it was thought that the printers ink... that he reacted, that he had an allergy to the environment in the print room, but that was almost an excuse for what happened because he obviously lost it – I don't know the details of that but I think it was quite clear that he was so totally frustrated. He'd got no outlets & Mum came along and decided that the only thing that would do him any good at all was to get him away from his mother, so that she virtually seduced him and got me! And of course that meant they had to marry, when it was obvious, and that set up the entire circumstances for the rest of their married life. Because it meant that my grandmother, Dad's Mum, never forgave Mum really, and it meant that my mother believed implicitly that the sins of the father shall be visited upon the children of the third and fourth generation and never, ever, lost that sense of guilt. She was totally convinced that something terrible would happen to you, because of what she'd done.

And then Dad too, although he also loved Mum, felt he was trapped...it was too soon to get married, he hadn't done what he wanted to do...he was in his early twenties. They lived in Dartford for three months and brought me, a three month old child, to Swanley where they got a council house and Dad had to do a bit of gardening, and then he took on being an insurance agent. But he wasn't happy, he just never, ever, fulfilled his potential. Although he did when he was in the army. I think he found it an invigorating place to be - he ended up in Germany editing the battalion magazine 'Brewcan'. And when he came out, I've got writings of his – he was trying to get a course in journalism, he was trying desperately to write, and getting furious at the comments that were being made about his writing. But there were some pieces about the nature of the return of a soldier into an environment that had no idea of what he'd been through, and which had been this mixture of strong bonding and horror, he carried with him to the doorsteps of the people he had to collect pennies from...

He always gave us the impression that he was not happy with people, and yet when he died it was quite clear that he'd got an unbelievable number of clients who doted on him. We had the floor covered in wreaths from individuals and from groups of people he'd collected from, and it looked as though when people were in difficulty, that he would actually lob them a bob or two, and make up their premium himself, we never knew that side of him...

Of course I was only just beginning to be taken into his companionship for a couple of years, because he'd not known how to deal with me really. He doted on Jenny, his reaction to Jenny's birth, he just adored her... and then that was it...**that was the accident**...yes, and all these things drop into place. At the time it was almost as though he was blamed for being too near the centre of the road, and Mum had a long, long compensation claim, and when it did come it was only about £400 and that was fought over. He didn't wear a crash helmet or anything like that, but the car that came out from behind a bus and wiped him up, that, on the face of it, looks as though he must have been too close, but he was going to turn right, the bus was at the bus stop and just the other side of the bus was a road junction and he was going to turn right, so he was taking up position to turn right and the car must have almost just swung out from behind the bus and that was it...I always feel that justice wasn't done there really...in those days accident investigation was fairly basic. Anyway Dad was dead and he couldn't say anything...

At one time I seem to remember you saying that he may have had a bit of manic depression or something like that...

It's possible, although if it was manic, I was never aware of the highs, it was just that generally he was quiet, he was withdrawn, he appeared so. I mean, he didn't like socialising and he didn't like digging the garden, because of the people who might stop to talk to him. So he was a loner...his highs, if they existed, and they did at times...there were a couple of occasions when he was looking after Chris and I and he'd do dinner, and he had dozens of unbelievably appalling jokes that he'd make up, he loved word play, and if he let himself he gave us, when he was on his own, a really enjoyable time... I can remember we upset Mum a bit because he didn't know what to do for a pudding, so he put a couple of white slices of bread into a dish and poured some milk over them and spread some jam on and we thought that was fantastic, and it became Daddy's pudding. And Mum was so pissed off with this, there was she slaving over... trying to get us meals and Dad threw this together...it became a real special treat - Daddy's pudding, so he was a bit of a mixture...

In those days how did you tell, what did you do about it? He and my Mum used to have flaring arguments, mainly over money and things but that was always the other side of a closed door....

And I think they were fairly happy ...what I think is interesting is that brother Chris found himself in similar situation having to marry Jenny. He lived an echo of Dad's life to a certain extent, only he decided that he wasn't having anything to do with duty, and would do what he felt like doing, bless him....

And I suppose with this business of a sort of mental condition, that I've been aware of conflict to a degree in me ...that I've had to deal with...and I've been fortunate that nothing has ever been pushed too far...I've been aware just through a couple of occasions that I've bottled up anger to the point at which it's been dangerous, and a couple of occasions when it blew...do you remember me upturning the table in the kitchen **...not really no...vaguely...**it was the whole business of shift work and doing everything we were doing in the house... and the underlying ...If I had the chance to go back and change a major aspect of my being, it would be to have actually accessed the freedom to talk about sex, openly, and not to have been totally shut down by bloody ridiculous embarrassment that surrounded the whole business...and of course you can see where that came from with my Mum and her attitude and nobody ever talked about it...I had never any experience of my parents talking about anything to do with that at all ...

Changing roles Steve – you've become the counsellor...

It can be so destructive not to be able to speak, not to be able to access the frustration or the anger or express it...and I know why I wasn't, and that's partly because my mother was the one who exercised the discipline when I was small and consequently if I said anything out of place, to your Mum or to any woman, virtually, and there was an element of the possibility of rejection, I would not do it – it scared the bloody pants off me...

I have always had a fascination with the way that we are, the way that it works, you know, and also the fact of my father's death - I refused to cry and that didn't happen till I was forty odd, when it really broke through. But also I was aware of a certain guilty sense of relief, because my father had held a strong control, and now I'd got a life without him, but that was balanced against the fact that I'd clearly lost the opportunity to have got him to know more about me in a way... But it meant that I shut down and to a degree I know that I can actually shut off from severe threat completely, so that it doesn't actually unnerve me. So that when it came to prostate cancer, that I had to get through that, I was able to enter a place where I could see what was necessary, what was happening from a detached point of view, and I was not worried. The fact that the poems came and I had sense of complete freedom in which to just get this sorted. So the same thing applies in a way to you, that I could actually go through the whole experience but still have this place to put it where it wasn't going to seriously undermine me...

I'm just gobsmacked by the fact that just twelve years later you've been able to put it to such fabulous use, you've managed to be as open and vulnerable as you need to be...

Talk about confession being good for the soul...what you did at Edinburgh... stops it from being a canker...

'It's stopped raining' the kid exclaims, raising his hands palms upward to the grey sky, as he steps out of the porch onto the silver, mirrored path...

REFLECTION

Mum and Dad, what can I say? Here you are at the opening of the book as you conceived my beginning. Through many difficult times you have always shone through with love, for which I will be forever grateful. Of course, we all have so much more to learn...

This is the first of many conversations with my former psychotherapist, Jenny Bloomer, reflecting on the content of the stories, in this case that of my parents coming to terms with what I was going through...

What did you learn about my relationship with my parents that could also apply to many other people's experience?

JENNY: Well Mum and Dad! They are just so consistently there for you, aren't they?

I've always felt very sorry for families when they're bringing someone into psychiatric care, because they do not recognise that someone.

You mention your grandfather. I wonder whether he may have had some bi-polar difficulties.

I just think your parents are marvellous; they're so supportive. They must have felt desperate. You'd know from your own experience with your own children that if they're hurting, it hurts you.

I wonder whether it affected their relationship. Problems, and especially problems with children can cause all sorts of difficulties, because people often deal with situations quite differently. Equally, people can be drawn closer together, often because they communicate their feelings to each other without fearing any negative consequences. Perhaps when you're chatting with them sometime and the subject comes up, you could ask them. It's another interesting aspect of us humans.

I like the bit where your Mum confirmed about the tablets. I thought that was so mother-like.

Many years ago in the late 80s I saw a couple with one son who'd gone out with a friend against their will on his 17th birthday and the car had gone into ditch and the son had been decapitated! The husband and wife came in to see me; the wife just wanted to cry and talk about it, while the husband sat completely mute. He didn't know what to say to her, he couldn't comfort her, they couldn't get near each other. They were both suffering in their own way. People doing my sort of work often forget that two people who happen to live together, as partners, may grieve or express emotions differently and they need help to get into the other's frame of reference to bridge the gap that may be forming and become a chasm.

Which could apply to any experience?

JENNY: Yes but it sounds to me as though your parents were very close.

Yes, I think so, very much so, they were both with me in Brighton

JENNY: To feel so helpless, particularly where your own child's concerned because you're used to making it better aren't you?. Having to walk away and leave someone who's terrified must have created a mixture of feelings – relief that you were being cared for when it was evident you needed that care, but possibly also a feeling of having betrayed you and left you at the mercy of others who didn't know their son as well as they did.

It felt a bit like that with Sue, Liz's sister, (as we'll come to see) leaving her in the psychiatric ward...

Yes, general psychiatric units are not quite like Ticehurst[fta]

It's good that your Dad felt you were in a position to hear his story and share his experience, that's really nice. They're great parents.

Yes, they are.

Many parents, or partners (as we'll see with Joyce), are in that situation of looking after people they don't recognise. I think it's a mistake made by many in psychiatry to forget about those who are close to the one who is suffering because they're suffering too...

Yes I've seen that with the psychiatrist for Sue who's been very understanding for Liz and actually listened to her.

JENNY: It's so important to allow people to gather their thoughts together and talk. So important! We'll hear more about Sue - I hope she does well!

TRANSITION: Heading West

 Our internal landscape evolves minutely, incrementally, the thunderous firing of neurons, making and breaking connections across a cerebral sky. Each shift in the backdrop of time marks a subtle change of perception, a gradual awakening, a new footstep in paradise. From even before our birth, as the embryo forms, we absorb the rich experience of the womb, heartbeat, muffled voices, movement, walking, reclining, drifting in an amniotic world.

Red. Red. Bright red. All he can see is red. Nothing but red. All he can hear is the drone of the engine, a hot mass of purring metal, and the rush of air pummelling at his silver crash helmet. He is in the outside lane of the motorway, heading west, the sun blazing on his face, filtering through the capillaries of his eyelids. 80. 85. 90. All that faces him, when he opens his eyes is the sun-filled sky and, unrolling at speed before him, the open road spread wide. The other carriageway is jammed, packed with traffic. 90. 95! He whoops with delight at the sheer exhilaration of the moment's freedom – Yee-hah! – then closes his eyes again, for one, two, three more seconds and begins to sing…

I never knew my grandfather on my father's side; he was killed in a motorcycle accident when my dad was only fourteen. But, some years later, my uncle, Dad's younger brother, bought a motorbike. And yet, I felt that my choice to buy one was breaking some unspoken taboo.

And I strip her ...all night she stands naked even through the dawn waiting for me to ride her, to fire her up and ride her hard...

The river of the fast lane draws him towards the dying sun. He arrives at his brother's in the Forest of Dean. His brother calmly tries to explain that things might not be quite as well as they seem, and that it's not a good idea to ride on to the writing course as planned. His brother speaks to their father and arranges to take our biker back to Kent, to Sussex, minus bike, where he is to spend several days in Ticehurst hospital, as he had done almost two whole years before.

The sun has gone and yet the pale sky keeps her arms wide open for him...

3 - SHOWING THE WING

From Parting Horse Mane raise your right hand and bring your left arm down, pointing your left hand towards the ground, your right palm facing forward as if making a stop sign, so that your upper arm is horizontal, out to your right side, your left hand beside your hip. Keep your right hand high, your left foot pointed forward just touching the ground half a pace in front of you, with your right hand, palm facing forward, you are Showing the Wing.

As if invincible, bold, brave, ready to take on the world, able to move from this position quickly to any other, prepared in case someone, or something, were to try to take you down. Yet this open movement also shows vulnerability, as if in surrender, revealing the underbelly, a point of display, of confession.

Trying not to notice the brush of the barmaid's fingers on his palm as the teenager hands him the change…

Showing the Wing was the last of my opening Tai Chi moves on stage, in Brighton and Edinburgh at the Festival Fringe events, standing facing the audience with my right arm raised, palm facing the audience as if in surrender. As the moves began Steve played an extract on his acoustic guitar from Pink Floyd, Brain Damage: 'The Lunatic is on the Grass.' Holding the position, my right hand begins to quiver, it seems to be a combination of nerves and alcohol (or lack of it) and lithium and olanzapine…and the show begins.

What follows, before more interviews, is a thread of reflection connecting creativity and sex and their roots within me – a common theme...

So much of life is shaped through childhood, and through school. I was in primary school when I started writing a diary, aged 10. Miss Gunn, an elderly, tall, gaunt, yet friendly teacher, inspired us to keep a record of everything that went on over the summer holidays. I bought an Aladdin notebook, and used a Venus HB pencil. I've kept on writing notes and poems ever since.

Careful you don't tear the fabric of space-time...

From an early age I was concerned about Man's reckless disregard for the environment. This came through most strongly when I moved to secondary school. So many of my essays were about the damage and destruction that Man was bringing upon the world. By the age of 14 I'd read all of Joy Adamson's books including Born Free and Pippa's Challenge. I was immersed in the Serengeti plains in Africa and deep into the oceans, which included reading Dr J C Lilly who wrote Man and Dolphin. I discovered that dolphins' brains are about a quarter larger than ours and that they can hear frequencies up to 200 kHz, as opposed to the 20 kHz at the threshold of our hearing; such endearing, intelligent beings. I also read Jane and Hugo Van Luwick Goodall, more tales of Africa, of wild dogs, chimpanzees, gorillas.

In my early teens, I wrote about species destroyed. Nature. And Nature was amazing, God-like, infinite, mysterious, majestic and wonderful. Man could never be forgiven for what he'd done to her. I would write: *The beautiful roaming creatures of the world, chatter and wake, every new day.*

Man wakes and walks his dusty streets...a small domestic dog whimpers at a dark, filthy station...a knife sinks into the back of a sleeping young man...a huge Polar Bear plods up and down his open cold, cage bored of his very life...

A significant step in the transition from childhood at about the same time could have been my school ski trip to Austria. On 19th February 1975, I passed the British Junior One Star Ski Test at Gerlosstein. However, unlike my schoolmates, I was not to experience the local schoolgirls, but instead to witness, to observe. With my friend Peter, one evening at a disco in the hotel where we were staying, we assessed the behaviour of our schoolfriends as they made their moves about the dance floor, getting together with some local girls. I was still fourteen, it was to be several years before my life was focused and driven by the opposite sex.

Fascinated by the silver pentacles dangling from the zips on the cheeks of her tight, black denim jeans...

Apart from kiss chase at primary school, my contact with girls in my early teens was mostly limited to the girl down the road, who I won't name to save her embarrassment. Our most special meeting was our annual walk with the dog on Christmas Eve, and a few days later she would come up with her family to visit on New Year's day. I was completely smitten, and when we met I was entirely dependent upon her moods and favour for my emotional well-being.

The seagulls half laugh, half cry. Do they ever sleep...?

A lifetime later, I was visiting exhibitions while in Edinburgh during August 2007, researching potential venues for a show based on my book launch. (I'd held a launch for the *Fast*

Train Approaching... e-book in the Cellar Bar in Tunbridge Wells for friends and family in Autumn 2006, and then again when the paperback was published in Spring 2007, at my place of work in Westminster.) The show was to become 'An Acute Psychotic Episode' in Brighton a year later.

My whole trip to Edinburgh, staying on the university campus, was accompanied, and lightened, by the hit *Hey There Delilah* by the Plain White T's, which I was singing and humming to, transported in my romantic fantasy of one day having a show at the Edinburgh Fringe. The music was another link through woman, anima, to my desire to create. But I would do it – I would have a show!

Even the toggles on her donkey jacket seem seductive...

The Naked Portrait

I visited the Edinburgh National Portrait Gallery (15th August 2007) and I was moved by an exhibition called the Naked Portrait. It held a tension and a delight, as if it were at the edge of the very real. Here are some of my favourite extracts:

'Men and women are 'irrevocably strangers to one another' and 'have different emotional realities and speak a different emotional language' yet 'there is an intense need for coupling in spite of it all. Even if relationships are destructive, people cling together.'

Nan Goldin, Self Portrait in Kimono with Brian

Book: Ballad of Sexual Dependency (1986)

'I think the naked human body brings up so many intense and important psychological issues in all of us. It is at times both vulnerable and strangely threatening when stripped of its façade, mask, persona and signs which clothing provide us with.

So a lot of my work attempts to explore the complicated feelings that we all have when encountering the naked human body, our feelings of delight, shame, amusement, embarrassment, or indifference.'

Melanie Manchot

And sex; creativity tied up with sex, the body, lust.

Come Play With Me, early porn, soft porn, playing in certain rather seedy, Sheffield cinemas; entertaining for a teenager and other doubtful characters. I was later surprised to discover that I saw the film the year its star Mary Millington died, in 1979. And she was born in Walton-on-the-Hill, not so far from Walton-on-Thames, where I'd been born nineteen years earlier…

Her white, cashmere cardigan high on her waist, her bare back, her tight jeans revealing an edge of her purple banded knickers, the rise of her buttocks as she looks at me over her shoulder, her brown hair tumbling…

On discovering a g-string on the doorstep…

River Lawn Road

I wait for you after class, at the corner
leaning against a red brick wall in sunshine
smoking my last cigarette. And on each
drag I cough - the same red box of Gauloises
I'd held onto ever since
the fag I offered you on our first date.

Later that evening, I notice the slight perfume
on my fingers, remember back to the crushed blue
packet I kept with me in my stripy jacket,
twenty-five years ago, when smoking was cool.

You take your last filter tip by the front
door, sipping a glass of rose in the light
of the disappearing sun. Then in the morning,
someone else's knickers on the doorstep
where the milk bottles used to be,
'Dirty old man', you say, catching the glint in my eye.

**

They're laughing so loud, it's got to be a joke about men…

TRANSITION: Crinkly pyjamas

I would sit and watch TV with my Mum while my Dad was out working late shift. And when the time came, I'd stay up to watch Miss World - every year we'd choose our winners - looking for personality of course. I was even too young to understand what wank would later come to mean...

On the road to puberty (and I took a while to get there), I would bring myself off at night before I went to sleep while wearing pyjamas. They were the best way to mop up the stickiness inconspicuously - the white marks got lost in the pattern. In the morning, the front of my pyjama jacket would feel as if it had been starched, crinkly like cardboard. Scrunching the material soon made the pyjamas flex again, ready to absorb the next wad the following night.

My imagination would run riot. I had nothing then to use as fodder, no magazines, no videos, no internet. Just glimpses of girls during the day - perhaps the curve of breasts, buttock, thigh - or even just the sensation of bringing it hard, the bed covers propped high with one hand so the sheets wouldn't be stained, rising to the moment, and at that point bursting beneath the sheets, soaking into the paisley, patterned cotton.

Pale blue shutters, the still reflection of the river in black windows...

4 - BRUSH THE KNEE

From Showing the Wing twist your body gently, rotating at the waist reach your left arm straight out behind you, your right arm bending across the front of your chest. As you do so also turn your head slightly to your left to notice the tips of your fingers behind you. Then step through with your right leg and bring your right arm forwards in a curve as if to lightly brush your right knee while your left hand now faces to the front, palm up, as if to halt an attacker...to defend against the unknown, darker elements, a strong, stable position.

This move, before the main interviews begin, reveals an undercurrent, affecting and resonating with my appreciation of life on earth.

Unearthing the Green Man

Dorset, June 12-14th 1992

Twenty years after writing about the destruction of nature as a child, I find myself exploring the meaning of the Green Man, on a weekend for men. I had been on a couple of Mens' Weekends before this one in Dorset; first at Lower Shaw Farm near Swindon in the late 80s. This extract describes what the weekend was about. What follows is a selection of simple poems that track my encounter with the Green Man.

The Green Man is a mythical figure both vegetative and human, who teaches us the cycle of birth, death and renewal. He is a powerful, male image who reminds us of the interdependence of all life and of the marriage of spirit and matter. Intimately of the earth, a lover of the Goddess, he can be seen as a model of masculine obedience to the wisdom of nature.

Through body work, ritual and imagery, we will seek to awaken the Green Man within us. Participants will be guided through a journey – both inwardly and in nature, involving our bodies as well as our minds – to experience his archetypal energy.

Playing between the high wooden sides of the biggest groins in the bay…

Before the ritual

I am not here
to be given answers
but to know
the roots within me
and to scream
when I know there is more

After a night of fire – Colmer Hill

The night of the Green Man

burning by firelight
on Colmer Hill

the blood, full, hot
rounded

the gorge through sandstone
a slice of life
between a woman's thighs
soft, sweet, wet.

Drumming on roots
crying by a lake.

Stone

heavy
angular
dark

mud-encrusted

dark enough to kill.

thumped against the roots
of a maple, straddling
the rock above me

we made music
stick and stone on wood

stroked the silvered legs
of a woman
lithe, supple roots

her cunt
arched open above me.

...From the Green Man and the roots of Mother Earth, to the voice articulating concern for Mother Earth: GROUNDSWELL. It's 1995, the Millennium is approaching, and with it my middle age. 40. Both a deadline and a wake-up call...

The weight of his balls in their sack shifting, like the weight of her breasts as she walks...

If you're like me you'll care passionately about our home, planet earth. It grieves me that the everyday things I do damage the environment: whether consuming energy, or directly contributing to waste. From the moment I flush the loo, switch on the kettle, travel to work, buy my weekly shopping, my ecological footprint is stamped all over the Earth. And there are so many millions of us. Together we will need several more Earths if we are all to share the standard of living the west has to offer - this could mean over four more Earths (see www.myfootprint.htm) We cannot continue consuming and wasting so much as we do now. It is not sustainable.

And it came silk and sticky at the back of his throat...

Groundswell

I'd long had a desire to do something, to make a significant contribution to the world, but had never worked out exactly what or how. I was looking to make a statement, to share something special at the close of the Millennium. As I mentioned earlier, in 1995, I thought of an idea to celebrate the transition to a new Millennium in a real, profound, even spiritual way. I reserved the Royal Albert Hall for a week of events: Groundswell week to run in September 1999, 100 days from the turn of the Millennium. In the Spring of 1995 I began writing to potential partners including: The Friends of the Earth, Greenpeace and the Association for Creation Spirituality (now known as Greenspirit).

Groundswell is '*a broad, deep, undulation of the ocean…a movement, as of public or political opinion or feeling, which is evident although the cause or leader is not known*'

Chambers Twentieth Century Dictionary

The restaurant is lit with red lampshades, and there is blood on the plates…

Here is a reply from St James's Palace on behalf of Prince Charles which I was delighted to receive (even though it is turning me down) among other correspondence from the potential partners and the group of people who, working with me, supporting me, came to share the vision. For - as I realize now - it was a vision, although some would simply call it a crazy idea!

ST. JAMES'S PALACE

LONDON SW1A 1BS

From: The Assistant Private Secretary to HRH The Prince of Wales

28th February 1996

Dear Mr Walter

My colleague Richard Aylard has asked me to thank you very much for your recent letter, with its account of your interesting initiative "Groundswell 2000". I am sorry that it has taken a while for us to reply, but we have been overwhelmed by the response to His Royal Highness's recently published article.

His Royal Highness is delighted to hear of creative ideas such as yours: his purpose in writing the article was to stimulate debate, and encourage the submission of bids for practical projects of social regeneration which might make a genuine difference to the quality at all levels of people's lives. Many of the organizations with which The Prince of Wales is formally associated are preparing bids to one or other of the Lottery distributors, and His Royal Highness is energetically supporting these organizations.

There is inevitably a limit, however, to the number of specific projects to which His Royal Highness can give his personal support. I hope that you will therefore understand that it will not be possible for His Royal Highness to become involved in the way that you suggest, although he would be glad to know the result of your endeavours. His Royal Highness has asked me to say that he wishes you every success in your bid.

Yours sincerely

M.W.

Sometimes just a glimpse is enough to keep me going for hours...

In 1996 we began meeting - a team of eight of us, to plan for real: Steve, Jan, Max, Jane, Perry, Peter, Rob and myself.

'The end of 1999, like every New Year's Eve, will be a time of reflection, and a time for new resolutions – even more so for marking a new millennium. There will no doubt be global celebrations. But what of our resolutions and action for the future of humanity and planet earth?'

Vision: To awaken and unite spiritual concern for the Earth and its people

The Royal Albert Hall is reserved for a week in the autumn of 1999 to provide a focus for peace, drawing together people concerned for the earth and for the health of life on earth. The week will be part of Groundswell 2000.

Take the number 9 bus to the Royal Albert Hall, from Trafalgar Square...

Groundswell *2000*

A festival project for the Millennium celebrating Life on Earth.

The purpose of the project is to provide a deep-rooted spiritual focus for people at a time of change.

I have a photogenic liver, according to the nurse as she slips her cool instrument over my belly…

CHARLES CONDEMNS GODLESS MILLENNIUM

Prince of Wales and Archbishop unite to force through a spiritual celebration

Independent on Sunday 1st December 1996

Pictures taken by men for men, by women for women…

And what became of Groundswell? Things were beginning to shift in a positive direction, but on June 25th 1997 I was admitted to Ticehurst hospital, for what turned out to be a month of psychiatric care. This extended into two more months of convalescence and recovery at home before I could be phased back into work again, over the months leading up to Christmas.[fta]

Collect yourself, fold your sky into birds and let them fly…

Street furniture, Newcastle

Although the project faded, I believe in 2000 there was a shift in more popular concern for the planet. This has been seen particularly in the global concern for what is happening to the climate. In its way *Groundswell 2000* represented a deep undercurrent of desire for change.

There is a large bubble expanding from the top of my half empty bottle of Peroni, just poured by the waitress. It is growing as the air expands from the chill of the fridge, to match the June tainted warmth of this not-so-cool cool room in the Charing Cross Hotel. The high ceiling, with four large chandeliers, is decorated with 36 white plaster roses set in pink. There is gentle conversation, background music, the occasional chink of bottles being disposed of, and the odd word overheard from one or two louder voices...

TRANSITION: Ribosomes

 Tiny, intracellular, molecular machines which translate the genetic code. I found them fascinating, how they take sequences of acids and bases on messenger ribo-nucleic acid (mRNA) and translate them into corresponding sequences of amino acids, constructing proteins (such as enzymes) intricately creating our bodies with the building blocks of life.

And the age old question: nature or nurture, which influences us the most? Does the seed of mental illness solely reside in our genes, or is it simply a product of the influences on our growth from our environment since birth?

I took a trip when I was a student from university to the Lake District, with a group from the faculty of biochemistry at Sheffield. The long weekend was to learn about, to discuss and think about, the latest research on the role of ribosomes in cell biochemistry.

But, finding myself walking with colleagues over the fells in Spring sunshine, my interest for the sub-microscopic evaporated. All I wanted to do was to breathe in the air lifting from the Lakes in the valleys and stay high, high on the hills, to write, and write, and write.

Young enough still to be excited by her own nakedness...

At other times experiencing the wide-open energy of the place, vital in every breath, the wind sweeping across miles of town-free space before reaching us, diminutive at the edges of the land. So much more the richer with close friends, bonding even when walking without speaking, sometimes even more so. Finding greater depth, a profound unity in the shared experience of these wild moments.

Breathe. Breathe in the air. Even when asleep her naked body gives nothing away...

From childhood, the roots of memory, the Lake District held a special magic for me, ever since we met our gorgeous cousins there at their home, Loop Cottage. The first time, we were on a family camping holiday in the early 70s, my father driving a Volkswagon Beetle, with a tent. I would return there to walk with my aunt, after her separation, and her companion Bob, King of the Fells.

Stepping out of the car, away from tarmac, onto grass, onto earth, instantly we are enveloped by the huge, transcendent silence of green and rocky hillsides; the space and scent of breathing fields and trees and water over stone. As if the soul leaps with the moment, the intake of breath, of open moor, the head of the valley, dry stone walls, clusters of silver birches, angled oak trees wrapped in their thick, furry coats of moss and lichen.

To be so far from the congestion of the city and the town, and free from the mass of airborne, respirable particulates (microscopic bits of unburnt petrol and diesel which can penetrate the tiniest airways of the lungs) was sheer delight.

It's Remembrance Sunday. I switch on the radio to listen to two minutes silence…

5 - PLAYING THE LUTE

Every move in Tai Chi flows smoothly from one to the other without stopping. However, for me, this is one where even only an imagined pause seems to invoke the music and inspiration of the Troubadours.

From Brush the Knee bring both hands round in front of you pointing forward at an angle, as if you really are playing the strings of an invisible lute, or harp. Here you need to take your weight onto your right leg and sit back so that you're supported by your thigh, as if it were a spring, your left leg straight, resting in front of you on the heel.

The moves flow into each other, smoothly, evenly. Here is a natural pause although the position is never frozen, to play the music which accompanies the ever changing flow of form.

From the beauty of imagined music, to the reality for an attractive and intelligent asian girl in her early twenties. It's a hot summer's day; we're on the balcony of the St Ermins hotel, enjoying a barbecue.

Amisha

Amisha is a good friend who I first met at work. She is a lively, vibrant and caring person. Here she tells her story of depression as a result of the untimely death of her father.

What has been your experience of mental ill-health?

In terms of my own experience, what I've been through personally - I don't know what the actual medical term is, but I think its called mild depression I've been treated for by counselling. I guess it's all in some way been linked to losing my father. It was the grieving period, basically a reaction to that and all that had happened before I guess - there was a sense of not being able to cope with it, not knowing how to react. I just couldn't get my head round what had happened it was really hard to accept that he was gone.

My Dad was diagnosed with his illness in August 2000. I remember it vividly, it was just a couple of days after we had celebrated my unexpected success with my GCSE results. I remember that day he was so happy never did he think that his rebellious pain in the ass of a daughter would do so well. I saw tears of joy in his eyes that day...little did I know that it would be short-lived and we would have tears of sorrow within the few days that followed. I went to the hospital with my Dad that morning as we were picking up his test results. It was an x-ray I think of his lungs and bloods etc. We went into the consultant's room and he started going through the results. We couldn't understand what he was saying but from the tone in the room we knew it was serious. They said that we should come back with my mum and they would talk to us in greater depth as we were in shock. The ten minutes in the car from the hospital to the house felt like ten years. I was crying and my Dad was crying not because of what he had heard but because I was crying...so unfair. At the time there was a sense of...almost a sense of denial really, not dealing with what was happening. He had fibrosis, which in some ways is a bit like a cancer because it basically takes over the lungs, then the rest of your body starts to collapse as well. It was watching him…watching him die, and slowly, which inevitably affected the three of us. Me, my mum and my sister. A man that was so active, had a love for food and drink (as in booze!) – not being able to walk and completely losing his appetite. At the end he was so thin that we could each carry him in our arms.

On 18th April 2001 Dad died. He was finding it hard to breathe so we called an ambulance – that night he didn't come home. The house has never felt the same again. We scattered his ashes the following year in London because we wanted him close to us. And then we went to India on a short pilgrimage that summer to commemorate him. So it's been a few years now, but the effects of it are still pretty current. And that's what encouraged me to become involved in your book. I think that, in terms of mental illness, there's no time, there's no just straight 'here's an illness and here's a cure for it, and that's it, it goes away. It's not something like the flu or a cold where you take tablets and it goes away. It's an ongoing process where you really have to work to get your strength back and to get your inner self back. From my experience, when I was depressed, I wasn't myself, I lost a part of myself in the way I thought, and having counselling and doing something about it was finding my strength again. It's weird because even when I talk about it now it's like I'm reliving the emotions but the difference is I am able to cope with it. I don't think that a loss of this kind is something you can get over. Like I said, there is no cure – but you just find a way or learn to live with it. And the experience becomes a big part of who you are.

And I think that often there's a view that people who have mental illnesses are really, really weak and they're almost stigmatised because people assume something is fundamentally wrong with them, and they're not normal. But I think that's really, really wrong, because doing something about it makes you a stronger person. It's like confronting a drug addiction; you need to admit you are addicted and dependent before you go about quitting and getting help. And it takes a certain person to admit that you need help. I think it shows great strength in character to admit that you have a problem, to seek help, and then to maintain that way of life. I doubt that anyone new that has come into my life can tell what I have been through. How miserable one's existence can actually be. I don't know whether or not them knowing would change their perception – you can't be sure. There is a stigma I think attached to people who seek help (of any form really be it pills, counselling, turning to religion or anything else).

Would you be happy to expand on how you first slipped into depression?

My father was 'the man of the house' and all of a sudden he became incapacitated. We had to take care of him, me and my Mum, my sister was away at university – she had to finish the last part of her degree. I really felt for her, she put a lot of pressure on herself. She wanted to get her degree, and get a job to start earning so she could take care of us because Dad couldn't anymore. I had been this girl who didn't have any responsibilities, who was at school. I would always be gossiping on my mobile phone and would come home late, since I used to go dossing around with my friends after school. I was around 16. Now, all of a sudden I was expected to come home so that I could look after my Dad while my Mum went to get the shopping, or do the cooking, or other household chores. My Dad needed to be watched at all times, he was really on edge. I remember sometimes I would come home from school and the journey would go really slowly because I'd wonder whether there'd be an ambulance outside my house: is my Dad OK? Is my Mum crying? Is Dad still alive? And I'd get home and then my

Mum would open the door and there'd be a look in her eye, then I'd have a sigh of relief because I'd think, 'No, today, everything's fine'.

My Dad was diagnosed when I was around 16 and he died when I was just turning 17, so it lasted a couple of months, living like that. I was resentful and angry that Dad was ill. It wasn't fair why this was happening to me. I was scared of losing him and sad that he was suffering. And I was tired from hiding what was going on at home from my friends at school. And I think my depression came in the sense that I was living almost two lives. We never really discussed what was going on at home at school.

At school, I was who I usually was, but at home I was this completely different person, not knowing how to deal with it. In retrospect, even though deep down inside I knew that he was eventually going to pass away, until it happened I didn't really accept it. I never really imagined living in a world in which my Dad didn't exist. I almost lost sense of what was real. Was living my normal life at school, real? Or at home, real? And it was really, really difficult. I was very mixed up. After he passed away I didn't give myself a chance to grieve because I was trying to support my mother and my sister because they went into complete shock. Everyone thought I'd be the worst, but I was actually the stronger one. For them that was it, they were bad. My sister didn't properly speak for about three months. My Mum practically lost her senses, she was there but she just went into herself, so we clearly knew that something was wrong.

I think for me it was more gradual because I could still cover it up, and button it inside, so my depression came later. I think it was an escalation of things I hadn't dealt with. I had to sit my A level exams and I didn't do very well in them; my predicted grades were nowhere near what I got. I ended up moving away to a university I'd never intended to go to. That affected me as well, I had to move away from home and do things for myself. It was just this escalation of things that I hadn't thought about or dealt with before which made it really difficult. Also there was my brother as well. I didn't know I had a brother until my Dad was diagnosed and we had to inform him. So it was also about having this big, key figure enter in my life and not to have known of him. I also tried to build bridges there. But I became so introverted. It was a gradual build up over two to almost four years. It got worse and worse and worse, things kept on adding up and I didn't seek help until the last minute when I definitely needed to. Had I sought help at the beginning, maybe it wouldn't have got so bad.

They said it was mild depression, and it was recommended that I see a counsellor. I think counselling really, really helped. Even now I feel that I need counselling sometimes, I wouldn't hesitate in taking it I think it's really important. I wouldn't make the same mistake again and let it escalate. I think talking is really, really important.

More recently (2008) I started to see a homeopath and spiritual healer which has been good for me. Meditation really helps too. I think you just need to do whatever helps you. Now laughing, trying to keep positive and happy has become a part of my life. It's like I worked to get that person that was there before this happened back. I got my sense of humour back which I thought at one point would be impossible.

I had counselling sessions for around 18-24 months. When I started I felt weak as a person. Even when I stopped I don't think I was as strong as I am now. I think it was a sense of need. I felt at that time that I needed it, and when I stopped I felt as if I'd taken control of myself and I was able to deal with things. I just desperately needed someone to speak to, someone that would understand. I didn't want to burden my family as they were trying to cope too. I think because you appear to be quite strong-willed or extrovert, people think that you are dealing with things. And when you try to talk to them they just assume that it's a phase and you get patted on the head, and they think that it will be ok. But I think for me it was just a desperate, desperate need to talk to someone, just to get my thought processes in line because I just couldn't deal with everything.

If I would stop thinking about my dad I would start thinking about my exams and why I didn't do well, or I would start thinking about my Mum and her sorrow. My Dad's family added to the distress as well. I couldn't understand how my perfect little world had been turned upside down. It didn't make any sense to me. I was really angry as well, and I just couldn't deal with being angry and miserable at the same time, because fortunately I hadn't been there before. Not having anyone else to understand that makes it all the more difficult.

I didn't start my counselling as soon as my Dad passed away. I think I must have waited about another couple of years and then taken on treatment. I finally faced the fact that I had a problem and something needed to be done about it. And I think the counselling really, really helped me. It made me realise that no amount of medication in the world would have helped me. Relying on other people couldn't have helped me. My Mum giving me a cuddle and saying everything was OK might have made me feel better and safer, but it would not have helped me. It was something I really needed to work on and deal with in myself. And I needed to accept what had happened, because I think a part of what it was, was thinking 'Why did it happen to me? It's not fair'. And you almost try to find a way to blame yourself, like why is it happening?

How did you feel while you were seeing the counsellor?

It was really hard getting through the day. If I'm completely honest and brutal, getting up to face another day became so, so difficult. I think even physically, I just felt constantly drained. I had anchors at the ends of my feet. I know it sounds really weird, but I was dragging myself through the day. At the beginning it was really like that. It sounds awful, and this is what came out in my counselling as well, there was so much good in my life at the time. I know I'd gone through this trauma but I just couldn't see it, all I could see was the bad that had happened. And even the littlest things like my hair getting wet in the rain – I know it sounds really silly – or my umbrella breaking, it's a small thing but for me it'd just be another thing that had gone wrong. Life just felt like a burden. Feeling happy, or laughing at something seemed miles away, it just seemed out of reach. I just didn't see a way of going back there. What's worse was I felt I was going to be like this forever. My Dad was never going to come back – it was a void that would never be filled so how can things ever get better?

How long did you feel as bad as that?

I think it was at the beginning when I felt I needed help and then as the counselling progressed it got better because you start processing your thoughts more – talking about it, then them throwing it back at you, helps you process your thoughts more.

Another thing that really helped were special groups at University. I can't tell you how valuable that was because I met people, who maybe didn't go through exactly the same experiences but felt similar to the way I did due to other things. Then there were people who'd been through similar things and had started feeling better. So I realised 'I'm feeling like this now, but it won't last forever.' And I started to accept that and I started to accept how I was feeling as well. Also a bit of belief, a bit of hope as well that I would regain my life. I accepted that my Dad was never going to come back, but I also realised that I could have a life without him, it would be different but I could. There comes a point where the focus of the counselling changes - instead of focusing on why you're feeling negative, you focus on how you're going to make things better. And I think that transition came across and that's what I worked towards. I got to a point where I thought 'Enough now! I can start living my life', and 'I'm ready to go back on my own without any more help.'

How did you contact the counsellor in the first place?

I went to see my GP about it. I'm very, very fortunate in the sense that my GP is situated in a hospital where almost everyone is in one building. And there were all sorts of groups. They ran bereavement groups there as well, and you have loads of people in the community that come to help you out. I've got a really good relationship with my GP - he's very supportive. When I went to university, I took the initiative myself because the students' union provides services like that as well. So I had one on campus as well that I could go and talk to whenever I needed to. Even to the present day, even though I'm not taking counselling anymore when there are group sessions anywhere I tend to go and talk about it because I think that it's an experience that can be shared, to help other people. I know that sounds really cheesy but I really believe that because it helped me, listening to other people. So it's still something that I like to be a part of. I think the journey begins after you talk about it. And now I think it's normal, I think it helps to talk about it. I think I'm a lot stronger now. I think, if any good can come out of it, I'm a lot stronger.

How do you think people can go about reducing the stigma associated with mental illness? If it exists?

I think stigma really does exist. In personal experience, and maybe cultural experience as well, I think that stigma is so detrimental to so many people because it prevents people from getting help, because it's the stigma that almost makes people believe that once you seek help or admit that you have a mental illness you're excluded from society and you're never going to get accepted again. You're never going to be seen as normal again, and that's the stigma and it's so detrimental because people want to put it off just so they don't get 'outcasted' almost.

And I think there needs to be more awareness, because if people were more aware then they would notice that somebody close to them is going through issues and they would seek help earlier on. And I just think it's such a hindrance. It seems such an obvious point but I think it's not one of those things to dismiss and say that's how it is. I think people need to be aware of the effect it can have on someone's life. I feel really strongly about that. Because with counselling and psychotherapy 'you must be mad' - people just assume you're going to be slung into a mental institution and have electric wires shoved on your head, you know – a psychopath! It's ridiculous, sometimes, things happen, circumstances happen which are out of your control and you just can't deal with it and you need help. It's a fact of life. It just happens. And the stigma associated with it, is just a real hindrance. I can't find the words Steve, but I think you know what I mean.

On a rather banal point I wondered what you're take is on the little presentation I gave on my book? How do you think people responded?

I think the people that were there were very much interested in the issue to begin with. And I think that because your approach was so real, it was so raw, if you don't mind me saying, because it was, it was bold, it was raw. I think it shocked quite a few people, and I don't mean that in a negative way, I mean that in a raising awareness way. I remember a passage which really stuck in my mind. It was something to do with a cockroach, and it was that sense, that reality, this is what it was really like. I think people must have gone away from there, having just swallowed it in. Thinking about your presentation in retrospect it was so real. I just can't quite explain myself properly…

It was your suggestion…it's not something openly talked about at all…

It just seems like such a taboo subject sometimes. You almost tread on eggshells all the time, you tell someone that you've been through it and people are so sensitive about it. When you've been through an experience like that and have come out of it, it's part of who you are. It touches a part of you and it changes a part of you and people think that that's negative, and maybe for some people it is, but I've seen it in my Mum, my sister and me, and it has all been positive. We're very different to the way we were. Maybe if it hadn't happened we'd be different but you know, it's just the way it is.

But I think it's great. I was always in support of your book. It's people reading about real issues. Reading someone else's book that they're not in contact with maybe detaches them a bit. But you're a colleague, people see you day in and day out. I knew about your past because you'd told me before and we'd been working together for almost a year, but there were people in that room who hadn't and it was almost like, well 'Hang on a minute Steve's been through this.' It's that awareness and that's what's so valuable to people that are going through it, especially at the same time.

Is there anything else you'd like to say?

A couple of years ago my best friend's mum past away in a very similar predicament to that which happened with my Dad. I see her going through what I have been through. She says to me that when she met me she couldn't understand why I would cry (for what seemed like no reason). She couldn't understand why after how many years had passed since I lost my Dad I was still grieving. She says she understands now – it makes me sad to know that we feel the same pain. She doesn't have a counsellor but she has me. For her talking to someone who has been through it helps. I see her become stronger and stronger like we did and that makes me hopeful. I think its important to remember that everyone has different ways of coming through adversity – what's important is that you take the step to find what will help you and do it.

Thank you for listening to me. I hope I didn't ramble on too much and I hope I did make some sort of sense…It's not something you talk about everyday; I haven't spoken about this in a very long time. But it's good, thank you so much for listening…

POSTSCRIPT

Amisha joined EEF as temporary admin support and became a fully fledged Climate and Environment Policy Adviser having successfully achieved her Masters in Environmental Policy and Regulation. But in January 2010 she was made redundant, along with others in the team. This is her parting email (headed Goodbye Everyone) on the day of the decision.

Hello everyone,

This is just a short note to let you know that I have been made redundant today and this is my last day.

I wanted to take the opportunity to say goodbye to those of you that know me and to say thank you to all those I have worked with over the last four years. It has been a very useful experience and I feel that the things I have learnt here will set me in good stead for my future roles.

If any of you want to contact me my personal e-mail is ... I am sure I will see some of you around.

Best of luck.

Amisha

Redundancy: the looming and sudden finality of it like a death in the family and the grieving of those left behind, which I was later to come to realise too.

REFLECTION

Most of us will experience the loss of a loved one at sometime during our lives and most likely the death of our parents. However predictable, it may still come as a shock, the loss, the grief. When people die young it is all the worse. Amisha explores her journey through grief. She is shown the value of counselling. As a school child, she never knew whether death might greet her on arriving home from school each day. Then she was also handling the grief of her mother and sister.

Jenny, how frequently do people come to you because they are having to deal with the loss of a loved one?

JENNY: A lot of people do come because of the loss of a loved one and they come with different feelings; feelings of guilt, feelings of anger that they find it hard to acknowledge because they can't really be angry with someone who's died. They are angry because they've been left behind. And feelings of helplessness and of fear, so many feelings... Yes I have had a lot of bereaved people with just the feeling of emptiness, particularly after a partner, husband or wife has died. It's a feeling of disjointedness really, of being removed from their place of comfort, suddenly they're on their own. Or with a parent, I've had several younger people with the loss of a parent, and they try to step into the parent's shoes, they'll almost adopt what the parent used to do. I could see this with Amisha. As if she were trying to be Dad, for the rest of the family, for her mother and her sister.

And of course if it isn't normalised that people should feel these things it can become an illness like depression. It's very helpful, I have found, for people to come and to voice their feelings and then to have it normalised – why yes, why shouldn't you feel that way!? It's OK. Then they don't feel so peculiar, so bad, so wicked. Whereas if feelings and emotions are kept under wraps and life continued as if nothing major has taken place, very often these will emerge later on.

In what sort of way?

JENNY: Depression. Depression is the most common thing and not being able to forgive themselves for feeling how they feel. It's one of the big things actually Steve, because Death happens to all of us somewhere along the way, we're all going to lose someone, but for each person it's a very individual experience.

Was there anything else that struck you…?

JENNY: I felt for her that, quite naturally as a young person, she didn't want to be dragged down by this. She could be ok with her friends and then she'd come home and it would drag her down and then she'd try to make it better for her mother and sister and eventually it dragged her down. Then she was able to talk about it and it helped no end that she could.

With playing the Lute…in contrast to your introduction, Amisha actually felt frozen in time from the pain and disruption in her young life, while keeping her sister going. Yet with support flowed new strength, overcoming the taboo of death, of talking about it…

TRANSITION: Something in the water

He is in a dilemma, as he reaches for the kettle for morning tea. Is the water that has been sitting in the kettle for three days while he's been away, any better than the water that has been sitting in the pipes for the same three days? He asks himself, how long should he run the tap? How much water should he waste? How many plasticizers are suspended in the water from the new mains plastic pipes they laid last year? He remembers how the clay-brown water spluttered and gurgled out of the cold tap.

Written in chalk on a blackboard by guys on the factory floor - Oral sex: a taste of things to come…

And what about all those halogenated organic compounds he'd heard of? Not the same organic as the organic carrots or organic chicken he had last night, but the organic, the carbon, of plastic and oil. The organic which, as organic chemists speak, means every molecule that contains carbon bonds. And what news of metaldehyde from slug pellets filtering into the water. How many chemicals exist in the world now that have never before been part of nature? Thousands. We can detect them everywhere.

Bunking off work to read the Glass Bead Game in Kensington Gardens…

He empties the kettle, runs the tap a little, waits as the electric melts the liquid, pours it boiling over the perforated panels of a tea bag, leaking the colour of iron. He surrenders to the tannins and bergamot of Earl Grey tea.

And then she laughs and the world is beautiful again…

Chemicals. The chemistry of life: biochemistry. Reflect for a moment on the workings of the brain: 100 billion nerve cells, 70 different neurotransmitters, molecules which act as messengers between the cells (including serotonin (which affects mood), dopamine (reward), endorphins (pain relief)).

What she said made absolute sense to him as if it were not only her speaking but a friendly spirit talking through her...

And there are as many as 10^{13} to 10^{15} (1 with 13 to 15 zeros) synapses or connections between the nerve cells which is about a million times the number of people on the planet (nearly 7bn) - only 100 times less than the number of seconds since life began.

Paradichlorobenzene lurking in the urinals; alcohol dehydrogenase burning furiously in the liver. The transparency of glass slowly, so very slowly, sinking to the table, super cooled…

6 - REPULSE MONKEY

Release the lute by taking your right arm back behind you,

notice the tips of the fingers of your right hand out of the corner of your eye as you turn your head a little, then with your left hand still in front of you, bring your right hand forward sweeping close to your ear and gliding over the palm of your left hand, as your left arm begins to reach behind you, stepping backwards as you do so. As if shaking off a tiresome enemy, like some persistent, clinging monkey.

From Repulse Monkey, to a foreign body I discovered in my mouth while drinking cappuccino[fta]. An obvious pun, yet clearly a position of retreat, steady, measured retreat to a place of safety and consolidation, although in this case also an uncertain beginning.

THE COCKROACH SAGA

So was it here that it all began for me - the descent, the shift into madness? Did the change begin from the moment I discovered that the gritty clump caught between my teeth from the cappuccino I was drinking, was a cockroach!?

I never have liked crustacea, seafood, not anything with a shell, from prawns to lobster, cockles to mussels (love fish tho'). I know a cockroach is an insect but it's got a crunchy carapace like a shell! An exoskeleton. My ex could never understand why I didn't like seafood. But I don't! It was made worse by university biology experiments, although I can now just about manage the occasional prawn from a fish pie. But *Not Everybody Likes Seafood*! I used this as the title of a performance of poetry (presented with the Knaphill Players in Woking in the early 90s); it was a phrase I often had to repeat.

What follows is my first letter of complaint to the café manager about the experience. On reading it again, I imagine how it might sound if Rowan Atkinson were performing extracts with exaggerated intonation and pauses, describing what happened in the voice of this unfortunate individual's complaint. Or then again, like John Cleese beginning the infamous Parrot sketch: "I wish to register a complaint!"

Somehow, it seems I've got through all these years with hardly any conversations with strangers…

Mr F M Z

Café Sante

17 Garrick Street

London WC2

19th January 1997

Dear Mr Z

On Tuesday 14 January at approximately 7.0pm I arrived at Café Sante with my friend Mr T. We had both eaten there before.

We ordered two desserts (a caramel flapjack and an apple pie), a tea and a cappuccino. This order was taken and delivered to us downstairs a few minutes later.

After about ten minutes, having finished the apple pie, I was drinking the rest of my cappuccino when I felt something unusual in my mouth. At first I mistook this for a lump of congealed chocolate powder but soon realised with horror that it was crunchy and had legs. Taking it out of my mouth I discovered that it was a cockroach, a German cockroach (confirmed by my friend who is also an Environmental Health Officer).

I felt physically sick at having this disgusting, insanitary creature in my mouth. I took the cup with the cockroach to the ground floor servery and handed it to 'Gealal.' He seemed rather dumbfounded. I asked for the manager but he said he'd just gone out. I asked him for the manager's name which he said was Fred.

He also said, along with the other waiter, that the cockroach might have been from the automatic cappuccino machine rather than the 'hand-made' cappuccino maker. Gealal added that I did not have to pay and offered a replacement cappuccino.

However, I am still concerned that:

1   the exact source and cause of the incident is discovered

2   thorough action is taken to prevent the same thing happening again

3   I receive compensation for the incident which has:

- made me feel physically ill and continues to sicken and upset me whenever I think about it, which is frequently

- put me off drinking cappuccino and all other hot frothy drinks (something which I used to enjoy)

- dissuaded me from using the restaurant; and

- encouraged me to tell my 'story' to many other people.

I look forward to receiving your written reply explaining what action you have taken to prevent a recurrence and what compensation you, or your insurance company are prepared to offer.

If I don't hear from you within 10 days I will be consulting a solicitor with this complaint.

Yours sincerely

Steve Walter

The sort of girl you just want to look at and look at and look at, and maybe move your hands some...

And during the exchange of correspondence with the Café Owner's solicitors my solicitors asked for a psychiatric report. What had been the impact of the incident? It was only a dead cockroach in my mouth after all.

I've gone 72 hours without a wank. The last time I did that I went mad...

Dr P

Ticehurst House Hospital.

Psychiatric Report

29th December 1997

1. This report was prepared at the request of K&F Solicitors. I was asked to comment on the effect of the incident at the Café Sante on 14 January 1997 on Stephen Walter's mental state. The report is based on my contact with Stephen Walter as a Consultant Psychiatrist at Ticehurst House Hospital. In preparing this report I had access to:

    a. A letter from Ws, solicitors acting for Café Sante dated 13 February 2007.

    b. A letter from Stephen Walter to Mr F.M.Zadeh dated 19 January 1997 describing an incident at the café Sante on 14 January 1997 when he drank a cup of coffee containing a cockroach

    c. A letter from Stephen Walter to Ws dated 9 February 1997

    d. Undated letter from Stephen Walter, written after his discharge from Ticehurst House Hospital, to R.R. solicitor.

Psychiatric history

2. I was asked to see Stephen Walter urgently by Dr B, his general practitioner, on 25 June 1997. Dr B reported that Mr Walter had been going 'downhill mentally recently, was thought disordered and having highs and lows'. He had appeared 'a bit depressed' and was not sleeping. Dr B also said in his referral letter that Mr Walter had been concerned about weight loss and rectal bleeding.

3. I interviewed Stephen Walter with his wife...at Ticehurst House on 25th June 1997. I found him perplexed, thought disordered and apprehensive. He had great difficulty giving a coherent history of recent events as his talk was jumbled and unfocused. He reported losing 1.5 stones in weight over the previous six months despite a healthy appetite.

4. His wife reported that since 1985 he had always been prone to misinterpret events and either get upset with himself or angry with others. She had learnt to 'tread on eggshells.' He had episodes once or twice per year when he became obviously more distressed. These traits had been more obvious over the previous three months when at times he had appeared 'out of touch with reality.'

5. I diagnosed Stephen Walter as suffering a mixed affective episode and arranged for his informal admission to Ticehurst House Hospital. Following admission he had to be detained under section 2 of the Mental Health Act (1983).

6. He was treated with antipsychotic medication to which he responded. He was discharged after four weeks and since then has slowly recovered his confidence. He was seen regularly by myself as an outpatient and was also seen by

Mr K, Community Psychiatric Nurse, from the local Community Mental Health Team at Pembury Hospital, Tunbridge Wells. He was prescribed the antipsychotic drug Olanzapine 10 mg once daily.

7. He made a gradual return to work and at the time of this report had been working full-time for about two weeks.

8. In a letter to me dated 9 September 1997 Mrs W summarised the development of her husband's recent psychiatric problems from her perspective. She first noticed 'subtle changes' in his 'mental state' around early February 1997. She wrote 'the changes in his personality reached their height once we returned from our holiday in America, in mid-April. It was as though a lever was being switched into higher and higher gear within him, making his response and sensitivity to outside stimuli even keener.'

Past Psychiatric History

9. Stephen Walter told me he had been treated aged 12 years, by his then GP, for anxiety with the tranquiliser diazepam.

Incident at the Café Sante 14 January 1997

10. Stephen Walter stated in the undated letter to R solicitors 'I believe that the impact of the incident may have been greater for me because of a combination of my sensitive nature and my experiences of enforcing food safety, infectious disease and health and safety law.'

11. Stephen Walter also stated 'I feel strongly about the incident which felt like an insult to me.' On 14 August Stephen Walter told me of the Café Sante incident that it had made him feel a failure in his profession as an Environmental Health Officer. He was unable to drink cappuccino again until 24 April 1997 and each time he would pass a coffee shop he would have a distressing image in his head of finding the cockroach in his mouth.

Family history

12. His mother and father are fit and well. He has a younger brother who is 35 years old. He was not aware of any family history of mental illness.

Personal history

13. He has been married to his wife for 11 years. They have one son aged eight years. He has an adopted daughter from his wife's previous marriage aged 21 years.

Drug and alcohol use

14. He drinks on average 2 units of alcohol daily. He does not use illicit drugs.

Opinion

15. Stephen Walter suffered significant emotional distress as a result of ingesting a cockroach in a cup of coffee at the Café Sante on 14 January 1997. This distress consisted of

feelings of anger and shame, intrusive images of the incident and phobic avoidance of coffee from shops, which he had previously enjoyed. This episode meets the diagnostic criteria for Adjustment Disorder (ICD 10 F 43.23). This episode lasted about three months and he made a full recovery.

16. He may have been particularly vulnerable to develop such a reaction because of pre-existing emotional sensitivity and his detailed knowledge of environmental health matters.

17. Stephen Walter suffered from a serious psychotic episode which has been diagnosed as Bipolar affective disorder, current episode mixed (ICD 10 F 31.6). The first signs of this episode were noted by his wife in early February 1997 about two weeks after the incident at the Café Sante. There were no other stressors reported around that time and on balance of probability the incident at Café Sante appears to have been the trigger for the psychotic episode.

18. The history suggests he may have suffered undiagnosed and self-limiting affective episodes prior to the incident over many years.

19. Stephen Walter has, as a result of the psychotic episode, suffered significant emotional distress and lost time at work. He has made a gradual recovery but has to continue taking prophylactic medication. This is in most cases a recurrent disorder and he remains at risk of relapse.

The impression of her body on every part of me...the two of us so new...

'He remains at risk of relapse.'

And I did relapse: two years later, in May 1999, and then again for briefer episodes in January 2002, and July 2004.

I gave her the middle finger…

How ironic then that fourteen years later (on the eve of Thanksgiving, November 2011) I should be nibbling peanuts in a dimly lit, but luxurious, hotel bar only to find that I'm chewing what seems like a sultana or piece of apricot in my mouth, but softer and suddenly more chewy, and to take it out and realise it was someone else's chewing gum!

Ugh!

TRANSITION: Broken shells

'Like walking on eggshells' is how my ex once described living with me. (But not the broken husks of cockroaches.) For her, it was the not knowing how I might react to what she said. As if afraid that I might erupt in a sudden temper, as I did one night in the kitchen, early on in the relationship, over a meal my daughter refused to eat. I chucked the meal away and stormed out into the bitter evening of strong winds and heavy rain. I was wearing a jumper and jeans with only slippers on my feet. I headed out along the canal towpath, walking for miles, swearing furiously, then muttering to myself, until I decided I'd had enough, cooled off, tired and wet, with only 10p in my pocket; I came around, caved in, found a telephone box and rang home for a lift. And she collected me.

"Being a man in 1997 means walking on eggshells. I don't dare tell a woman she looks nice anymore. That I like the colour of her dress or the way she's changed her hair. They'll have me up for sexual harassment"...

..."But," Dorrie says, leaning forward, "how much do you mind walking on eggshells?"*

Carol Shields, Larry's Party

I wanted to say something about the meaning of life, something noble and inspiring, instead I have left everything to chance...

For me, much emotion is rooted in creativity; the desire to express, to make something of the experience of the moment. And there are moments when the emotion is too vast to embrace, when a sculpture, a painting, an installation, triggers an avalanche of desire to express again what is the sum total of this life, in time, in space, in this place, this universe, and what it means.

The sun has no shadow...

Know our experience as beings: alive in every moment of an infinite yet infinitesimal cosmos, opening our eyes to the sun, breathing the scent of eternal skies, listening to the subtle heartbeat of the Earth as if forever almost touching the lining of a universal womb.

But realise how close the end is: tangible, inevitable, our dissolution in the planet, the molecules of our being recycled, appearing in other bodies, food, earth, animal breath.

Seen from behind: the contours of white denim jeans, a black leather jacket and shoulder length blonde hair...

7 - STROKING THE PEACOCK'S TAIL – (LEFT)

Imagine the shimmering, spread feathers of a peacock. After repeating four paces backwards of Repulse Monkey, turn to Holding Ball back into Parting Horse Mane and then bring both hands round high across your front, first to your left, and draw them down close together, not touching, as if running a peacock's feathers gently through and between your fingers.

The fine structure and beauty of the peacock's tail leads to the craft and art of the sculptor. Sculpture which may not outwardly always be obviously beautiful, but is beautiful in the nature of its original, inner sensibility.

Jenny Parkes

Jenny is my aunt, my Dad's sister. She is some fourteen years younger than my Dad, so slightly closer to my age than his. She is an artist, a sculptor, and an inspiration. She hasn't experienced a breakdown but feels that she has come close. She has worked through so much of her experience in her art. I particularly remember a very powerful and moving piece, which she'd created at Farnham College, and which I saw at an exhibition there in Spring 1997, called The Kiln Door. It held the intensity, the fire of creative inner tension, which moved me to tears.

From the outside the door appeared relatively plain, innocent, unblemished. From the inside it was blackened, burnt, having sustained all the ravages and violence of intense heat. And yet, it was the one door, as if symbolising the whole person, sane, normal from the conscious exterior, through the logical left brain, yet driven, raging with a violent intensity of desire, to express every level of emotion, through the more creative right brain, and subconscious.

In 1999, ironically a few months before my second breakdown, I helped her to organise an evening of poetry at The Keep in Reading. The tall, solid, brick and concrete building was once a munitions store but now accommodated artists' studios. Jenny had her studio there. Her exhibition this time, which I'd first seen some weeks before, entitled Mind the Gap, was a powerful exploration of destruction, demolition, and decay. Here's a brief note I left for her following my first viewing. I'd spent over an hour in the small space, reflecting, writing and once more moved to tears.

Dear Jenny

I have to say that you have excelled. Magnificent. I'm so pleased I took the time to come over here this morning. And to have the privilege to spend time alone in what has become an energised sacred space. A chapel. A room of remembrance. Of Peace.

I almost cannot believe the power which you have created between these pieces, Frames of Mind, Coming Apart at the Seems, What the Eye doesn't See, and what is Untitled.

I long now for the words to express this. This whole, complete moment.

love Steve

Here, among other things, she had window frames suspended by wire, motionless in the centre of the room, salvaged from demolition, broken glass, screaming out the ceaseless process of death, of decay. A mattress ripped open, in part exposing torn filling, springs, a cruel reminder of comfort disrupted, of the inevitable end.

What led you to seek psychotherapy?

It was through beginning to do an art degree course at Farnham - the Surrey Institute of Art and Design - something I'd really wanted to do all my life. Then finding that I had a severe lack of confidence. It was as if I'd discovered a gap in myself, and I got to a point where I felt as though I was sort of losing the plot. Like going down into a deep pit. I'd also read about psychotherapy in books, the first being The Road Less Travelled by M Scott Peck. I decided not to see my doctor because I didn't want anti-depressants, instead I went to see a psychotherapist. Fortunately, one was recommended to me by my sister in law.

Almost immediately there was a sense of relief that I could actually talk to somebody objectively about what was going on inside me and know that they wouldn't be biased. She would ask questions which led me to find my own answers. But it wasn't a fast track process. Very early on we both realised it was going to take me sometime because I would talk about a lot of superficial stuff being unaware of the deeper issues underneath. So it took a long time to get to the roots of it. Each time I did get to a deeper area it felt like peeling back a layer of an onion to discover that there were still so many more layers to come, so much more to learn. It's helped me tremendously, to stay balanced.

I became quite fascinated with how the mind works. But at first I was just a bit scared.

How else did psychotherapy help you?

The best thing now is that I have a greater sense of detachment. Not always, but I'm more able to watch my thoughts and reactions, I'm building a place inside me which is a hiding place for myself and that's getting stronger and stronger, although there's still some holes. And I've understood why this has come about, why I needed therapy in the first place and why I still get hung up on certain things. It helped me with college, which was where it began, because it helped me to see myself in relation to other people and to realise that I could do what I was trying to do. It was ok to feel the way I was feeling, and even though I was nervous I could work through that. Sometimes at the college it would hit me like a block that I wouldn't be able to do anything, I'd be so panicked that I wouldn't be able to make anything. I felt invisible.

I suppose what psychotherapy did was start to help me build a coping structure inside…I'm working now with grids, which were there at college but I didn't realise the importance of the grid when I first found it. It's a metaphor. My work has always been a metaphor for what's going on in me.

I've done a lot of work analysing my dreams. I've learnt a huge amount about myself through my dreams. They're ways my subconscious communicates with me over things that I've squashed out, things that I won't acknowledge, or maybe that I'm completely unaware of. When I first went to see my psychotherapist, also called Jenny, I'd already had this powerful dream. It was about a little girl who was extremely angry but trapped behind glass and the glass was broken. It was coupled with another dream, a strange dream, of being with children as if I was in a foster home. We were fed up with the way we were treated and I had decided to leave because I felt trapped. The foster mother came in and this young child in the form of a spirit charged at the mother and winded her. She went to do the same thing to me, I could see her and said 'Don't leave'. This second dream came about a week or two after the first. My dreams have been incredibly important in therapy.

Basically my therapist explained that the characters in your dreams are nearly all aspects of yourself. Therefore I was the teenager who wanted to leave, I was the foster mother at the door and I was also the baby that was invisible and yet desperately needed to communicate. I was also the little girl behind the glass, which connected very much with the baby that was invisible. And it became clear, gradually, that it was to do with my grief as a child of one year old, over the death of my dad. The death had never been expressed or even acknowledged by any of my family then, because I was told over and over again as a child that I was too young to know. I was too little. But in actual fact it is now fully accepted that the emotions, the effects on us of loss before three years old have a massive influence on the child's psychological development.

For one thing, a one year old is separating from mum and starting to walk to dad, separating out from the mother and beginning to form identity. I didn't do that in the normal way. I did have two older brothers, but just through circumstances my eldest brother left home when I was four (to go to Korea) and the middle brother left home when I was seven. So the 'Don't leave' bit was to do with a sense that the baby part of me was always left, ignored. Not from anybody's fault, just circumstances.

So, although I thought in my memory that I had a very happy childhood and was quite often almost spoilt because people tried to compensate for me not having a father, there was a whole chunk, a whole gap in me caused by the fact that he died at that particular time. This realisation had been coming on for some time but there's a tendency to think it was all in my mind. I didn't realise how angry my one year old was. I didn't realise how much grief I still had to work through. I didn't realise the implications of growing up with just my mum. Although I had male role models, my brothers, I didn't have a normal marriage or partnership as role models.

And then I found that this had become a pattern in my life - the anger from it all. Because there was no room for it in my early childhood; because I think my brothers and I were both aware that my mother was vulnerable. So I would not get angry with her, as a child normally would. I didn't have tantrums. The anger, the temper got turned inwards on myself and became a huge critical voice which was always there and stopped me from doing a massive amount of things. I had no physical confidence as a child I still can't swim, can't skate, can't climb mountains...I did learn to ride a bike. But a lot of anxiety was caused because I would chew myself up about every action, I'd worry if I were doing the wrong thing or the right thing, my critical voice was omnipotent, like a little child telling you off. That's the voice I've had inside me all these years...

I found at art college that I wanted to work with eroded materials I wanted to work with demolition and vandalised surfaces. I was drawn to deconstruction and it was through working with those materials that I began to see how destructive the pattern was that was going on inside me. I still love rust, the erosion of metals, I love burnt wood, broken surfaces. I will erode surfaces deliberately. I would work with nitric acid and deeply etch printing plates and get a real thrill out of it.

I discovered something I truly responded to that was an absolute metaphor for me. My art was a way of communicating all of the feelings inside - I was putting it out there although not in a direct way. The materials became a vehicle for me to explore these buried feelings. I remember I re-presented an old, deeply burnt, deeply eroded kiln door in new girders, new brackets and new base. The base was half new and half eroded. And I remember a group of first year students were being brought round on a tour and the tutor asked if I would talk about my work, and I did and I explained about my response to the materials and the kiln door and that it represented me and was a metaphor for myself. I remember an elderly lady for the group said you mean you are the kiln door and I said yes! And it's how I felt inside.

How did the kiln door represent you?

I began to realise that the process of self-analysis, and the therapeutic process, was like going through fire and water. Facing buried emotions was like burning through the layers of rust and metal on the kiln door. It had been exposed to tremendous heat: on one side it was so corroded, it was almost eaten away in places, and yet on the other side it appeared to be just rusty, just ageing slightly. It felt very akin to how I felt. The work I was doing in therapy was like the new girder the new bracket that supported the door. And the door was actually very beautiful - the erosion and corrosion had made it so - and this felt like a great metaphor for life.

My work continued to be about eroded surfaces. Often this involved discarded objects that had been burnt, or shown other evidence of use. Sometimes rescued from skips or demolition sites. It's strange but every place I've worked in has gone through some kind of demolition or regeneration.

What lead you into art in the first place?

I think growing up with a brother who drew and painted incessantly. By 13 he was painting murals all over the house: an alpine scene up the stairs; a fairground scene and churchyard scene in the lounge; and a gypsy encampment in the main living room. My mother had run out of paper, so he painted the walls instead. He was nine years older than me. When he was painting the walls I would have been four. I grew up with this and I believe that what we're exposed to as young children is often how we explore our creativity.

I wanted to go to art school when I was 15. I wanted to get into illustration. My mother and my art teacher were seriously against it but very cleverly arranged that I had an interview at art school. But I had no idea about what was needed and had the most horrendous interview. There were four men sitting with their backs to a sunlit window and I couldn't see their faces. I had very little work and they pulled what I had apart, quite kindly and said you're too young, there's not enough work, come back in 2 years which to me felt like a lifetime. I lost a lot of confidence through this.

Then my art teacher and mum and other staff suggested teacher training and said I could do a main course in art, so I could still use my art but have a secure job. I went to St Gabriel's college in Camberwell. It was a very good college for art. I enjoyed it. As a teacher, you do put a lot of creative thought into teaching but you're not extending your own art practice, it's not about your own personal development, whereas exploring your own creativity is very much about exploring your own development.

The dreams are usually metaphorical so they're not about reliving an actual experience but more about giving me insight into feelings and emotions that I can't get in touch with any other way. I had a dream quite early on which was to do with my mother. I was probably a teenager, possibly 16 or 17, and we were in a house that was being attacked by a dragon. It was my job to protect my mother from the dragon. It flew down and I killed it. She gave me the knife and I killed it. And as I killed it, I realised that it was incredibly beautiful and I'd killed something incredibly unique and beautiful and although it was dangerous it was precious. And I'd killed it because of my mother's fear. Then I came to understand that the dreamer plays all the characters. I was the mother and me, and the dragon was associated very much with my creative drive and how I'd killed it off - I'd blocked it because it became too scary. I realised what I did to myself and maybe still do at times - how we block our creativity, we kill the dragon, because it becomes almost too powerful to deal with.

I usually try to record my dreams. Now, if I get a vivid dream in the middle of the night I write it down immediately because I've learnt so much through them. Another recurring symbol is to do with two children, two babies, two girls, sometimes boy and girl, it has to do with a feeling of being split inside between logic and creativity or two parts of myself. And I found recently through other work with my inner child, that she was closed off, definitely shut behind glass. I saw myself in a creative visualisation, a meditation, removing the glass in front of her - I began to have a relationship with her. I've always been very scared of her because she is much stronger than me. If you imagine a child that's never let out temper tantrums - she's got a lot built up inside.

It's been great! I now feel that I can at least begin to experience that release. It's scary sometimes, but I can at least begin to feel anger properly - I don't have to feel in work or dreams I can feel it directly. As a result my work now has become almost pretty and I'm actually working on construction rather than deconstruction. The latest is a metal grid from a barbecue that's become rusty and fragile and I'm weaving it together with new copper wire. And it feels really good.

I was dealing with the pulling apart more at college, the erosion and corrosion and now want to hold and support the fragile eroded material and give it a new framework...broken glass, broken windows, broken doorways, broken window frames...all of that has been, in some ways, a metaphor for some deep seated emotion or something that I've not been able to express in any other way.

What have you wanted to communicate through your art?

Self-expression, emotion sometimes may have to do with the world around me, what's going on in the news, war, loss - one of my greatest fears has been loss - and also relationships. The materials and how they relate to each other is very much to do with how I express myself to the world and my inner relationships.

Have you ever experienced a breakdown?

No. Not completely, but I think I was on the edge of it a couple of times. I do feel that being able to speak to a therapist on a weekly basis has prevented me from having a total breakdown.

Are you having any form of drug treatment?

No

How does your spirit inform your art?

Now my work has led me to feel a much deeper connection with spirituality I suppose. I have trouble with the word spiritual, but by it I mean a deeper essence. And I've actually been on a course on spiritual development. The one area I have slight difficulty with my therapist is that I think we have different views on spirituality. I think there is unavoidably a spiritual dimension to any creative expression. I think now it feels much more just a natural part of my work, and of being creative. It's more about playing, a mixture of play and contemplation. I don't know which comes first, but I know that you can't have one without the other.

What do you believe in?

I believe it is all One. That there is a universal energy in everything, that it is there for us to tap into and we only have to ask. I could say I believe in God but the word tends to summon-up a bearded gentlemen on a cloud - that isn't it at all. I could say I believe in Christ, but I believe in some sort of essence that he represented. I could say I believe in Buddha because I believe in finding a still space inside if you can. So the essence, or the energy, is within us and around us. It's not external. It's not separated from us.

The course I'm on is a Satvic Energy course, meaning of pure, or highest balance. It's a sanskrit word, and the foundation part of it has been about harnessing my own energy through chi kung out in nature and other meditational exercise and a lot of group therapy work. I've finished the foundation part and I'm going on the next final year and going onto energy fields and healing energy. As part of the course you are encouraged to seek counselling so I've been able to discuss it in therapy sessions because it's a process of looking at your own history and examining your own issues. And it's helped me a lot. But I don't think I could have done the course if I hadn't already done the therapy. It's all the same pathway for me.

Apparently the infant has to feel anger or rage at the mother in order to separate and I think I internalised the fact that my anger was so powerful that it actually got rid of my dad! And that's another thing that metaphorically has come to me in dreams. So my anger to me is intensely destructive. I turn it in on myself and in the moment that I'm feeling angry, I cannot get angry with my therapist. It was an immense relief to have discovered this. I was able to be fully aware of the feelings involved in losing dad. The anger - and also the fact that I'd killed him, 'disappeared'.

I think we live most of our lives in an 'ignorance is bliss' state, only half aware, if that! So I'm much happier knowing why I've not expressed anger easily and avoid confrontation. I get over anxious about relationships. Better to know why than to go on blindly or continue suffering. For so long it was painful, but now it's not painful any more, now I realise it's just me behaving the way I do. The important thing is not to blame yourself and to realise that you can't blame anyone else either. The things that happen to you are often simply circumstantial, and often out of your control.

REFLECTION

Jenny, my aunt, has found herself through her art. She has rediscovered meaning in her life, and in the universe which shapes our lives. She brings this creative energy to heal the wounds which she was left with following the loss of her father when she was very young. She has found counselling and psychotherapy very helpful even though she never experienced the fragmentation of breakdown or the reality of depression. She has overcome her loss and continues to be inspired and to inspire others, as a teacher, in their art.

Jenny Bloomer, would you recommend psychotherapy as a preventative measure, a way of stalling, of halting the onset of a possible breakdown? Because my aunt Jenny never actually went through a breakdown...

JENNY: Someone's got to be aware that things aren't going right, that there's something wrong somewhere. But, yes if they can sense that, can feel that then yes, "better to know why than go on blindly or continue suffering" as Jenny says.

She certainly seems to have a lot of insight

JENNY: Absolutely, she has a lot of insight, she's clearly a sensitive, intelligent woman

So there are benefits for treating with psychotherapy in a preventative way...because if you take Amy's story later, in America, especially in New York, people are seeing their 'shrinks' all the time

JENNY: Yes, it's a sort of fashion, isn't it? I have a bit of a problem with the American way of doing it because I think perhaps they're too navel gazing. However, if people are recognising potential difficulties then maybe that's a difference in culture because they're far more outgoing than we are; we're much more reserved as a nation. But if people are recognising that something isn't going right in their lives that something is missing, then I think psychotherapy definitely can help, because it's an exploration isn't it? I think I said to you all those years ago, that I'll walk with you...psychotherapy is a walk with someone as they explore...

It's about self-awareness isn't it, and insight and understanding.

And of course for her a lot came out through her creativity

JENNY: Absolutely, yes, but not everybody is able to do that.

So if you can't express yourself creatively, then talking through things will help?

JENNY: Yes. Yes because a psychotherapist will go into family dynamics and what has happened in the past to build up a picture with the person that helps with understanding of possible reasons why certain survival mechanisms have been used.

I think she's a remarkable lady. She almost found her own salvation, but she just needed a little help to release her from some bondage...bondage of the unknown...that she felt could get into her art but that she didn't fully understand. Understanding helps you to make changes or not as you choose to, with understanding you can be more at peace with things...

For an update on Jenny Parkes' story see the Epilogue

TRANSITION: The Testing Pool

Every day, as a young teenager, I write in my notebook…

It is a hot June lunchtime in the early 70s, Clarke and Simmons are teasing me, trying to snatch my notebook. 'What are you writing, Walter? Let us see. Let us see. We won't do anything. Promise. Come on let's take a look.' I always keep my hard-back, feint notebook pressed firmly into the large, outer pocket of my black blazer. It just fits, snug. It's private. It's my friend, my companion. I share what I think and feel with its lined pages. But its top is showing from my pocket, red. I am clutching it tightly to myself. What have I been writing? I write about everything in that book. It is my confessional, the seat of all my aspirations, my conversation with the world, with what Man is doing to the world. Private. Nobody, but nobody was to read my diary.

Reading the first lines of novels in the doctor's waiting room…

And I had written about them, nothing damning or harsh, only mentioning their names. How we'd run round the field, or with Connell would leap sets of stairs trying to be the first to arrive at the next lesson, tearing through corridors, bashing open the swing doors. Or how we'd club together to form the Cupboard End Mafia. Of course being only thirteen or fourteen we hardly inspired fear as the young Mafioso. Not like the sixth formers - everyone listened to them.

The tree surgeon carving his son's initials into the freshly cut tree stump, to help it rot...

I was standing beside the Testing Pool, holding on to the railings so they couldn't drag me away. A Technical High Boys School; the pool was used to test whether the plastic motor boats we made were watertight, pond-worthy - would they truly float? It seemed almost the size of a swimming pool then, but of course it was only a few inches deep and a few yards in length and width. But we weren't allowed in. I'd made a boat along with my class, with a motor, propeller and rudder, and had set it free there.

He always wanted to be a writer...

But I couldn't hold on to the notebook any longer, they grabbed it from me. I tried to wrestle it back as they passed it from one to the other, Suddenly Clarke was throwing it high and long, into the water. I watched it floating for a moment, the pages turning limp. A lump in my throat, trying to suppress tears, but sobbing. I lashed out as they teased me. Somehow, a few minutes later, in what seemed an eternity, my friend Warren saved the day, retrieved it for me, handing me the lank pages, which I could barely see through my tears. Thankfully, the biro I'd used had hardly run, it was still legible.

Beautiful to see your smile this morning…

Back then I wasn't prepared to Show the Wing. Instead, I was rather like an oriental bird in a Royal Park - its wings clipped, pinioned, so that it can barely fly.

For her: the muscles of his chest and stomach, firm and flat, his tight butt. For him: the soft weight of her buttocks, her breasts. And the utter strangeness of each other...

8 - STROKING THE PEACOCK'S TAIL – (RIGHT)

From Stroking the Peacock's Tail to the left, turn, Holding Ball as you do so, and repeat to your right, stroking the other side of the shimmering fan. The ending of this move again involves a Push Forward and Roll Back, which is also repeated later on.

I met Cara on a Life Writing course and, after I'd shared my story, she said that she had previously been diagnosed with bipolar disorder.

As for Jenny Parkes, the same move to the other side and the graceful swing of the arms, the tips of the fingers stroking the peacock's tail. However, for Cara stroking the peacock's tail, is as if side stepping the oncoming energy of an opponent, letting them brush off to one side. Here she shares the reality of her condition, in a neat and good humoured way, side-stepping the darkness.

Cara - Long Grove

When I think back I can't remember if I stayed at Long Grove once or twice. It was an old, echoing building with extensive grounds and a winding path that seemed to go forever before it reached the road. At least it seemed so to me as I was making for the road, hoping to get home to Laurence my baby, who needed feeding. They caught me long before the road was even in sight and pulled me back to administer the sedating needle.

I remember asking a psychiatrist what was wrong with me. He said he didn't know, then sadistically added that it might be congenital syphilis. He gave me the jab of haloperidol without an antidote so that not long afterwards my jaw began to lock and I had the greatest difficulty in speaking and almost no chance of being understood.

It was in this condition that Dr S, the consultant psychiatrist saw me. A formidable lady with huge yellow, plastic rimmed spectacles. Angry and resentful I was unable to communicate with her and she spoke to me patronisingly, seeming oblivious to my condition. I had a measure of revenge the next day when, having recovered my voice, I was brought to speak to a couple of gentlemen from the Mental Health Review Tribunal. I was one of the token inmates they spoke to and was quite free with my opinions. I remember that they said my intelligence could not be called into question. What they didn't say was that my sanity could be and indeed was, as I was held under a section of the Mental Health Act.

Not long after being admitted I decided I wanted a drink but the kitchen was closed. I thought that if they could bring me here against my will there was no reason why I couldn't use my ingenuity to get into the kitchen. I slid up the white hatch cover and climbed over the counter.

My Dad had died a few months earlier and I decided that I was going to meet up with him in heaven and we would have something to eat together. Having just got access to the kitchen this seemed only reasonable. So I set a few tables. He didn't come.

John the artist, another patient, looked on puzzled as I tore the pages out of a bible that I found lying around. He was there because he had gone to A & E and said he would kill himself unless they admitted him. I don't think he had any idea what he was letting himself in for.

I remember telling one of the social workers that my mother had been taken into hospital, my Dad had recently died and my first son was born with a heart and lung defect and had been in hospital a few times already. She said that was a lot for anyone to cope with and until that point I hadn't really thought about it. It was just something that had happened to me and I didn't think about whether it was more or less than other people had to bear.

I was probably there for around a month. I don't know what we did all day, although the days were certainly long. There was a large day room and we sat about. I think there was some form of occupational therapy and I have a recollection of kneading clay which felt strangely soothing like making bread, and using the wheel to make a small pottery dish. If it was ever finished I have no memory of what it looked like.

My husband Peter sometimes brought Laurence in to visit and he would pull himself up on the filing cabinet in the nurse's office, in his little blue jacket, his chubby legs wobbling with the effort. He was nearly a year old but not yet walking. I'm sure I missed him dreadfully when he left but I would have been heavily sedated, my feelings numbed and diminished.

I'm not sure that anyone attempted a diagnosis[5] although I attributed my breakdown to post natal depression. I'd been psychotic and delusional but I can't remember the down side particularly. John asked me once to help a Romanian girl who had been sectioned by her husband - he thought that the husband was trying to get rid of her but, whilst I felt for her, I didn't see how I could help.

Long Grove was part of a group of Psychiatric hospitals outside Epsom – I suppose they were asylums. It was later to be closed in phases when '(who) cares in the community' was introduced. Many of the patients had spent most of their life in the institution and were completely unprepared for and unsuited to life in the community. Some would have ended up on the streets or in prison or at the mercy of unscrupulous landlords who were able to claim rent from social services for their sometimes squalid bed-sits.

There was an elderly patient, a lady who seemed determined never to smile and John saw this as a challenge. He said he would get a smile out of her before he was discharged. I'm not sure he ever did.

I was allowed out for Laurence's birthday party. There are photographs of me with thick dark hair, in a Laura Ashley dress with Laurence on my knee and some other friends there. Mum was in hospital then. She'd had a stroke while I was in Long Grove and had been admitted to Kingston hospital by the same Doctor who had refused to take her onto their books when she moved down from Wallasey. I was able to go and see her but not often as the well

---

[5] Five years later I was to be diagnosed with bipolar affective disorder in Australia, seventeen years after my first serious manic episode.

meaning and totally misguided Mrs W, the health visitor told me I shouldn't visit too frequently as it was tiring for me.

One day I took Mum some little violets that were growing in the cracks of the crazy paving at the pink house and some forget-me-nots. The violets are called heart's ease. She told me to give them to another older lady in the bed by the window. 'She never has any visitors' she said. The lady told me I was just like my mother which was a wonderful compliment.

The next week, on the day that she was due to be discharged my mother had a final stroke. She died in the afternoon just before my brother came to take her home.

Cara

REFLECTION

Cara's recollection is a powerful and touching take on her experience of hospital, which she read with a sense of irony. It says something of the mental health system, of the boundaries of patient-nurse interaction which still seems rooted in an almost Victorian mindset.

How would you say mental health care has changed since the 1950's?

JENNY: It seems this is written from a long time ago when psychiatry was different, and diagnosed 17 years after her first serious manic episode in Australia...

Since the 1950s...?

JENNY: Yes, really the 80s were probably the optimum time when they'd got so many things sorted out but then psychiatry went into the community without making proper provision first. This left people high and dry, without the care they had been used to. Poorly and elderly patients were placed into B&Bs which caused a lot of havoc.

But in the 50s and 60s they were still doing dreadful things to people, such as insulin induced comas, lots of different things that are now unacceptable. People were considered as crazy patients – they weren't considered as individuals suffering with the difficulties of illness but with thoughts and feelings, however difficult to understand.

They were also using medication without knowing what the results were going to be. Mad people looked madder than they were to start with - drooling and making funny jerky movements. There were still people who'd been put into asylums when children, because it was easier to have them out of the way. They should never have been there, some had stayed all their lives – it was very, very sad seeing them.

I didn't go into psychiatry until the early 80s so my knowledge is based on history. But I was seeing elderly people who'd been put in there as children, in the equivalent of pharmacological straight jackets, not real ones.

I particularly remember Cara's description of being given haloperidol without an antidote, and how her jaw began to lock. This was very common. CPZ (chlorpromazine) Haloperidol etc (major tranquillisers) would be given in vast quantities to keep patients quiet. They would then develop involuntary jerky movements – tardive dyskinesia. Things did improve in the 60's and patients were treated more as individuals and less as hopelessly crazy.

and not written off quite as easily

JENNY: Yes…and when I was there in the 80s then people really did see the asylum as the place of safety, and would come in of their own accord when they knew that they were ill.

Cara's father had died a few months earlier, then her boy born with a heart and lung defect and her mother dying…so much to bear.

Steve Walter

TRANSITION: Event Horizon 2007

13th August 2007, we visited an exhibition of Anthony Gormley's work at the Hayward Gallery. I was fascinated and in awe; he says so much that is true about the creative experience, profound connections with the root of life.

Event Horizon, an ambitious new installation commissioned by The Hayward, consists of life-size figures – casts of the artist's body – placed on rooftops and walkways both North and South of the Thames. This invasion of foreign bodies spreads outwards from The Hayward in all directions over a 1.5 sq km area. All the figures face towards the gallery's three sculpture terraces, which form the main viewing platforms for the project as a whole. Depending on the weather and time of day, some figures will be clearly visible while others will be sensed only as presences on the horizon.

'The title (Event Horizon) comes from cosmological physics and refers to the boundary of the observable universe. Because it is expanding, there are parts of the universe that will never be visible because their light will never reach us

Anthony Gormley,
2007.

Looking out through the thick walls of glass of the gallery I can see a man, an iron man standing on the edge of the roof. He is staring out across the Thames to another iron man standing on another roof, almost too distant to see. And with these figures there is a kind of longing, a desire to know the presence of metal, its connection with the furnace.

'You could say that there are two very discrete and almost oppositional places where a sculpture belongs. One is physical: in a landscape or a room, and the other is in the imagination of the viewer, in his/her experience and memory.

'Sculpture reminds everyone that we are human and that we are embodied, incarnate, that all your sense of self and being comes through the body which is only fully itself when placed, connected to an elemental world.'

Anthony Gormley, 2001.

Critical Mass II 1995

Five cast iron suspensions over the stairwell.

'Maybe there are two things identified here: firstly, bearing witness to torture and execution, the worst destiny of the dispossessed...The use of this material – iron – is associated with the deep underground that lies beneath our feet and emphasises that our body is on temporary loan from the mass of matter constituting the planet and to which, in some way, we give shape.'

Anthony Gormley, 1995.

9 - SINGLE WHIP

From Stroking the Peacock's tail, extend your right hand high at an angle behind you, the fingers closed together, all touching the thumb, as if holding a whip, ready to flick. Bring your left hand round to face left, palm vertical (you will be moving to your left) as if holding back the enemy, taking a long stance with your legs.

A prepared stance, at the ready, ready to face whatever life might throw at you. A stance of authority and potential; Abacus taking charge of her life.

Abacus

Abacus (not her real name) stayed in Ticehurst House a few years after me. Her experience as a teenager leads us to question the adequacy of Child and Adolescent Mental Health services. She seems to have outgrown the trauma during her earlier teens although sadly there still seems to be a risk of her harming herself...However, the Epilogue finds her well.

The medium of using poetry for self expression is another creative outlet and her poems and Sharon's give a good flavour of this.

Interview with Abacus

I first spoke to Abacus over the mobile microwaves as she was sitting on the common in morning sunshine under a blue, blue autumn sky. She had seen Fast Train Approaching...written about somewhere, she couldn't remember where, and had downloaded an electronic copy through Chipmunkapublishing.com. I am delighted that she should actually want to share her story with me.

What were the circumstances that led to your breakdown?

I was diagnosed 4 yrs ago when I was 16. The diagnosis hit me for 6. I had been abused in my family since I was 13. It got very bad around 16. I went to Ticehurst to see a child psychologist and was given tablets - citalopram (an anti-depressant) - and I got better. Then my grandparents both died within a short time of each other and I broke down.

They changed the tablets to ciprolex, on a stronger dose, plus neuroleptics (quetiapine) to stop hallucinations and delusions. I had been in trouble with the police and was done for assaulting a police officer. I was interpreting situations wrongly.

I have been sectioned 3 times in the last four years. Section 136 - mentally disabled in a public place. When it happened two years ago I didn't know I'd attacked the police officer. I was kept in hospital for 3 days then had daily appointments. And the crisis team at would ring me every evening. When I was sectioned again in February I was in for only a day and a half.

Recently I became an aunt to twin nephews. My twin sister is normal, she has no health conditions.

How would you describe the experience of breakdown?

In one way it was quite frightening, I was contemplating suicide. Other times it can be quite tough, difficult trying to cope with the way things are. I've wanted to change quite a few things, to go back, but I have to accept the past, to move on to the future, and let go of the past. It can be hard.

What have you learnt from your experience?

When I had the diagnosis I thought what does this mean? Can I lead a normal life? What's going to happen? Where am I going to go? Now I'm trying to be positive. I want to see my nephews grow up. I've something worthwhile to look forward to.

What advice do you have for others managing breakdown?

I've not really discussed it with my friends. They know I have some kind of problem though. What I would say is that there is a way out of it. It's not how it's going to be forever. There's a way out at the end. Try to keep going. And there are professional people to help or helplines like Samaritans. I've rung them but I've been too scared to go into their office.

What, if any, spiritual experience accompanied your breakdown?

I've not really had any spiritual experience. I wasn't a

believer in god beforehand. But I did feel on one breakdown that there was this super powerful thing next to me, surrounding me. This only lasted a week then it went when I was coming out of the experience. It was comforting to know that there was something with me.

How would you describe your philosophy on life?

When I was having the breakdowns I wrote quite a few poems, about twenty-five or so. Well, lines of words. I'll choose some for you and send them over if you like.

I'm feeling pretty good now, although at the moment my mum is in hospital having an operation on her spine. I'm happy about my nephews.

Abacus was happy with the transcription of the interview but in an email said

'I would like to add that I have been self harming for 2 years now. I use it to cope with the pain.' I don't mind telling you about it. What would you like to know? Things are looking better, and I have more control over it now :)

I replied... **I guess since I've never had any real experience of self-harm I'm wondering what it's like. How would you describe how you feel when you're thinking about self-harm (if you do) and then when you do it and afterwards? I don't want to pry and don't feel you have to answer but I think any reader would be curious if it is outside their experience, or indeed may learn something from your recovery if they're harming themselves.**

For me it's a release. Things build up inside (emotions, thoughts etc), and I struggle to find a way to deal with it. This is when I self harm. The pain and the blood is the release. The release of the pain I keep inside. This makes me feel better for a while, but not very long. Then things build up, and the cycle goes around again.

I don't like doing it, but it's the only way I can let things out. I wouldn't call it an addiction, but I know when I need to do it, and the longer I go without doing it, the worse it is the next time. After doing it, I tend to get really emotional, and sometimes even regret doing it. I know it wont solve anything in the long run, and I know I will end up with scars.

As advice to people, I would say that there are other options available. Self-harm is not the only way to release the pain. It's also not the solution.

Talk to someone. Anyone. You don't even have to tell them everything. Just share some of it. It will make you feel better in the long run.

How long is it usually between episodes of harm? Do you think of self-harm as part of your condition or something separate?

It really depends on how bad I feel at the time. Sometimes it can be days, and other times it can be hours.

I know that self-harm can come as part of the bi-polar disorder, but I wouldn't say that it is as a result of it. I was self-harming before I was diagnosed, so I think it's separate.

Can't Sleep Again

Can't sleep again
These shadows in my room
They laugh at me
And my head goes boom

Can't sleep again
This freezing cold heat
It eats away at my mind
Drowns every beat

So tired
But these nightmares
They play tricks
Tell me he cares

I can't sleep tonight
I have you on my mind
You're so scared
Yet so good and kind

Can't sleep again
He's running through my head
Grabbing my wrists
Laughing like I'm dead

Can't sleep again
Without you by my side
Will you protect me from sleep?
Whilst I run and hide?

I can't sleep tonight

He's here in my head
Making me re-live every moment
And cry in my bed
Wishing I were dead...

Save Me

The day I thought I'd lost all hope

You said you'd help me through

Every time I'd run away

I'd run straight into you

You knew it hurt to feel this way

And wanted to understand

So you helped me through the tough times

And let me hold your hand

When it seemed like I was slipping

You were there to break my fall

You stood by me through thick and thin

You've been my wonderwall

Only you can save me now

From this pain I feel inside

Your smile seems to heal me

And make this pain subside

No one's made me feel like this

Without you I can't live

You're the only one that matters

And to you, myself – I'll give.

As Abacus has said she also spent a spell in Ticehurst. Here's an extract from the very first edition of the Acute Newsletter, Acute News, of 11th July 1997, written by and for the patients on the wards at Ticehurst House.

ACUTE NEWS

Acute News consisted of a few pages of A4 stapled in one corner, including drawings, poems, minutes of group meetings, jokes and puzzles. Jokes like: How many psychiatrists does it take to change a light bulb? Answer: It depends if the light bulb wants to change.

And I'd submitted a couple of poems, this one followed a trip out from the hospital in a minibus to Hastings...Steve's Poem

Visiting Seatown

The cries of gulls - airborne...

or flat-footed on chimney tops -

cascade across angled slate

collect in pools, behind parapets

bubble, tumble and overspill onto

window ledges, sills, weave thread-like

through the fiery forests of her mind

come to rest in some grassy shade,

waiting for the day to rewind and replay

echoing inside caverns.

And there was more, but it got darker – I think devolving into
bones and skulls – which they edited out.

But, a few days later on the 14th July, I was to receive a
poem from Sharon, a girl who was self-harming, as I
remember, addressed to Steve...

The brilliant rays,

of sunshine

cascading through

the rooftops, topsy-turvy

like battlements, slate, stone

slab, grey flooring

LOOK TO THE

SKY

AND SEE

from Sharon x

REFLECTION

How often have you had to confront self-harm in someone, and how do you tackle it?

JENNY: An awful lot. I think a lot of people who have suffered from sexual abuse often self-harm. As Abacus said, it was a 'release from the build up of thoughts, release from the pain inside, the only way she could let things out'. And that is so usual I'm afraid

A very common pattern then?

JENNY: Very common. I don't think Abacus said & it may not have happened, but lots of people who've suffered abuse hear voices in their heads: 'If you tell someone, you will die', that sort of thing.

I worked with one girl who stitched her lips up with wool and glued her eyes together, she didn't want to be seen, wasn't going to say anything and had to let the pain out some how…

It's a lot about pain, deep, deep distress and sensitivity. and of taking some sort of control through self-harming. Self harm takes place when it isn't possible to put the blame where it belongs for various reasons; for example people might be un-believing, the perpetrator may be inaccessible, possibly dead or fear of possible consequences.

…How do you tackle it?

JENNY: The way I work with people, is to get them to gradually realise and really accept that it was the other person who was at fault and not them. This takes time, sometimes a lot of time. Self-harming is actually turning all the helplessness, anger and disgust felt on oneself because it has to be put somewhere. Because people are told all sorts of tales such as, 'because I love you so much' or 'it's your fault, you are making me do this', that's why it is happening or has happened. I saw one girl with beautiful hair who said "if I hadn't brushed my hair perhaps he wouldn't have hurt me, he wouldn't have done that to me." She was convinced it was her fault. I've worked with a lot of self-blame.

There must be some very harrowing stories

JENNY: Yes, you think you've heard the lot but you never have.

For an update on Abacus's story see the Epilogue…

TRANSITION: So many lives

Through these stories weave pain and recovery, pain and loss and so much that is underlying it all. Why thread in my story, if it matters at all? Because I still try to make sense of all that happened, that is happening. As if I face a multi-faceted mirror, which is reflecting many new truths, many older truths, and I need help to piece together larger fragments of reality, to reach some resolution.

So, in spite of the huge backdrop of death and cancer, I will tell of the circumstances surrounding the performances of my story and the stage, the moments which brought it all alive, and which connected at some deeper level with so many people in the room.

Nothing an hour in bed together wouldn't cure…

10 - HANDS IN CLOUDS

For me this is the highlight of the 24 moves. If you're listening to the authentic Tai Chi 24 music, it changes again here, markedly, reminiscent of a fairground, as if imitating the sound of some carousel, a lazy merry-go-round. Now you release the Single Whip bringing your left hand slowly up in a circle, anti-clockwise across your body, in front of your face. As you draw your palm across your eyes, your face follows and at the same time your right hand is circling, clockwise, first protecting your belly. This sense of hands high in clouds, both rotating in opposite directions, conjures spirits, a sense of the invincible.

Try this move with your eyes closed, it seems to give you a power of moving through space, totally in control, and command as if, many times faster, capable of deflecting a volley of arrows - overcoming fear.

Brighton Fringe 2008

I had planned the trip to Edinburgh in 2007. 2008 was to be the dry run in Brighton. We know how quickly a new day approaches, the time is constant – we live the repeated revolutions of the Earth spinning on its axis, and its cycle around the sun. But there are those days that, for whatever reason, assume greater significance and whose approach seems to hasten with rapidly increasing speed. Sunday the 18th May 2008 was one such day.

The pain of breaking sunbeams crashing through the trees…

The date began to materialise through future mists as I came closer to pinning down a venue during the Brighton Festival Fringe, for a show based on my book *Fast Train Approaching…*. Brighton, February 2008, I'm visiting prospective Fringe venues: the Ambassador hotel, New Steine; The Coach House, Middle Street; The Mad Hatter, Montpelier Road; Pokeno Pies, Gardner Street; Upstairs at Three and Ten, Steine Street. It's not until later, with suggestions from my partner and friends, that we hit upon Komedia. They have a slot at 3pm on Sunday 18th May. Money exchanges hands, and it's booked!

Little Venice

Before the big day, my singer/songwriter friend, Steve Antoni, and I had the chance of a dry run. I'd contacted Nutan Modha who co-ordinates a London based mental health support group. She invited us to do an extract of the show at a pub in Little Venice. It's the first May bank holiday of 2008. Arriving at the canal: the bunting, the boats, the ice cream, the children. Finding the Bridge House Bar; Guinness, tables reserved, and a small group of half a dozen willing volunteers. We introduce ourselves and explain that we're going to the Brighton Festival Fringe in a couple of weeks time. We perform extracts of the show against a background of mumbled conversations and muzak from the other half of the bar. However, all of the group are really positive, and seem to admire our courage - they wish us well.

The day I'd planned for months arrives in all its glorious finality. I woke up on the morning, edgy, even before I opened my eyes. I couldn't hide it any more, it was going to happen - this thing would be born. I'd told my friends and colleagues at work sometime in March, only to be met with silence as if to say, surely he's not going through with this? What held me to the date, apart from a contract and the exchange of money, were the kind words of those close to me urging me on, and the stubborn belief that it simply had to be done.

Fill my heart with song and let me sing forever more…

(Fly Me to the Moon, Sinatra)

My lover had helped me to find the venue. But even then it wasn't completely real, until the morning and the rapidly shortening hours. Thankfully though, I did have the opportunity of a very brief practice run, for five minutes of street theatre on each of the three previous Saturdays at Fringe City. They were cause for concern in themselves: how was I to attract an audience in the street without appearing to beg or, rather ironically, seeming actually to be mad?

Girls wearing tiaras of flashing penises on springs…

Brighton Fringe City - Street theatre

Busking. At least with busking you have music. I had signed up for a few five minute slots at Fringe City. This consisted of several streets, around Brighton's North Laine, dedicated to showcasing the acts which were appearing in the Festival Fringe itself. I had five minutes to draw an audience, to tell them about the show, to inspire them to come along. And yet the show was centred around my madness, my confession of psychosis. I decided that to start with silence would be my best ally, to hold a pose in silence, almost a mime. I began with karate style warm up exercises, standing, bending, stretching long stretches, and then the opening moves to the yang style 24 Tai Chi, from Holding Ball to Showing the Wing.

Amazingly, although I was focused on the first moves, I noticed that some people had actually stopped to watch. Was I already looking slightly mad? I moved from standing still to Holding Ball, to Parting Horse Mane to Showing the Wing. Hidden behind my thumb in my raised hand I held a plastic cockroach, for later.

I struck on the idea of laughing to begin with: "It's not my fault. I mean, I haven't done anything. Don't blame me. It just happened!... repeated once but seriously the second time. And I recited:

"So, so you think you can tell, heaven from hell, blue skies from pain?

Can you tell a green field from a cold steel rail...? (Floyd)

Then I told the story: "Picture a café in Garrick Street in London's West End, over ten years ago, on the14[th] January 1997, Café Sante, Café Health. I was drinking cappuccino with my friend, an Environmental Health Officer, as I had been. Let this poem speak for itself:

Teabag in a wineglass

There are many dainty rules

of etiquette intended to avoid

the incongruous, designed

not to upset, like picking up

a bone china tea cup between

thumb and forefinger

with little finger cocked...

or tipping a soup bowl away

from you, to finish

the very last drop...

But when that gritty clump

of chocolate powder (...is it?)

caught between your teeth

turns out to have legs,

etiquette can go stuff itself.

Waiter: there's a fucking

cockroach in my cappuccino!

...And there really was! I picked it out of my mouth from between my teeth... At which point I pretend rather cleverly (not) to extract the plastic cockroach out of my mouth, making a face like the one that appeared on my flier for the show. 'Ugh – here, look..! But then it was real!'

Naturally, I didn't swear in public, in the street but these few words and first moves were to form the beginning of the show. And I followed this, rather oddly, with quotes from the performance: Chief Seattle on connections, and Nelson Mandela on Our Deepest Fear.

Rocking horse on a wheelie bin…

Komedia

On occasions I like to think of myself as an actor. I've played in several amateur performances to very welcoming local crowds in a village hall and I've taken part in lively and challenging classes in improvisation, I have even performed some of my poetry, but until today it's never seemed particularly important.

She is licking her face and swallowing…

In the last few weeks, I doubted whether I'd have the energy to go through with this. Why would I want to put myself through it? I am sad, disillusioned, so many friends can't make the show. Forget the hype, it's not a big story. When I'm finished I will simply pack up my bags and think again, it's not fame I'm after, just applause, someone to say 'what a good boy you are. Well done!'

She still thinks he farts Johnson's baby powder…!

Simply say the word 'poetry' and for many people it's as if a light has suddenly gone out. They switch off, perhaps imagining lace doyleys and tea at the vicar's with crust-free cucumber sandwiches. Most people are unaware of the raw, vital energy that can accompany mastery of the spoken word - the rhythm, the imagery, the resonance.

So now we have it. This moment was to be the first time for me to go public, a Fringe virgin, under the spotlight in the Brighton Festival. I was to share my personal experience of breakdown, and survival. My name and my picture were in the programme, I was committed – in a manner of speaking. So what was the performance called? It was to be '**An Acute Psychotic Episode.**'

Burning five pound notes to light the kindling in the grate...

It's the morning of the show: Sunday, 18th May. I'm petrified of being stuck in traffic on the way to Brighton. We have the Komedia Studio theatre booked from 2.30pm to set up, to get the lights and sound organised. Doors open at 3.15. We leave at midday. Steve Antoni, is staying over with us in Tunbridge Wells, so that we can leave together on time. We have our first and only chance to practice this morning - for less than an hour - just a technical run through of the links between what I say and when he comes in with the music and songs.

He knew every part of her, exactly how her bra gently restrained the weight of her breasts, how the elastic curve of her knickers held her...

I put a box of 'Fast Train Approaching...' books in the car, just in case. When it comes down to it I only take a few into the studio with me, too bulky to carry and I'm superstitious - I've no idea how many are likely to turn up, and I don't want to jinx the success of the show by presuming lots of sales.

On the pavement the remains of eggs yellowing the tarmac – sticky, like the drying protein of his come…

We arrive early and carry our baggage to the Studio. The place seems smaller than when I booked it, but intimate. Outside, it's a delightfully sunny afternoon. The Lanes are packed, everyone's enjoying the sunshine, chilling out with cappuccinos, and wine, relaxing. Liz is with Sue by the beach. I'm waiting with Steve Antoni at a café al fresco. I can't eat lunch, too nervous, only a bite of a sandwich. At 2.30 we're back at the Studio door.

Buddleia poised high on the old cinema building pending demolition…

The stage is small but thankfully they bring out extra sections from behind the curtain. Karen is an angel, making us feel at home, sorting out the warm red, orange lights, and the technician fixing Steve A with the sound, making sure everything connects with everything else... and works! Wires, leads, plugs, sockets, amps and stuff I have no idea of.

I can hardly believe it, it's already time to open the doors. Strangers walk in. Somebody other than my friends and family have heard of this! The front rows are already full. They are bringing in more chairs. It's feeling warm, cosy.

I hadn't even thought to have someone manning the door, to take tickets - money! The seconds steal up to the moment. This is going to happen. It's time to begin. Karen offers to help at the entrance. Afterwards I learn that she takes some 70 tickets, mostly pre-booked. Slowly, I stretch on stage.

Steve Antoni opens with 'The lunatic is on the grass' from Pink Floyd, Brain Damage, his inspired choice.

I begin the Tai Chi moves. Holding Ball to Parting Horse Mane, to Showing the Wing. As I recite the first poem, In Place of Silence, the energy is high. I did it! I so feared stumbling, forgetting my lines. I'm reading the prose, reciting the poems. And I recite all of them, something I can rarely do. The lights, the music, the event, the adrenalin takes me to some other place as I reconnect with how it was back then, with the guts of the poems - the experience of losing my mind.

In the group gathered on the street corner, the women are talking, the men are standing silent...

And applause. How grateful to be showered with applause. And for people in the Q&A session afterwards, when invited, to ask me questions about the experience, and even to thank me for speaking out.

And so many good wishes...the following quotes were recorded in a notebook titled 'notes from the couch', written by some of the audience after the performance:

> *"Loved it – sensitive – simple, beautiful, emotional – thanks so much for bringing your show to us"*

> *"Brilliant – thank you & good luck for your future performances – great message, keep spreading the word!"*

"I am rarely moved enough to leave words in a comments book. However, your performance was so moving and clear that I cannot go without saying thank you. Wonderful stuff"

"Thank you" x

"Well done! That was great…You are very perceptive of mental health and treatments! You are not alone!"

"Hey I'd like to say well done and I think you're very brave and are a credit to all us mental health sufferers out there. I was in Ticehurst with schizoid personality disorder & psychosis so you're definitely not alone"

"The performance was excellent and I found reassuring that people have the chance to hear such personal experience. Thank you for sharing."

And so, so quickly it's all over. I'm profoundly delighted, so high that the event went well, that it was by all accounts a success. What more do I need to do? That was enough.

There are many subtle energies which influence our lives and our becoming and may be inspiration for the sensitive…

Belly Dancing Diaries follow my show. This reminds me of earlier in the year when I was researching performance spaces. The first place I try is Upstairs at the Three and Ten. Entering the pub at lunchtime, I find the bar is empty. The theatre upstairs is occupied by a belly dancing club - if I could come back in a couple of hours, the barman said. I squeak in my motorbike leathers as I leave to check out other possible venues, including the Mad Hatter. On my return the upstairs is still occupied. I order half a lager, only a half for the road. There are voices, girls voices, gathering a crescendo as they laugh and giggle their way down the stairs. They don't know that I know what they've been up to. My imagination leads me astray, I imagine pole dancing, but of course it has been belly dancing fun. Are they the same girls now programmed to follow my show, as when our paths crossed that afternoon at the Three and Ten?

Hard to believe that giving such a little could bring such relief...

It's happening again...

Of little significance to anyone else, except my parents and immediate family – like my birth... But, a different kind of birth: I'd settled on The Vault, Annexe, Edinburgh; getting set for nine performances of '**An Acute Psychotic Episode (II)**' at the Edinburgh Festival Fringe, 2009.

The change in tone of her heels clunking on the ground as she steps from pavement to road from road to pavement...

TRANSITION: Caroline

We heard the news just after Liz's Dad had died, as the arrangements for his funeral were taking place, in February 2009. Liz knew then for certain. Caroline, Liz's niece, at only 36, had been diagnosed with bowel cancer, with the worst possible prognosis.

Tragically, it was the same cancer Caroline's father had died of six years earlier, yet her doctor had failed to diagnose it, failed to even carry out the right tests a couple of years before, when it might have been caught in time.

During the next two years, until her untimely and sudden death at Christmas 2010, I would see Caroline, cheerful as ever from time to time. But it was Liz who really knew, understood and shared her pain.

Darkness with a smile...

11 - SINGLE WHIP

The Single Whip is a second point of focus, formed in a similar way to the same poise after Stroking the Peacock's Tail, and now introducing a series of commanding moves.

Janet Hart

As with Abacus, I've never met Janet, only corresponded by email. She got in touch with me after reading my story on the HSE's website. She lives and works near Liverpool. She was very happy to share her experience which, as you'll see, has been profoundly disturbing. And, like Abacus she has taken charge of the anxiety inflicted upon her in childhood, and for her this represents a new beginning.

Janet's story

In order to fully understand the mental illness I was eventually to suffer from, it is important to look at my background. My childhood started off OK , but was to end abruptly.

The year was 1977. At 11 years old I was about to become a sexual abuse victim. I thought at first he would stop. When he didn't, I took the perhaps unusual step for a victim; I built up the courage to tell my mum. Still only 11, it took all the courage I had in the world. I naively believed that I would be helped and believed.

My mum got angry and said "Oh don't be stupid Janet, it's your imagination, now go and play." I still have trouble understanding how a child of 11 years old could have that kind of imagination. I will be haunted by it for the rest of my life.

My mum's reaction left me feeling totally alone. There was no hope, no one was going to help me. Fortunately the next time was to be the last, but it was the worst, as he pinned me down. I thought I was going to be raped that night. Naturally I then became withdrawn, causing my sister to question what was wrong. I kept quiet as I knew I wasn't going to be helped. Eventually both my sister and mum got it out of me. Their idea of help was to make sure he was never alone with me. This was a bit like shutting the stable door, after the horse had bolted. Worse still, he had ways of getting me cornered, even when people were around. He was never approached, questioned or prosecuted. He was still allowed to visit the house. I had to sit on the floor to keep out of his way, I daren't leave the room, in case he found a way to get to me. My dad would feed him whisky and his wife would get cups of tea. I felt absolutely worthless and unimportant to my family and still do.

I spent years locking myself up in my bedroom because I couldn't socialise, not if it meant having to deal with men. I lacked confidence and never pushed myself forward for anything. Unfortunately, the day approached that I no longer felt comfortable and safe in my bedroom, I'd started to feel lonely and like a prisoner. I had cut myself off from my friends. But I started to go out with my sister. The trouble was that if a guy approached me, she would have to do the talking. I couldn't deal with it.

When I met my first serious boyfriend, because of my background, it immediately put me under stress. We went on holiday to Rhodes. This is where I had a mini breakdown, but was unaware at the time. I would hear people talking about us and I was convinced that a camera was behind the mirror in our hotel room and that we were being filmed. I even went to the police about it when I got home and at one point became convinced my boyfriend was in on it. Eventually I calmed down and put my beliefs behind me.

Nearly a year later, in the spring, my father developed senile dementia. I realised it was unlikely that he would ever recover and that he would eventually die. I also had a lot on at work. I had stress coming at me from all directions. I approached my manager for help and was told I would have to manage as they were snowed under too. I was a typist at the time, working in a 2 man centre on my own. It's impossible for one person to do the work of 2, but stupidly I started work at 7.30 in the morning, worked through my breaks and barely stopped for lunch. Eventually I snapped.

What I went through, I can only describe as like being awake during a nightmare. Sometimes before my psychotic episode, (as that was how it was diagnosed) I would have dreadful panic attacks. Going to bed one night I thought I heard next door talking about me. Saying nasty things like, I was only with my boyfriend for the company. I didn't love him. I was pregnant. None of it true of course. Even though the chat went on all night and I didn't get a wink of sleep, I didn't question what I was hearing. I told my mum the next day and she refused to believe me. The next night was the same. I became exhausted.

The next day I started hearing voices in the car on the way to work. I was convinced my car was bugged and took time off work to get it checked out. The mechanic must have thought I was a nut. Still it kept happening. My Chief Typing

Manager began to worry about me and rang to check if I was okay. I had just experienced my first hallucination when she rang. I knew then that things were not quite right. I had been typing when I saw my next door neighbour appear in the seat in front of me. He materialised like something out of Star Trek. I told this to my boss and quite naturally I was sent home.

My mum contacted the doctors for an appointment. In those days you couldn't get an appointment straight away and I had to wait virtually a week to see someone. I had already spent two sleepless nights. I was to spend a further two sleepless nights before I was to receive any attention. I would keep mum awake pacing the floor. She would try to embrace me. A voice in my head told me that if she did I would die, so I would back away. I was convinced someone was out to get me. I'd leave my car keys in another room, believing that they would transmit where I was to my enemies. Sometimes I would get the smell of apples.

I spent a few nights in Wigan with my eldest sister. I took sleeping tablets to help me sleep, but I now thought if I slept I wouldn't wake up, so I fought against their effects and still stayed awake all night. I had my niece's walkman and lay in bed listening to the news. This is where it got really freaky as I had developed ESP and was able to mouth the exact words the newscaster was saying at the same time. I saw a wire in my back and then decided that my boyfriend had planted it there, it was transmitting to my enemies and if I had a shower I would be electrocuted. That was when I began hearing a crackling sound as I entered the room. I convinced myself the floor was live, and if I was left alone in a room I would be electrocuted.

Eventually I was admitted to Fazakerely Hospital on the psychiatric unit in Cedar Ward. Whilst being admitted I sat telling my mum and my sister exactly what my boyfriend and my other sister were discussing approximately two miles up the road. I was later to find out I was spot on.

I was placed in a dorm with other women who had various problems. They tried to calm me and convince me it was OK to go to sleep. The first lot of medication didn't agree with me and I was sleepy all the time. My family would visit and I would shuffle along to go and meet them half asleep. (The medication was affecting my liver and they had to take it off me while they checked my blood and discussed what to give me instead.) I was eventually put on Sulpiride.

Whilst in hospital, just to add to my problems, I developed a 24 hour bug and was throwing up. I had to be sent to bed and given an anti-sickness injection. I fought to get out of that place, some of the people there scared me. We had a guy who was sectioned by the police and brought in, he was very volatile.

Gradually, I was allowed home over a period of time. First for a few hours, then overnight. I hated going back to the hospital. Eventually, I was allowed home for good, to recuperate. My father had been put into respite to allow mum to visit me. He was due home a week after I got home. He never made it. We received a phone call to go to Whiston Hospital where we all waited round for dad to die. I was sent home with one of my sisters as my mum didn't think it was wise for me to hang around.

Although I wasn't getting the voices anymore because of my medication I was extremely tired all the time. I would get up in the afternoon and be asleep again in two hours. I started to suffer from depression. It was really difficult to shrug it off.

Eventually, I began the road of recovery and went for a weekend break to York with my boyfriend. Things didn't seem the same. I didn't feel the same about him, although I felt confused at that time. Shortly after our trip to York he was diagnosed with a brain tumour. He had to go into hospital to have it removed where they then found a shadow on his lung. Six months later my boyfriend died of lung cancer. Even though I didn't feel like we had a future anymore, I was still devastated.

I went in to work to discuss my return to work plan. I was lucky enough to work for a company who recognised that I needed to do things gradually. I returned on reduced hours, building up gradually week after week, until I was working full time again. The problem was that I had acute tiredness and found work difficult. I would be in bed by 8 o'clock. I was off work for 3 months in total. Eventually they reduced my medication and I found I wasn't as tired.

I still had to visit the hospital though, as an outpatient. I would go back twice a year. I was eventually discharged in 2007. I have since run into a few problems though, in trying to get life insurance. It was then that I discovered through an insurance company, that I had been diagnosed with Schizophrenia. I was very angry as I knew I didn't have this. I went back to my doctor and complained. Unfortunately, it meant I had to go back to the hospital to be re-assessed. Thankfully, the doctors agreed with me. Unfortunately though, it appears I can't have it erased from my record but just a note added to say it was wrong. Apparently what I have is called "Acute and Transient Psychotic Disorder". As a result I was told the dose I was taking was only like eating a smartie a day. In fact it was doing nothing. Sometime around October 2009, I was taken off the tablets all together and I now just keep a stock in my medicine cupboard, in case of any further attacks.

Thankfully I have my disorder under control now. I mostly recognise the signs, if not my partner does, so I just take a tablet and speak to a doctor. I have been told to keep away from stressful situations as this is what causes the attacks

I feel that my family have contributed to my stress, and I think that if they had helped me when I needed it as a child my illness may not have happened, or would have been less severe.

I hope that writing this piece and having it published will help me get some kind of closure.

REFLECTION

Janet is still trying to overcome the legacy of abuse as a child. Sharing her experience is cathartic for her, a way to take control. Abuse can of course profoundly damage the psyche, it disorientates - the victim is shaken through the loss of confidence in those they trusted and respected.

Child abuse is all too common it seems, what can you do to overcome its effects?

JENNY: Is it surprising with all that happened to her that she reacted in this way?

It's a similar situation to what we've said for Abacus...

**

For an update on Janet's story see the Epilogue

TRANSITION:

Edinburgh - approaching day zero

 The prospect of nine performances at the Edinburgh Fringe Festival is beginning to feel a little daunting, to say the least. What if!? God! How I hope for an audience! And then… will that have been enough; to have had the opportunity to be heard, to have raised my voice, to have been loaned the stage, to have overcome the fear, as if in freefall, waiting for the parachute to open?

Thank you God for a happy day, please take care of me tomorrow…

This is something I could do. Not quite the Albert Hall but still making a stand, an opportunity to express my point of view. Drinking coffee. Day zero looming. Time for a haircut! After Edinburgh I will look after my body better, and write poems, and finish the book, and love, love ever more deeply. Watching the profile of people passing the dark café, as if I were some kind of creature lurking in a cave, looking out into the brilliant sun.

Later, the newspaper headline: PC faces G20 death trial. The news is that papers have been passed to the Crown Prosecution service. I find myself still shaking slightly, the tremor in my hands, my fingers, eased by a good pint.

Fearing that I might forget my words, but pleased to have found black linen trousers which tie with a cord like a martial arts outfit. Preparing to take on and repel any negative spirits. Now all I need is a black t-shirt. Instead I buy 5 metres of VGA cable, for an LCD projector and a PowerPoint presentation to introduce the show, which in the end I never used.

I guess this experience will correct my misguided vision of success – nothing like an empty theatre to cure a rash dose of optimism! How did I think it would be any different? And all the expense is for what? For the sheer hell of it! The freedom! The life!

Bees on the lavender, making honey outside the Lava Bar by the main road in Tunbridge Wells, while Rome burns. We have measured their plight - what if all the bees die? We die! What can I do that actually makes a difference...?

EDINBURGH

Day 0, Friday 7th August

In the Edinburgh Festival Fringe in 2009, there are 2098 separate shows, 34,265 individual performances playing at 265 different venues. And we're on at the Vault, Annexe (Venue 29, lucky - my parents' house number) for nine shows, two evening previews on the Saturday (8th) and Sunday, then seven afternoon performances at 2pm each day from Monday to Sunday 16th August. I'd chosen the times, 14:00 hours, a lucky number for me - the date of my birthday.

Steve Antoni and I arrive at Waverley station in a mixture of apprehension and excitement. But first what will the flat be like? Carrying our bags and Steve's guitar up the steep stone steps to Princes Street, we walk rather than forking out for a cab, it isn't far. Anyway, Princes Street is fenced off for the length of the gardens, it's a construction site, preparing the way for the Tram. I wanted to be central, to be able to walk to the venue, not to have to rely on transport to get us there on time for curtain up each day.

We leave the fantastic view of the castle on the mound and head for Rose Street. Lots of pubs, bars, restaurants and buskers - it's a busy quarter of town. A few hundred yards and we're there. The door to the bare stairwell is standing open, we climb flight upon flight of stone steps, a mattress stuffed on one side. The cold, dark, grubby stairway feels like a terrible mistake, but behind the double locks to the top floor, front door, resides a comfortable, relaxing two bed apartment in the sloping roof space, roof-lights opening out across rooftop views. The room furnished with dark leather armchairs, decorated with ornaments from the thirties.

All at once it's nearly midnight, bordering the first day of the performance. We've had our get-in. Rediscovering the place was terrifying, not remembering the venue very clearly from two years before, not really knowing what to expect, doubting my choice, my decision.

As we negotiate our way over King George IV bridge and down Candlemaker Row, it feels like a backwater, as if no one could possibly find their way there. There's no sign for the venue. The Vault, Annexe, is tucked away in Merchant Street, the other side of a dark bridge, or underpass, off Candlemaker Row, past Merchants' restaurant with its red doors, in a dead end, beside a collection of commercial waste bins, opposite the seemingly empty Irish pub. A place where refuse vehicles turn, the sound of glass cullet being collected, and in the middle of a performance too!

Her long hair and her skirt blowing in the wind as she waits beside the kerb for her man...

At first, the venue is like an untidy garage: a concrete square of a stage about four paces deep by four paces wide. No backdrop, vaguely organised chaos, mayhem, but run by people committed to making a success out of the experience including those who seem to be volunteers. I'd taken a gamble having not actually seen this part of the venue before - it was the first year for the Annexe.

So, with one of the Directors and kind technicians from Paradise Green taking us through every step, everything needed for the set up, the warm wash, the spots on each mike, each position. Steve Antoni had his mike stage right, with me on centre mike for the main script, and then taking a mike stage left for the poems. This third mike was space solely for my poems learnt by heart. The idea was to create some imaginative as well as physical distance from the narrative centre stage while emphasising the strength of the narrator. These differing dynamics are like the effect of studying different points of view in NLP - looking at a psychological situation from physically different positions. Setting the mike levels, SM 58s, industry standard...we're reassured.

Afterwards a chance to chill, to take it all in at Maxies Bistro and Bar, high on the terrace, overlooking Victoria Street and Grassmarket, the rooftops, and the Hogwarts castle-like, George Heriot's school. There is the sound of rubber beating cobblestones as cars drive up West Bow. The kitchen blowing its heat over us, the downdraught from the fans, billowing grilled steak smoke out of the window, warming but almost suffocating at times, lager, wine, whisky, lager. And the live sounds of Edinburgh at night, as we head back to the flat, negotiating a Meat Loaf impersonator, singing outside a bar in Rose Street.

Returning to the flat we feel safe, cosy, in spite of, or because of, the night-sounds of singing and shouting, of bottles smashing, of seagulls disturbed.

Because there is more to a hand job than simply the rhythm...

Lying awake I ask myself again, what is it I want to say? It's written in the poems and the play. And yes, I guess it is a journey. I'm still looking for the answers. I think part of it is finding them here in this experience, as if I am putting my life on the line. Not literally, but psychologically.

Asylum: 'a place of safety...'

12 - HIGH PAT ON THE HORSE

Or Pat the Donkey. Moving from Hands in Clouds through Single Whip, this is a short move, both hands making a circle over the left knee as it is raised then lowered, as if in a prelude to a small kick.

This move is a reminder of our companion, the horse. In this case an almost untamed spirit, learning through cruel life experiences. This, almost playful move, is one of transition in preparation for the subsequent change, the big kick. For Jane, it was the beginning of three months of sabbatical, of transition, before perhaps, heading out in a new direction.

Jane

What's your experience of mental ill-health?

Well, lately I've had quite a lot of experience with it: I've spent a stint in the Priory in North London; I've been under the care of a psychiatrist and a clinical psychologist; I've had CBT therapy and I've been to South Africa to spend time in an addiction clinic!

How did you end up in the Priory?

I guess it was from suffering depression related to one particular event which led me there. Really out of desperation, I did a very stupid thing - I took an overdose and ended up in A&E and subsequently got put in the Priory. I had about 8 months with depression before the Priory (it had started last January). It was mainly about the issues I had with myself, and my ability to do my job. I always questioned myself and compared myself against everyone else and just didn't feel I was good enough. I'm a perfectionist and I wanted to be the best in my job and in my team and I constantly put myself under a lot of stress. Although the office is a very stressful environment anyway, so I didn't need to add to it. I found myself working quite long hours and not sleeping, just generally neglecting myself and worrying all the time about work.

In the end I went to see my doctor who signed me off with stress for a week and referred me to a psychiatrist who recommended that I'd benefit from Cognitive Behavioural Therapy, CBT. So I had six sessions doing that and I found it unhelpful, but I think that was more because of the lack of rapport with my therapist. I don't think she got me and I certainly didn't get her, and I do think that how good therapy is very much depends on what psychologist you have. I've also had different reports from different psychiatrists on what diagnosis they would give. One says I suffer from the disease of addiction while the other one says I don't and that it's just a lack of self-confidence, general depressive episodes to do with myself, but not addiction. I might have obsessive propensities such as going to the gym all the time and things like that, so I might suffer from extremes, but I'm not sure it's addiction. Maybe I'm in denial.

So I'd been doing therapy for a while but stopped that and continued working and feeling very down, often crying before I went to work on my partner who I was living with, and often getting home late, very despondent. Then in March last year... we had a great relationship, it seemed, there didn't seem to be any issues at all; I was aware that I wasn't happy in that time but he seemed to be very supportive, he said he'd pay for my therapy. I turned thirty. Two weeks before we split up he bought me this (diamond) necklace and then the week after, he turned round and said he wasn't happy. It was the first I knew of it. We'd planned to get married and have a family - we were properly planning our future together. I felt like I'd been massively led up the garden path – but it was such a clean break.

He literally went back to his parents' for five days to make his decision, came back to break the news to me and left me in utter devastation. The following week he came back to collect all his clothes and stuff when I wasn't there and I didn't hear from him for 9 months...it was brutal - you spend every night with someone, wake up with them...I guess I went through a bit of a bereavement process...

When did that relationship end?

13th March 2009. My birthday was on the 1st March. So, he'd done a surprise party for me, bought the necklace, took me away for the weekend, and the week after we'd had a great week. On the 8th we had a bit of an argument and he said he wasn't happy. He went off to his parents and came back on Friday 13th when we broke up. In my eyes you work these things out. He was saying he was still in love with me but couldn't see us working forever. He said - which I think is so harsh - that I was from a divorced family, so I was more likely to be a divorcee myself...a statistic...

For the next 9 months I didn't take a day off work. Whether my attendance at work was any good to anyone, probably not, I was often very late. I wasn't eating, I lost a lot of weight

…getting pissed almost every night, not sleeping and that's what resulted in my breakdown and overdose. I'd often get so drunk just so I could sleep and not think about it, I'd pass out but wake up religiously between 2 and 4 in the morning just lying there and I would never go back to sleep I might drift off for an hour before I woke up and then I just felt horrific. On one of those nights I allowed myself to think about suicide. The more I thought about it, the more attractive the option seemed …That's why I can't even allow myself to enter into those suicidal thoughts now…

Were you drunk at the time?

Well yes, I got in pissed and passed out, woke up about two, tossing and turning for 2 hours but thinking, contemplating…I knew I had enough medication and enough bottles of spirit so that's what I did. I was gagging and I was making all sorts of concoctions of vodka with a lot of paracetamol and sleeping pills. And that's what brought me into the Priory.

So the fact that you had all those spirits probably saved you, made you sick did it?

No it didn't, basically nothing was happening, I was so scared. I sat on the sofa and waited for myself to lose consciousness. I was crying with it. When I was drinking a lot there was a gag reflex but I was looking at photos of my family, my brother my sister, my Mum. And there's one photo of me and my sister and I thought fuck! Fuck! What have I done? I crawled to my neighbour in the flat next door. Her door's always open, she could obviously hear me really crying and this was about half five in the morning and she called an ambulance …so I ended up in A&E

Had you ever had a similar experience before going to the Priory? Had you ever thought about suicide before the end of the relationship? Had depression or been on any medication?

I'd never been on any anti-depressants before March 2009. I was often quite troubled as a teenager but more because of my parents' divorce. It was a particularly nasty divorce. I had an awful argument with my Mum and I smashed the window to try and jump out of it, but I don't think I would've done. It was dramatic effect really, but I cut my arm quite badly.

You mentioned about your hemiplegia and you'd said that's affected your body image and your day to day persona. Do you want to say a bit more about that?

It's basically a birth injury, a weakness in the right hand side of my body. I look perfectly normal to everyone else but I do things quite differently. People often raise their eyes and make assumptions. I always worry about what other people think, it does bother me - half of me wants to tell them that I have it so they don't continue to judge me as if I'm drunk or just clumsy. But then I know if I tell them about it they'll look for it even more, so I always struggle how to tell people for the first time. It's become more of an issue in my working life, being in a professional environment, even if it's a simple handshake I struggle to do that with any authority and it's very much about first impressions…

Psychologically it's really affected me. Physically it's affected me on a day to day basis but I work around it. Obviously there are certain things I can't do like drive a manual car, I've had to learn an automatic. But I have adapted a lot. I've never been able to learn how to ice skate, balance is a real issue.

And you're a perfectionist?

Ironically one of my real dreams is of being a professional gymnast, an athlete, or a dancer. I don't know why that is. Is it because I can't do those things? But being a perfectionist, it's really hard to deal with it because I know, I'm like 'damaged goods'. I'm not kind to myself. Probably a lot of people are very kind to me and admire me for what I have achieved, but I'm a bully an absolute bully to myself.

And you've had to live with yourself being a bully? is it something you've ever had any help for?

In my childhood I've had lots of physiotherapy and several operations on my leg. I had all the support in terms of everything physically to give me the best chance, but I didn't get any psychological support. Hindsight's a fantastic thing, but perhaps my mother's approach wasn't the best way because of all the psychological issues I have now. She thought I should just hide it. My dad just mollycoddled me, which didn't help.

How would you describe the psychological issues that you have now?

The problem is that now I think I've lost my identity. I had it all mapped out. I had my life planned with F. I wasn't very happy in my job, but after another year I was planning to get married and have children and go and work in a smaller high street firm that was less pressurised. I am good at what I do and it pays well...maybe that would've suited me better than a large city firm.

F can no longer be the focus that he was when my career was secondary. Now my career is the focus and ultimately I haven't been very happy in my job and that's made me more depressed - I don't feel as if I have any purpose any more. The reason my career doesn't work for me is the culture of no praise. If you do a good job it's not acknowledged. If you do a bad job you're soon told about it. So that's also consolidated the depression because I'm working and not getting recognised for it and this only confirms my belief that I can't do it.

So I think the depression revolves around my loss of identity. I don't really like myself at the moment because everything I've worked so hard to achieve is all falling apart around me. If law really isn't for me then I need to be making some headway to find what I really want to do career-wise.

And you've got time to think about that now in your sabbatical?

Yes, I have three months sabbatical, and I signed up for this writing course only a week ago. This is my first week of leave. But obviously with depressives I know I could potentially waste all that time. If I drink, the insomnia and all that shit... I know I need to be completely productive with my time. This week has been quite difficult it's been the perfect environment to do nothing. I've resisted so hard the temptation to put my 3G on my laptop and check up on my emails because I know there will be so much to go back to.

I really want to get my sleep back. Sleep is absolutely crucial. I think lack of sleep led me to do what I did, because I was so tired, surviving on two to four hours sleep a night, not proper sleep. I think I have a better perspective at the moment because I've managed to sleep while I've been here.

Do you think the writing's helped you?

Yes it has, when I've been able to engage my mind. My concentration is absolutely shite! That's something I've never had to struggle with before - I've always been so focused and so hard working. I hate not being able to commit and focus – it is not me. But when I can focus and get into something it really helps. But, as you know, it's hard to stay on that line of concentration. I'm really grateful to Carole SJ because she's been so encouraging.

Any message you'd like to give to crystallise where you're at or where you hope to be?

Nothing is forever. Where I've gone wrong over the last five years is that I've devoted myself to someone else and I've been co-dependent - a carer who wants to make everyone happy. I absolutely devoted myself to him, when he'd gone I had no identity. So now I'm very cautious. I need to have hobbies for myself; I need to know what my passions are and what I want to achieve.

If a man does come a long and they make me happy, great, but I need to be in a happy place. And that's what I'm doing now, exploring the things that do make me happy. In my mind it would be a failure if I were to change from being a lawyer; I'd let down my mum and dad who are so proud of me. Perhaps it's now time to give that up and to focus on fulfilling my life - it's not about being loved by everyone. This time is for working out what I really am passionate about such as writing but also possibly helping others through psychotherapy.

I am confused. I have a real problem of letting go of my career as a lawyer – I've worked so hard to get there and I'd think myself a failure if I gave it up. But perhaps I should be true with myself, and kind and stop pushing myself. I then think about other options/careers. One minute it's teaching, the next a psychotherapist, or a nutritionist, then a writer, an entrepreneur. I don't know what would make me happy. I have lost my passion – I blame the medication. I just don't feel me anymore.

How are you going to get over the negativity with your bullying self, is it a case of making friends with your other half?

It's a case of being positive about it. I try so hard but it seems impossible. I think it's the way I am naturally tuned. I have high expectations, which sadly means that nothing will ever be good enough.

Any other parting thoughts?

I'm desperate to get off the medication... I'm on fluoxidine 20 mgs anti- depressant and in the evening 100 mgs trazadone...

REFLECTION

Jane has shared her open cry for help in fighting her demons. We have come to know that the fracture of a close, loving relationship has been profound. And yet has been doubly significant because of her shaken self-image and lack of confidence. It's frightening how much damage we can inflict on ourselves without realising.

How much of ourselves do we project onto other people and how do we overcome excessive dependency on those we love?

JENNY: Big question! We project an awful lot of ourselves on others and until we recognise that's what we're doing we go on doing it. That's where psychotherapy can come in useful.

How do we overcome excessive dependency on those we love? Very often people who've got problems of one sort or another find people with similar problems and it can become quite a destructive symbiotic relationship. It's almost like a see-saw - when one's up the other's down, and vice versa each feeding into the other's weakness. And then if one gets strong the other can't cope with it because it's not the same sort of relationship, it's not a needy relationship...It's very common, when people are low or poorly (and you see this in hospitals) they'll strike up relationship with another poorly person. One might then recover while the other is still poorly and it can cause havoc because everything changes.

Everyone's hurting, all the people in this book, they're all hurting. It's frightening how much damage we can do ourselves. Most people hurt at some point in their life, it's very rare to find someone that's been able to shrug off all the hurt in life. All of us, to whatever extent, can hurt on occasions, feel fragile and maybe have self-confidence or self-esteem eroded.

Have you heard of Tim Knott? He's quite a well-known radio broadcaster who became psychotic when younger and he writes in one of his books something like 'life is chaotic, it's never going to be smooth, and the chaos can be manifested in all sorts of different ways.' His mother hung herself, but he became ill before she did that...And those who are supersensitive are going to feel it more than others.

It seems to me that there are two crosses that intelligent, sensitive people have to bear and they are just that: intelligence and sensitivity. We have to learn how to deal with them and how to manage ourselves, knowing we're always going to think deeply, to feel deeply...But the other side of this is, like you with your poetry, you can feel good things deeply as well, and fully appreciate beautiful things...

Sometimes I imagine a whole new continent of loving...

TRANSITION:

Edinburgh Day 1, Saturday 8th August, 2009

 Morning. Today's the day. Breakfast out at Gastronomic Grub...leaflets and posters for other shows on display. I chose not to have the expense of paying others to distribute leaflets beforehand, except for some of the main fringe venues in London. Instead I paid to have a 'button' on the Fringe website for people to click-through to my micro-site and the booking page.

I take a walk, while Steve Antoni practices the songs. There's a guy with an electric guitar and backing music playing outside the flat. I make it to the Royal Mile, there's a sea of people giving and accepting flyers. Those first few words 'Can I interest you in An Acute Psychotic Episode?' somehow don't seem quite right! But my postcard flyer's great – at least as good as any other. I make it to Fringe Central, which doesn't feel central at all. Erin, a Press Officer, is delightful as she interviews me, coolly, calmly, sensitively, bringing out what the show's about for the press...part of my journey.

I resolve to stay on for the Meet the Media at 2pm. I get to see the Scotsman and leave my details, they say they'll aim to write a review and will contact me. Later, I meet Liz from the station. Only a few hours before we're on. We have a light meal. The show is on at 8.30; we get in at eight. Liz, acting for the first night as technician, has no trouble sensing the tension, as she says, feeling for us – 'like being a parent at their child's school play'.

You're my pride and joy, et cetera… (Elenore, The Turtles)

Difficult to describe those first few moments before the show begins: standing in Tai Chi plimsolls on bare concrete…No going back as the audience of complete strangers builds one by one from the door behind the last row of seats; and saying 'Welcome' as a way of breaking the ice, inviting them in. The first night: a dozen. And a dozen is enough! Those moments when I try to remind myself why I'm doing this but I'm too close to fear to know the answer.

It is time - a move has to be made. So I move to stand with my back to the audience, while Dad's introduction plays across the PA, and I stretch, not having to try too hard to give the impression of someone under tension.

And so the show begins to an audio recording of my Dad, setting the scene:

> *"Testing…testing…one…two…three…O.K.?*

> *Hello. I'm Ted Walter, Steve's Dad. I'd be a kind of warm up man if I was here with you. As it is I'm just a warm up voice. But knowing what you will be hearing shortly I wanted to make a couple of observations.*

> *Firstly, the journey Steve is going to describe was never a descent. He slowly climbed higher into a world that his mother and me took pretty much for granted because of his enthusiasm. He would book the Albert Hall in which to celebrate the Millennium….Fine. He'd clearly got the energy and*

the vision. But it did not happen. Then on the evening of a poetry Slam performance I knew that he had moved well away from my familiar world. That was the first 'breakdown', a good chunk of that experience you will be sharing soon.

Secondly, the second time Steve entered that alternative world, my wife and I were much more closely involved, having to care for Steve overnight while waiting for a bed in the unit he had been to before. We were taken into his reality and I, in my rather smaller 5'6" frame, had to somehow manhandle him back to quiet, as I refer to in my poem 'The Burren[fta]*.*

So; enough from me. If this is being played then there must be someone here. Steve came through his experiences and is here to tell you how it was. That makes this a very positive event. It eases the terror of An Acute Psychotic Episode to recognise that he was there but he is now here, well, and able to report he's well and I thank him for the reassurance, and for the opportunity to introduce you now to my eldest son, Steve Walter…"

Then turning at the mention of my name, moving into warm-up exercises and into Tai Chi, as I was in Brighton. Moving from Holding Ball to Parting Horse Mane to Showing the Wing, accompanied by Steve Antoni playing *The Lunatic is on the Grass*, from Pink Floyd's *Brain Damage*…

Interspersed throughout the narrative Steve sings *Small Blue Thing* by Suzanne Vega, and plays the *Bookends* theme by Simon and Garfunkel, then *After the Gold Rush* by Neil Young, Steve's own song *In Your Dying* (about discovering his brother-in-law dying on the kitchen floor having committed suicide) and Steve's upbeat finale *Lifeline*.

And I recite: In place of silence; Teabag in a wineglass; Alive; Corpus Christi; Asylum; The laying of hands; Biology practical; Washing up and we play Dad's recording of The Burren [fta] and together close with the pair of us reciting Prayer on Ward 10.

Connect with all sentient beings…

13 - KICK WITH RIGHT HEEL

From High Pat on the Horse straight into a big kick with the right leg: raising the leg smoothly, horizontal, or higher if you can, pushing out the heel, holding briefly, then stepping forward into the next move - Boxing Ears.

One of the more obvious martial arts moves, this kick to the side, reminding me of my kick to the door of the hospital, breaking out, breaking free, early one summer's morning[fta].

This is the first real test of balance, and a powerful move. Jonathan took on the world and founded the first charity to bring together those with mental health problems in the name of eradicating stigma. As well as running the charity, of course, he has his own health to manage.

Jonathan Naess, founder, Stand to Reason

How would you describe your experience of mental ill health?

I had my awareness of mental health thrust upon me! I had no knowledge of manic depression at all. So when it was referred to as a diagnosis I was very sceptical. I thought manic depression meant being extremely depressed but because I'd been experiencing an exuberant life I didn't see myself as having been depressed at all! So I thought manic depression was a misdiagnosis. I now much prefer the term bipolar.

What were the circumstances of your first experience?

I was training as a psychoanalyst. In Psychoanalysis the injunction is to free associate - anything goes. As I was becoming increasingly manic I was associating more freely and thought I was really getting the hang of it - I was able to make interpretations easily. This deep personal work may have been a trigger for my breakdown. So I've been cautious about doing such work ever since.

I was in my early 20s, a recent graduate, and it was a very horrific experience. I was physically restrained several times. When I came out of hospital I was determined to see it as a blip, not something for the rest of my life. I didn't find out about manic depression much at the time. To say I under identified with the diagnosis would itself be an understatement. When I left hospital I chucked my medicines away as I walked round the corner. A rather brutal senior nurse had said most of our customers come back sooner or later, and usually sooner. I thought I'd get as far away as possible. In a few weeks I'd gone back to Spain living with my girlfriend (now my wife) and started working, and she helped me to recover. Although I didn't realise it at the time, work helped me get better.

The second time I got ill I realised there was a pattern emerging and that I had to take on board that I had an illness. So it was more than 10 years afterwards that I had my second breakdown. I had a stressful job in the city, and the obvious culprit to blame was the stress in the job. When I left hospital and went back home I was really unsure as to whether I could work again. I could see my life falling apart.

It felt like, if I lost the job I'd lose my house and marriage and end up on a park bench.

But actually what happened was that I was able to negotiate a return to work, and for the second time I realised that work was a key part of getting better. Both times I was in hospital I found that a lot of socially excluded people are in there, with fewer resources than I had, and very noticeable in terms of numbers of people visiting and the lack of flowers. I was described as being a ship that passes in the night by a psychiatrist. He examined me while I was going through a tribunal to have my section over turned, as it happened successfully. I felt if only I could do something...that was when I made the decision to try to help people with mental health problems. I didn't feel I was treated fairly or properly in hospital. It seemed to me that people with fewer resources would get stuck there, raging against the system, in the way that they shouldn't. Having been back there again recently and seen some of the same people still there in a much worse, drugged up, condition is awful.

Before my latest breakdown, through talking to people who were activists in the service user movement, I learnt that recovery is an ongoing process even when 'well'. I also learnt to see mental wellbeing as an evolving process. In all honesty, having recently come out of hospital for the third time, my self confidence and self efficacy is much lower than it would be when I'm well and I have to have a certain amount of faith that I will continue to get better in the way that I have done previously. It's only a couple of months now since I was last admitted to hospital.

The previous time I was unwell I remember taking 9-10 months getting my confidence back to normal and recovering from my cognitive deficit, particularly the loss of short-term memory; although it's difficult to separate confidence from memory because the two go hand in hand.

Does 'treading on eggshells' resonate with you in terms of mental health?

Treading on eggshells has a resonance with me as it was a phrase my mother used to describe relating to me when in a manic phase. It was one symptom I wasn't able to acknowledge. In hospital I acknowledged them all, even grandiosity, but irritability was the one I wouldn't accept. My wife and family strongly identify with that symptom. Particularly in the manic phase - when I feel good - I'm less understanding of other peoples' needs and the way they need to take time to catch up with how I'm thinking.

I think now having a bit of humility regarding my irritability has opened up an opportunity to improve my personal relationships. But it's painful and very frustrating to think that people have to tread on eggshells with you. It opens up the question how much mental illness is personality and how much the illness itself. At times one feels huge frustration because you want people to see you rather than the illness but, by the same token, there are other times when you'd want the people you love around you to understand that things have happened because you're unwell. So, a real fear of trying to have your cake and eat it at the same time.

When I was struggling with anxiety and depression last year before this latest episode, I kept on asking myself whether I'd made a recovery, I still felt wobbly. It felt as though I was walking on sinking sand. I couldn't rely on the recovery that I'd made. I felt wobbly as if my legs wouldn't hold me up. My recovery was fragile. I felt great disappointment and frustration that progress was slow and that I had new symptoms I wasn't accustomed to, and I had to learn how to deal with them. I'd come to terms with the sense of stigma in having bipolar disorder, from the first time I was in hospital, by sharing my experiences with other people with bipolar (and going on to find a charity to tackle the stigma associated with mental illness). But I still found myself stigmatised, weak and vulnerable and full of self-loathing because of being unable to deal with my problems which were the apparent cause of my depression, in a more grown up way. And I'm still unsure, at the time of this interview, whether I've let myself down and failed by being ill for so long.

My challenge is to find forgiveness in myself, to find acceptance for my condition even as it changes and new symptoms appear, like anxiety. In a way it feels like a new start, a new beginning. A true understanding of recovery is that it's an ongoing process, and while challenge has been a useful spur to recovery, I think I also need to be more kind and understanding of myself. It's important to see mental illness as a no-fault illness, it's very empowering...but it's one thing thinking it compared with knowing it in your gut.

What message do you have for people who are partners, relations, or other carers for people with mental ill health?

I think there's scope for similar work as Stand to Reason does with employers. Tackling stigma is another word for education, since stigma is made up of ignorance, prejudice and discrimination. So the interventions we hope to provide in Stand to Reason can best be described as education rather than tackling stigma. When it comes to relationships between people with mental illness and their partners, there can be a lot of fear and misunderstanding on both sides and in relation to the illness. And commonly people who attend self-help groups, where they could bring their partners, will not do so because they don't feel they could possibly do so.

I think it would be wonderful if there were more carers' groups where carers and people with mental health problems could work together to break down fear and misunderstandings that commonly exist between couples or parents and children or friends. And instead of just having separate carers and service users groups it would be good to bring them together.

There's an analogy here with the work Stand to Reason does with employers and employees; most of our work is about getting them together. Perhaps this will be an area for Stand to Reason to work with in future.

What message do you have for the government?

I think my main message would be to continue supporting the move to let people with mental illness have say and control over the decisions that affect them, particularly in terms of the services provided.

REFLECTION

Jonathan continues to wrestle with his bipolar disorder and the toll it has taken on his home life. And yet he has been a visionary, inspiring others to come together, to stand in solidarity in mental health and to help bury stigma.

What would you say to people who wish to present a united front to help tackle stigma?

JENNY: it is so difficult because people are scared of difference they don't want to see difference or hear it. They want everything in the garden to be lovely and they want to hide away everything that isn't nice.

It can be over done, sometimes gay people over do it to present a front …I think what you're doing is great, out there…saying that actually we're all just people, everybody has a hiccup in life, but perhaps through good fortune, it doesn't turn into an illness.

My advice is to keep trying to spread the message in whatever way you can without over doing it…

What do you think of Mad Pride?

JENNY: I think that anything that educates people and helps them to understand that people who have psychological differences aren't frightening they're just going through a difficult time is a good thing…I don't mind what people do as long as they're not hurting anybody…

What we're really looking for is acceptance – yes, that we are different, that there's no two people the same…difference I think is the big problem with stigma…

TRANSITION:

Edinburgh Day 2, Sunday 9th August, 2009

We wake early enough to go to see Sylvia Plath's Three Women, round the corner at 11'o'clock, at the Assembly in George Street. We bump into Simon, the Finance Director where I used to work, on his last day in Edinburgh, and also two who came to the show last night, both Community Psychiatric nurses. We hand out some flyers, everyone very reflective after Plath, powerful performances. I guess you could say in a marketing sense that they were warm leads! Then we're off to the Iris restaurant in Thistle Street, for a delightful, classy lunch with two bottles of Rioja (El Coto, the Red Deer Stag). Afterwards we have free tickets, making up places for The Sociable Plover, very entertaining and again brilliantly acted. Neros for a cappuccino then a chance to chill with the web and writing up notes while Liz walks round the craft exhibition at a nearby venue; St John's church.

This evening we have the largest audience of some 30 people.

Day 3, Monday 10th

Even on waking it's there – the slight signalling of nerves, the build up to the 2'o' clock matinee performance. But already nearly a third of the way there! A couple from my old drama group Actor Sharers and their 12 year old son (will the show be ok for him?) are coming along, having been staying with friends in Newcastle. They all seem to really enjoy the show. It took them a while to find the venue, as I feared. But we meet just beforehand at the Under the Stairs bar: dimmed lighting, cosy upholstery, perhaps a little drink, perfect to steady the nerves, first choice pitta bread and dips. Gradually increasing our alcohol and food intake before the show during the week. Afterwards we chill out at the Oz bar at the end of the street, in a blaze of sunshine.

At five-ish we watch Kataklo Athletic Theatre's 'Love Machines'. I have to admit I was attracted by the suggestive nature of the publicity but, unfortunately, the show didn't live up to all the semi-naked elegance of da Vinci that the posters suggested "performers dazzle with their beauty and grace" – interesting yes, but not moving, nor passionate.

There is still the apprehension, the fear which increases in the hours and minutes closer to the show. Last night a giggle from the audience at the beginning set me wondering was I going to lose it, lose them? But they came round, included a psychiatric student in his first year. (I think it was him who afterwards warned me about Lithium toxicity, my hands shaking with the script, which others, including a reviewer, had taken as being nerves). Four books sold, like the night before. Luke did great on the lights fading down and spotlighting the poems. Except almost too bright for the centre mike, unable to see the audience, when I want to. Tall Luke Meredith, with his ginger tache and an edge of being gay. We watch his show Dragged, Kicked and Screaming, a wild wacky, and even madder experience..!

She's wearing a little red coat, which reaches up high on her neck, princess…

14 - BOXING EARS

From the Right Kick with the Heel bring your hands together behind your back then swing them round at head height together as fists to box your opponent's ears with both sets of knuckles.

This is a distinctive martial arts move - fitting for a former member of the armed forces.

Matthew

I have known Matthew (not his real name) on and off for many years. I'm delighted that he's been prepared to share his story of bullying and harassment at work. He's a tough, fighting man, competing in triathlons, having first worked in the RAF. Here he describes how his personality was affected as a result of the behaviour of his boss, and his boss's boss, at work in civilian life.

How pressure and stress affect people in different ways - fight or flight. Matthew describes wrestling with his demons, struggling to resist the temptation to beat the living shit out of his pompous bullying manager.

An anonymous story of the impact of bullying at work

I now see how bullying and stress affects people in certain ways. In terms of the way it started to affect me I had always been a highly competitive individual and demanded a huge amount of myself and my career, being successful in all that I do, like competing in triathlons. Up until the problems started occurring, everything I'd done before I'd been successful at: university, sport to a professional level – I could have probably played professional football, cricket (for Lancashire), and squash.

For my first job I trained as a helicopter pilot. I went through officer training, and survival courses but had to come out after 2 years because I got a stress fracture of my right arm (which had been broken three times before). So I was downgraded and I chose to come out. I ended up with a public affairs job for a small trade body in 1990. Gradually, because they were a small organisation, I had an early opportunity to do all their PR & became No2 to the Chief Executive. By the mid 90s I'd been there 5 years. Up until then everything had been a success! In the mid 90s I was headhunted to do a public affairs role for a large PLC. When I started I knew on the first day that I'd made a big mistake - there was no real job. The lady I was reporting to didn't particularly want me there. I soon wondered how I was going to pass 7 hours in the day... it became very difficult, so quickly I started looking for other jobs.

I found one with another other big industrial company in Manchester, doing their PR, working with all the major car companies, and their markets in Europe and the States, which involved constant travel. There was at least one European trip per week...very long days. It was a fantastic job, I got to see all the major car plants, and had some time to myself. Although, partly because of what happened in my previous role, the relationship I'd been in fell apart. I moved to Manchester in May 96. Then, just as I got settled the company was taken over (in early '97) by an American company and they closed the corporate function and I lost my job. So, in 18 months I'd gone from everything being excellent with job in the South, moving to a third and losing it. At the time I thought it wasn't a problem, but looking back it was probably the start of a huge period of the rug being pulled from under my feet.

Having lost the job in Manchester I got my current job and felt that I'd landed on my feet. But I soon realised that I'd ended up working for a couple of psychopaths! Overall in the building there was always a very threatening atmosphere and a massive blame culture. The management concerned always adopted a constantly threatening, aggressive, bullying attitude to staff at all levels. The other senior staff were performing a combination of either keeping their heads down or were plain scared by those two individuals. It was very clear that my boss had a pattern of behaviour towards his staff on a more or less daily basis of bullying and harassment. It began to affect me very quickly - there was constant criticism of my work to the extent that I doubted whether I could string two words together. I would draft a press release and he'd ask me in for a word and it would be covered in blue ink with whole sections crossed out and picked apart, not in a constructive way, but as if I didn't have a fucking clue what I was doing. And if I had a difference of opinion, I'd get volley of abuse 'Who are you to question me - I'm the director!' he'd say.

This was constant behaviour from early on. I take the view that if you only witnessed this occasionally, or if you were in another part of the building and only visited periodically then you wouldn't see the full effect of it, but when it happens every day, constantly, it begins to feel like being mentally punished all of the time. I began to question whether I could do my job and it began to affect the way I operated. It was easiest to keep my head down and do nothing…so I'd stop doing the job properly, I'd be less proactive, no way would I put a quote in any one senior's name. The answer was to do nothing, to avoid getting a bollocking for doing my job. This happened over a period of time.

Very quickly after moving back down South I met someone and got engaged. Everything was fine for a year but, and I guess it was a combination of how I was changing as an individual, my confidence was shot to bits. I'd gone from having a successful career, to feeling that I couldn't do my job...career wise I felt everything was falling apart because of the two times when things had not worked out in the previous year.

It got to the point when I was constantly on amber alert everyday. I was just waiting for something, even the smallest thing, and the red mist would come down on me, not fear but scared that because I hated him so much I'd hit him and wouldn't stop hitting him. I'd be on edge all day, everyday. I started in April '97, but this change didn't happen overnight. The first time I noticed it was the summer of '99, it took just over two years to come to a head. I remember quite distinctly the first time I realised there was a problem. I'd gone for an interview and for some reason I was really apprehensive about it and had wondered whether to cancel it or not. I was walking to the company in the morning and was overcome with a massive sense of fear and I said I couldn't do it. I cancelled and walked back to the tube and got a coffee and was in absolute bits & crying - I had an overwhelming sense of fear, of panic, that's how it was. I learnt later it was to do with the fight or flight syndrome.

Then about six or seven weeks later another job interview came up. It'd been arranged for me to fly out the eve before...and in the run up I became really apprehensive. At the airport the same thing happened, I became terribly hot, started sweating, terrified...and that's when I knew there was a problem. It had also started affecting my relationship. I would fly off the handle so easily. My fiancé had moved to Kent for a new job. I'd begun to avoid certain situations - I would avoid meetings at work or going to parties, I would rather stay at home. It was towards mid to late '99 that I knew there was a problem.

If I consider my background: I'd always thought I was mentally quite tough and then all of a sudden to be in a position when I thought my career had fallen apart, my engagement had broken down and to find I was too scared to go for a job interview! Over a period of time the legs on the stool were just gradually pulled away.

I'd read stuff about panic attacks, fight or flight, stress... I'd always been close to my parents and family but I found I was arguing over the most trivial things, things that would never have bothered me before but because I was constantly up tight I would fly off the handle at the smallest thing...

Then there were a couple of changes - my boss got the sack. I was still in touch with my former girlfriend who worked in HR and offered counselling to those made redundant. I told her how I was feeling and she offered to have a word with her contact. I went to see her and relayed my story and she arranged for me to have some sessions with a counsellor. When I told the counsellor what had happened she explained the fight or flight syndrome, and symptoms, and said that this could happen from three or four things happening simultaneously or over time. She said I'd be amazed at the seniority of those who go to see her – their fall is so great when come off their pedestal, their status would plummet. Over a period of time I'd also fallen a huge distance from a very successful career to a point when I couldn't string two sentences together, and my relationships had fallen apart. Something between my ears had just gone bang. Seeing her for a few sessions helped, my boss not being there helped, his boss moving on also helped. The new boss lead to a better atmosphere, touch wood things are fine now.

At the worst time in '99 I had some very dark thoughts...I felt suicidal...on two occasions.

As for my boss's boss I remember on one occasion a BBC producer came into interview him. He said to the interviewer 'You have 5 minutes to set up your gear or you can fuck off!' I remember that quite distinctly and the producer said to me 'How can you work for a f-ing bastard like that?'. And I remember a colleague who did some slides for him and he came marching down and laid into her in front of everybody, bringing her to tears. My boss would do the same thing in open office. My colleague and others had made complaints about my boss but nothing had been done about it. He destroyed another colleague...He would be full of bonhomie with other people, he could be very charming, but when nobody else was around he was just off the scale. Gradually more people became aware and eventually he was sacked.

I feel that personally and professionally I lost three years of my life...from 97 to 2000 which I'll never get back.

Partly because I kept my head down and kept things to myself. Our personnel manager would talk to me about it as if I'd have an objective view...but if they knew how I was feeling they wouldn't have felt that I was putting on a face - underneath it was exactly the opposite.

I now realise that, even though I thought I was mentally strong, the brain is like a muscle and it can be damaged and it can happen to anybody.

I went through 9 months of officer training where you would be bullied as part of the training and I got used to it, so I had learnt to cope with it... I was trying to handle it in the same way. Normally I have a long fuse, normally most things don't bother me but with him even really trivial things assumed massive importance and became a real issue.

I'm now far more cautious when I'm dealing with people. It takes me awhile before I'll trust people, and it was sometime before I let my guard down and was prepared to start a new relationship. My engagement had broken down in '98/'99 and it took six years before I could start a new relationship, whereas before I was far less reserved.

Someone said to me of my boss's boss, 'He's the 'only person I've ever met who I could sit and watch be tortured...' I wouldn't go that far, but close to it.

I wouldn't want to go through the experience again, some of the lessons might sound a bit shallow but looking back on it now I have a fairly sanguine view of life. It's not all a bed of roses - you have to take the rough with the smooth. I'd never had to go through a really difficult period before, now looking back on it, in the cycle of life it was one of those bad periods. I think I probably appreciate stuff more now, I have strong beliefs about ways of communicating with people on whatever level. There's a way of treating people and I have strong principles on this, I realise how it can affect people's lives. I think you have to be pretty daft not to learn from your experience whether good or bad...

In pilot training, when doing acrobatics, you have to hold the joystick to your chest until you rise to the point when you stall then you have to release your grip and let gravity take the plane back around...you have to overcome the fear of letting go. Then to discover that I couldn't even go for job interview! Huh!

REFLECTION

Matthew has been a fighter. He continues to show physical prowess and yet he describes how his confidence was eroded through continual bullying and intimidation. Any of us are susceptible at any time.

How common is it for 'strong' people, physically tough people to be affected by mental health problems?

JENNY: It's as common as in other people. I've seen policemen, great big, huge men who've come and cried because people think that because they're big and strong that they don't feel things and that they have to try and keep up this pretence. People don't expect them to be affected at all.

I was interested by the bullying, that he was more angry than anything else.

JENNY: Yes, he had to internalise his anger, otherwise he could hurt people quite severely, but bullying does have a huge effect on people. That's something that's come to light more in recent times, thank goodness. I felt very sorry for him actually...which doesn't help him at all.

At least the perpetrator left and he could get on with his job

JENNY: Yes. How is he now...?

When I last saw him he was fine and has since been promoted...

TRANSITION:

Edinburgh Day 4, Tuesday 11th August, 2009

 My brother and his wife are coming, we manage to meet them briefly beforehand in the Under the Stairs bar. But our day begins with a delightful man, Paul Cairn who does a Burns breakfast at Henderson's Vegetarian restaurant in Hanover Street. A superb entertainer, very warm, friendly, natural and fun and 80! His rendition of Burns is a delight.

The show goes well, 12 in today and the technician with OCD really enjoyed the performance and even bought a book.

Excitement: a phone call - we're invited for an interview with Radio 5 Live on Friday night.

We visit the Gilded Balloon and the Turret Room to see Elvis McGonagall. He gives a fun, commanding performance, quick-witted, sharp, and some great lyrics. Then we're off to Café Marlayne, Thistle Street for another delightful meal. Rich Hall was on the menu later, 10.30 at the Assembly, a bundle of fun, playing his tricks on the audience.

Day Five, Wednesday 12th

Over half-way through the week today. Bach for Breakfast at the Royal Overseas Lounge in full view of the castle. Piano, guitar (he was only 17) and saxophone, like I've never heard it played. All crystal sharp, spot on, such mastery of their set pieces. We take a cab to Merchant Street because of rain and there are delays on set as they try to fix a blue light. A glass of wine to steady the nerves, becoming a habit. But only three in the audience and one of them with his A4 pad in front of him, clearly taking notes. It's a tough call with little reaction to the humour. But still, overall a very warm response. And the sun breaks through. Afterwards I buy black shirts on Princes Street, and then we're off to Cuban Rumba the other side of town. The darkness rumbling on.

Day 6, Thursday 13th

Unlucky for some - there are tensions between us. It's a difficult morning, after a difficult evening. I was being a real shit, no excuses, except tension and disappointment that it seemed we weren't going to be getting a review. We choose a dodgy, Scottish breakfast at a pub in Rose Street that insisted we ordered at the bar, the other diners having pints of lager at 10am.

This afternoon's performance felt a little shaky at times. We'd passed an old guy in the street who I'd overheard say to someone, 'speak slower', and afterwards Steve A also said I had been speaking quickly. But Hallelujah it went well, and even the girl from Sylvia Plath (one of the three actresses we'd seen and met in the Under the Stairs bar) enjoyed it and said it was powerful and I think she added, 'a privilege to share the experience!' Luke is becoming more experimental with the lights and consequently the show's looking even more professional.

Later, that evening it was a delight to see Mark Watson - excellent, fantastic fun. He's on for two nights only at the Assembly Rooms, then we're back to the Iris restaurant for dinner - superb cuisine. A visit to the Salsa bar but it's dark, there's hardly anybody there and they seem to want to bleed us for money.

26GG – Petite? I don't think so...!

15 - KICK WITH LEFT HEEL

From Boxing Ears bring your arms round, cross and push out your hands as you kick out with the left heel, again holding briefly, horizontal, or higher if you can.

Repeating the previous kick, this is the second main point of balance, in this case the dynamic between father and son. Parents take on the system that seems to fail them and their son, who is eventually diagnosed with schizophrenia.

Peter & Ross Wilson

I first met Peter through work. He ran a business specialising in engineering solutions to noise and vibration problems. We met for the interview in the garden of Waterman's pub in Eton just prior to the Funny Farm comedy club evening with his son Ross who was due to perform stand up.

Ross had over two years' experience of the mental health system. As a musician he has done several events with his Dad against the stigma so often associated with mental health. And just the previous day they had both been interviewed on Radio Berkshire as part of the station's mental health awareness week.

Something very powerful about father and son; father trying everything to save his son from himself, to save him from being lost, his crazed notebooks, diagnosis of schizophrenia, injections of risperidone. The experience of places that just didn't care about the trouble they put people through - when a little humanity would've helped.

What is your experience of mental ill health?

Peter: Ah Déjà vu from yesterday morning. For one thing you never like to admit it, because it's a big thing. To begin with Ross was at Reading University and going mad, not in the obvious sense, but he was doing...everything. He'd got the BBC down because the university weren't doing enough on recycling, he did a radio show, stand up, open mike, the lot. It started to get a bit odd philosophically, as it were. But then, when I was that age, I was obsessed by Luke Rhinehart's the Dice Man (which tells the story of a psychiatrist who begins making life decisions based on the casting of dice).

For about three months when I was at university I'd be throwing dice to find out whether I was going to go out and what I was going to drink, or something. Everyone was doing it at the time, and I thought what Ross was up to was just one of those things. But it started to get a bit more serious when I saw his journals and some of the pictures and what he was writing, which he was proud of. He'd say Dad look at this and I'd say - Shit!

Then it started to get really weird. He'd sit reading these books by Eckhart Tolle who's a manic depressive and has made millions out of being a manic depressive; it's cultish, very cultish and Ross got really into it. One of the things was living in the moment; he was trying to be aware of every breath he was taking. And he'd sit and stare at you for a long time or go away and stare at his brother who was trying to take 'A' levels. So I realized there was a problem but it's still difficult to admit. This was February 2007. And Ross, you started doing weird stuff, like putting books in sinks.

Ross: Yes, I put my Dad's science fiction book in a sink and turned the tap on and soaked it. Then when he came up and said 'What are you doing?' I launched into a tirade of shouting at him, 'When are you going to wake up?' It's all part of the philosophy that's in the book by Eckhart Tolle, A New Earth, and it's all about the ego. I was trying to shock his ego in order to dissolve it, or something, some kind of spiritual thing. I was trying to pierce through the shell of his ego, a healing experience for him, by screaming at him!

Peter: Hmmm, didn't really work. Ross had been down to the 'Walk-in centre', (A&E) (at about the end of February, beginning of March) and said he needed a break because he was stressed. He filled in some forms but they said you're not clucking enough, go away but they made him an appointment to see a psychiatrist about two weeks later.

What they should've done, and this is something I know now, because I'm on a mental health committee, they should've immediately phoned the early intervention people and got a crisis team straight away, because in two weeks Ross was no longer. They might have saved two years of our lives if they'd done the right thing at that time. It got worse and worse, and more and more difficult to deal with. He wasn't at home all the time, he went off to Reading for a while. But what really triggered the decision to take action was when in about the middle of June, aged 21, he came to say 'I'm going to America because the Universe is calling me: I will heal the Universe, I will heal the planet'.

It was a Saturday or Sunday, and when he told us it was a family shock. We knew nothing about mental illness, we didn't know how to react, we just got angry and upset. We were in our extension, which is quite a large room, and looking back it was horrible because it was like an inquisition: why are you doing this? Why are you doing that? He was going to New York specifically to become destitute - because that's the way you do it. He was going to go and sit on a park bench for two months; that was the plan. I remember he was sitting against the radiator, it was quite cold, quite a long meeting. And he'd also deleted all his friends off his phone for various reasons, some which were quite bizarre, like they were judging him.

Ross: I was judging them; they weren't spiritual enough. They drank and drinking wasn't spiritual. It was to do with them not being enlightened in the way the book was describing.

Peter: No one lived up to Ross's standards basically; he was the only one who knew. So he'd deleted all his friends, and we all had a long chat with him. When we were talking about friends he went quiet for quite a long time. It was almost like a plea for help, as if he was not really sure why he'd done it. I went out into the garden with him and sat on the bench, trying to be really calm, and trying to get to the bottom of this, saying it's not a good idea and so forth. Then Ross said I think you've got a point there Dad. He was almost on the point of agreeing or thinking again, then suddenly he leaps up and shouts at me 'Why are you going to hit me?!' 'Why are you going to hit me?!' I think it was because of the challenge, he'd got to the point where he'd felt very threatened and thought it was physical violence...

Ross: No, no, no. It was the 'pain body'...which is apparently a reservoir of pain within the human psyche,

which gets activated under certain circumstances. And I was
activating his pain body

Peter: I didn't realize this at the time, I thought I was talking
sense and getting somewhere…

Ross: And I felt a wave of violence coming from him…and I
knew he was going to hit me.

Peter: No, not at all. It was quite startling, quite shocking.
Anyway the next day I thought I've got to do something. I
made an appointment to see the GP and took one of Ross's
journals down with me. It had some very scary pictures like
the Scream by Munch, and lots of violent things, like
stabbings, all sorts of things. I knew this was serious and I
showed the GP and she actually said 'Shit!' She immediately
phoned mental health services and set up to do sectioning.
Ross wasn't living at home at that point he was living at
someone's house in Windsor. Someone he'd met through
busking. She'd seen him busking and quite liked the cut of
his jib…

Ross: She fancied me, gave me her card and said, 'Call
me.'

Peter: So I found out the address where he was, I can't
remember how. But this was a big thing - the idea of having
to section your own child. And I didn't want anyone else in
the family involved, I didn't want us all to all be tarred by the
same brush. So I didn't tell them about it. It was some of the
four most stressful days of my life…building up - I was
thinking if my son goes to New York, destitute, I'll never see
him again.

So it was all organized, I turned up, his car was outside, so I knew he was in there, and the social worker turned up, and the doctor, and we waited for the psychiatrist, and he's late, he's late, so I was standing there stressed. I spoke to one of the other two people who I'd met and I showed him the journal and he said 'Shit!' too. Then the psychiatrist arrived. But it turned out to be a gated, secure development - there was no way in. We spoke to the security guard and said we need to find this flat and do you know where it is? 'No' he said. Is there a plan of the place? 'No.' Can we come in and look? 'No.' So we explain and he says, ok I'll phone him up, and we say 'No!' It was like something out of bloody Monty Python, scurrying round the outside trying to find a way in, four of us like, 'No one expects the Spanish Inquisition!' Exactly like that, except without the red. He refused to let us in. And I'm so stressed, I feel like I'm going to pass out, my chest is tight and getting tighter.

Then some dustbin men appeared, there's a door in the wall to get the bins out and it's got a combination lock on it and they're walking towards this, so I walk towards them. I can't remember what I said, the first thing that came into my head: something like, 'Excuse me do you know where you can get colour coded bins?' And all the time I'm looking over the shoulder of this bin man. He must have noticed this bloke staring past his shoulder asking questions, but I saw the combination, 4314, kept it going round in my head, 4314.

And after they left I got in, we all got in. But it was a big development and we couldn't find the flat. We asked this young woman coming out of a flat with her daughter in the pram, but she said there was no plan, the only plan available was on the internet. So I explained a little bit and she, bless her, went back into her house and got her laptop, with WiFi online and found it. I climbed over the gate, up to the flat and Ross opened the door. Hi Dad. I was standing with a row of people behind me. He said can you give me a minute and he went upstairs and meditated for a bit. Then when he came down and let us in he was so fucking polite, with his middle class charm: can I get you a cup of tea? Anything special? So he goes on being charming and humorous and I'm thinking You Bastard!

So the interview went on for an hour and a half or something like that. But when I went downstairs with them afterwards they said we can't section him. He held it together. He's got very, very serious problems, he is psychotic, but we can't prove it. And if he did this and went into hospital and appealed and was like this, we'd be roasted by the solicitor. But, by the way, if he doesn't get treatment soon he's going to get worse! The longer he goes without treatment the worse it's going to get. I really didn't want to hear that. I'd been so tense for four days. I went back up to him and had a cup of tea and he was so nice to me, after the bastard I'd been to him, the guilt I felt.

So I drove home. I started walking round the house and I had a mini breakdown. I drove off somewhere and found myself at Stoke Poges crematorium where my grandmother was buried and I ended up curled up on the grass next to her grave all of the afternoon. I can't remember getting there. I phoned a friend because she worked fairly local and I freaked. I had my first breakdown. It lasted about a day.

After that there was no chance to stop him going. We tried everything. We tried to find his passport. We called the airlines. And in the end we gave up, because he's an adult, he has a passport, you can't stop him. So Gillian spent a long time organizing the trip so that we'd know where he is, and where he's staying, to try to make it as safe as possible.

So, at the time Ross, how did you feel in yourself?

Ross: I'd just done a gig at a local heart centre...

Peter: I have to say that was one of the best gigs he'd ever done, well he's cyclic, and he did this gig and he was fantastic...

Ross: No you weren't there...

Peter: That was an earlier one then - you were brilliant!

Ross: I was staying at a friend's house, and I was just normal, I thought I was normal. I didn't like my parents very much at the time. But there was great purpose to it all, I was going to heal people. There was a strong sense of, I've got to do this, because I thought the Universe, or God, was talking to me through signs. I had a big thing about signs. Like overhearing someone else's conversation and reading into it meaning that applies to your life. So I might be listening to them, and if they say something in particular, I might go, Ah that means this, and I should do that.

And the reason I chose New York in particular was because the person I was staying with in Reading at the time I made the decision, randomly went off on a ten minute chat about how he'd been to New York and how amazing it was. I took that as a sign that I needed to go to New York. And then I saw a pair of my pants that Mum had got when she went to New York once and it said I love New York on them. And I wanted to move there, to live. I sent an email to the immigration people, asking them, telling them that God has told me to come and live in your country, would you give me permission to stay. I thought, well, they're American, they believe in God, so...!

Peter: He flew out at the beginning of September. We had a few emails from him while he was in New York...He put his card into a cash machine and saw his overdraft limit and thought 'Someone has put a thousand dollars into my account – it's a present from God I'll go and spend it all on guitars! So he bought himself two guitars and then lost one, left the other...

Ross: I didn't lose it, I left it with a homeless person while I went to the toilet and when I came back it was gone. ☺!

Peter: But he got chucked out of the hostel, and had no money. I think he begged money to buy phone time and phoned us to say he needed money. We'd been talking to my brother who had a friend psychiatrist in Spain, who just said look, one of the big problems is, if anyone with a mental health condition doesn't suffer the consequences of it in some form, nothing's going to happen, you're just prolonging the agony. So, basically the message was don't support the behaviour that's causing the problem. That was a really hard decision not to send him any money. But we managed to get him a ticket to go to someone he'd met, in New Orleans.

Ross: I was begging for food and money for the phone. I got picked up by a strange man who offered to let me stay at his house one night. And then I woke up in the middle of the night with him on top of me. So that was...interesting! I got down to New Orleans on the Greyhound.

Peter: Making the decision not to send him money was so hard. We'd already sent him some money to begin with and he'd bought a CD player and then lost it. We managed to get him back in the end. But he skipped his first flight home so we had to book another one! Then we had an email from the girl he was staying with asking for money. When we asked for her details she said 'Ross has gone, he's been picked up by the police'. We contacted the police but they were completely unhelpful. So we just waited to hear from him, imagining that he was living under a bridge with tramps.

Ross: Yes I was, just near the girl I'd been staying with. She'd kicked me out and the police came because I was randomly knocking on peoples' doors asking if I could stay with them. I think an old lady wasn't too happy about that, knocking on doors at 9'o'clock asking to stay with people. They took me to the bus station. I was supposed to go and stay with another friend. But I decided to skip that bus and stay under the bridge instead. Somehow I managed, after a long walk, to find my way back from the police station to where I'd been staying before…(under the bridge).

Peter: A homing loony! Well we got him back in the end, miraculously. He turned up looking like a hippy. From the top he looked like a daffodil because he had a yellow poncho …

Ross: I didn't have that then

Peter: Well you'd sent us pictures of it, I just remember you looking like a real hippy. It was a big reunion at Heathrow, for his return in December. But very shortly afterwards, after a hug he said 'If you ever try and section me again, you will never see me again!' Oh hi Ross, nice to see you too… I think he was scared that he'd turn up and there would be a load of doctors ready to arrest him.

So he then lived at home for a while. But he had what he said was a simulated breakdown which was really horrific. We called the CRASH team, because we had all the numbers by that time. They came round and suggested he take something to calm down, and he did (you were all very cuddly then). They came back and said he'd need anti-psychotics, so he promised to take medication, otherwise they'd section him there and then. But he lied, he spat it out. I'd say two thirds of the time he was shouting and then being completely silent, and a third of the time, it was like having my son back again. It was cyclic. But it just got worse and worse and worse. He'd move out, stay with friends, then move back. When was it you did your dance on the bridge? He saw someone attempting to commit suicide off the bridge at Slough and tried to demonstrate how dangerous it was to him by walking backwards along the parapet above the railway line.

So, all these happened at the same time as I was trying to work, and to run a business. Over the spring there was more. One day I came home to find all his stuff in the hall.

Ross: I went on a massive giving away things spree, because I didn't want material possessions any more, they were beneath me. I saved one guitar, I thought I might need that, but I gave away another guitar, and smashed my acoustic guitar.

Peter: Yes, you killed it…on New Year's Eve. We'd spent the whole day decorating it, and he went out into the woods and killed his guitar. That really freaked me out because music is his thing. He did an album before going manic and even just before going to New York he did some fantastic stuff. And to kill his guitar was like committing suicide, I thought - an iconic moment really.

Later he got arrested and taken down to the police cells. I thought I'd better not see him, Gillian went and sorted all that out. They let him out again. He went and lived with someone else, then was lost and got picked up at Stanstead airport, trying to leave the country.

Ross: I asked them how much it was to go to Australia. They said it was £3000. Oh dear. I stayed there a day or two. In one of the books I was reading, by Deepak Chopra, it says any area you're experiencing more creativity in then you'll grow in. So if you want certain areas to grow you should try and be more creative in those areas. I wanted money to grow so I thought I'd be creative and create a new PIN number every time I used the machines. Obviously I didn't remember every PIN and the machine sucked my card in.

Peter: So I got a phone call from him, this was after he's been missing for several days: 'Can you come and pick me up from Stanstead?' But, when he was off the line, I thought to myself if I go to Stanstead he won't be there. He'll be hiding watching me, and he won't come out. So Gillian went instead. And got there and he'd disappeared. He was picked up a mile and a half away by the police. He kept on threatening to jump off the train on the way home. Then he was living at home, and was really non-functional so we thought he needed to be sectioned. There was this one late afternoon when Gillian had arranged for the section to happen. But his girlfriend was coming to pick him up to go to a Christian healing centre in Birmingham. So they left even though Gillian had tried to delay him, and five minutes after they left the team arrived.

And the next time, the next time it worked. I chickened out - it was stressful enough the first time. But I got a phone call, the police were there. Ross would really like to talk to you, come home. So I did and Ross just gave me a hard time in hand cuffs. So he got taken off to Wexham. Unfortunately it was a Friday and they didn't handle him well at all.

Ross: I just got left in a room basically, after a little introduction with my care nurse from the community mental health team (Peter: she was brilliant). Then they all buggared off and I was just left there without really knowing what was going on, what the treatment plan was, or anything. How long was I there for, 6 days? (Peter: only about 4 or 5 days). I was refusing to take my medication. And then I escaped.

Peter: The only security it had was that it was on the first floor, but there was a lift.

Ross: I just waited for someone to come up in the lift. (Peter: he had his bag over his shoulder) And I just got into the lift as if I was a visitor.

Peter: I was away running a training course and I had a phone call, coffee break time – Ross has escaped...and there was nothing I could do...then a bit later another phone call to say he'd been found, he's at home. Thank God! Then another phone call half an hour later, he's escaped again.

Ross: That was a classic action film escape that one. I'd escaped from hospital, I'd gone back home. And then they'd come to take me back to hospital with the police. I said to the community mental health team who were there before the police arrived. Can I go and play on the drums? So I went to play on the drums in my bedroom. I hadn't pre-meditated that I was going to escape...Then a policeman came up. I think I was on the phone to a friend of mine to ask can you say I'm not mad? (Peter: you said you were on the phone to everybody.) I was on the phone to Sam and said could you talk to these police officers (who were knocking on the bedroom door) and say I'm not mad. Then I just jumped out the first floor window and ran down the street.

Peter: Getting these phone calls was like hope one minute, despair the next, hope, despair. And then he went missing for a month. We went round all the hostels, youth hostels, Salvation Army. And I spent my weekends cycling around Slough and the surrounding area, looking in parks and accosting policeman. Because we'd reported him to the police as a missing person, but there's several missing, I wanted them to remember Ross, so he wasn't just one of the usual morning briefings – I'd give them the leaflet, photograph and phone numbers. And the second weekend I was walking in Slough and thought: that looks like Ross. And it was. When he saw me he turned round and ran off, like startled deer. I can't catch him. I phoned the police, I phoned everybody, but he'd just disappeared. That was so depressing.

Then 29 days after being sectioned, he turned up at home. The section runs out after 28 days – he wasn't stupid! He was in his friend's car, and said I've come to take my stuff. It was a real shock. I freaked out, Ross went upstairs and I grabbed the bag he'd brought in with him (Ross: I still don't know where that bag is) and stormed off. I got a chance to look through his notebook and found a couple of addresses. So when he'd gone we phoned around and found out where he was living.

Thankfully, we'd also found his passport. But later that night, at about 11, he rang up asking for his passport. I said come round tomorrow morning for a coffee and we'll talk about it. He screamed down the phone, so I put the phone down. He phoned back. I put the phone down...then left it off the hook. 20 minutes later, quarter past midnight, bang bang bang on the door, screaming outside on the street. I let him in, he was furious, went to his room and started banging on the drums.

I'm standing in his doorway, trying to be really calm, then he starts slapping me. I couldn't do anything. I couldn't defend myself. I just stood there. Owen came dashing in and leaps on his back and says stop hitting our Dad. That broke the spell. Gillian called the police. So I had to think how I was going to keep him in the house till the police arrived. He didn't seem to realise the significance. But as soon as the police arrived it was really horrible. There was this violent metallic smell. They don't know what the situation is, they come in ready. They've been told, assault, mental health - it could be anything. It's the smell and chinkle of the hand cuffs. I chickened out. I have this memory of Ross being terribly middle class and polite.

Ross: 'Excuse me, that hurts rather, you don't really have to do that you know.' And that was the beginning of the end.

Peter: Then a couple more police arrived, and we had to start filling in forms at 2'o'clock in the morning. Would you like another cup of tea officer? So, in bed at half past two, then at 4'o'clock the phone rings. He's in the cells. The police doctor wants some information. The doctor was saying things like, he seems fine. He slapped you - are you hurt, was there any damage? Have you been to A&E. And I'm thinking no not again! So I said if I email you the pictures I showed the mental health services? But the police system wouldn't accept attachments. This girl on the phone was an angel, she said send them to my personal account, I can access that, so I did. Dawn was breaking and eventually they said they were going to get the mental health services and he was sectioned that morning.

Ross: I'd stayed the night in the police cell. I didn't get much sleep because it was a bit uncomfortable, and I had a guy watching me the whole time. First in the cell with me, then maybe when I was asleep no one was watching, but there was when I woke up in the morning. And then I went to have the interview with the doctors and told them all about the spiritual 'nonsense' and I think that's when they decided to section me.

Peter: I think I remember someone saying that he didn't maintain his quiet demeanour anymore, I think he freaked out a bit and got very angry. So they sectioned him and sent him off to Heatherwood because Wexham Park (where he'd escaped from before) was full. He ran into a doctor there who he spent an hour talking to. So something gelled. This guy was into Buddhism so they were chatting about stuff. He didn't want to be there, there was 'nothing wrong' with him, it was 'false imprisonment' but...much better than Wexham.

So we went over the next day, saw Ross briefly, and they said we're going to send him back to Wexham as soon as there's a bed available. Ross said, if I go back to Wexham you'll never see me again. So we spent an hour and a half talking to the doctor and the senior nurse. They just said it's policy, it's all in the patient's best interest. I said explain how it works, he's made a connection here! That evening I got a message on my mobile to say they've kept him at Heatherwood. Such a relief. We opened a good bottle of wine. But then a text next morning, we're sending him back to Wexham. That was Friday morning. I emailed everybody, I got the patient liaison service, no one would have the grace to get back to me and explain why it was good for him.

So I said this is wrong, and unless you get back to me I'm going to the media. I did a piece at the local radio station and on Monday morning I was on Radio Berkshire. About 7'o'clock, forty minutes later, I had a phone call from a senior person in the NHS –there's been a misunderstanding. I'd embarrassed them into it. All sorted.

Two days later they start pumping him full of anti-psychotics, which is horrible, you turn into a vegetable, until they get the dose right. And yet within a couple of days he'd put in for a tribunal. I didn't know what that meant, but I discovered that if Ross convinced them he'd be free of the section. I remembered that the case nurse throughout had said the system's really poor for someone who's articulate. They are bending over backwards not to section people. There's such a paranoia about sectioning someone against their will. According to the Mental Health Act: don't get mad if you're intelligent.

I was scared about the tribunal; they do a 20 minute, half-hour interview, and it would be so easy for him to be out. So I sat in the tribunal, they upheld the section it was such a relief. I had another breakdown. I just shut down, I'd forgotten how to drive. We visited him everyday. Later, we'd organised to pick him up and take him out for a bit and they said, no, he can't go. Gillian had to wait for ages before a doctor would simply sign a prescription.

Two weeks later, it was Ascot week. I was due to collect him. A journey that would normally take 20 minutes took an hour and a half. We'd phoned up two days ahead to arrange it, and checked again the day before. But when I turned up they said he can't go because the release form hasn't been signed. I completely relaxed, I said this is not my problem it's your problem, I'm taking him as arranged. 20 minutes later it was sorted. Some people are so patronising; 'we're the mental health professionals'.

He'd gone into Wexham in April 2008, escaped, then into Heatherwood in May for 9 weeks until July 16th. The day after he came out we went to France and we had to arrange for him to have his depo injection in France, so we took the stuff with us in the fridge. We were staying at a friend's house, a quiet secluded place. Ross was up and down, one minute hating it, then enjoying it. We wrote a song together (Song of Sickness), which I thought would be good therapy.

Then the main problem was depression: suicide thoughts; he wanted to crash the car and stuff. So that went on for 6 to 9 months. I'd read a lot and realised that you need to talk about suicide, you don't just ignore it. If I sat down and talked to him for about an hour and a half, by the end of that time he'd be feeling almost up. But I found myself double thinking all the time, what do I say next, I don't want to say the wrong thing…I just got so tired, I was only working half days. (**Ross:** where have we got to now? (he'd been distracted in conversation with some friends at the pub))

Peter: We were in France with you being cyclic, manic, depressed, one minute saying No I don't want to play tennis, then yes I do and cycling off furiously up the hill…Gradually he got better as he remembered to take his medication.

What sort of stuff were you on?

Peter: He'd on the minimum dose every two weeks, the lovely Sandra injects his bottom.

Ross: Risperidone

Peter: More recently - Ross and Owen are now in a band. Owen's A level results were not what he should've got, with all the turmoil, but fortunately for him enough to do what he wanted. And Ross earns his living teaching guitar (**Ross:** not really a living, a part time wage) and he got a stipend for a while to teach guitar as occupational therapy. Since last autumn, we've also been doing visits to schools, a sixth form anti-stigma show, which has gone down really well. We're going to do more of those.

I went to see a woman in charge of the schools programme to ask for a list of service providers that I could let the schools know about. But she was like something out of Dickens; she wouldn't make a decision or provide anything, even though it was supposed to be public information.

It was a really good, interactive show. I'd ask them for what comes into their minds relating to mental health to begin with and they'd say psychosis, schizophrenia, bipolar etc. At the end we repeated it and it was all things like frightened, scared, sad, a complete change in the words they used.

So what is you're diagnosis?

Ross: Well the first episode was psychosis, bordering on schizophrenia.

Peter: It depends who you talk to a certain extent, like you Steve, they were vacillating between diagnoses ...X, with some aspects of...Y, like they have these pastry cutters and some things don't quite fit inside the pastry cutter. So they could bring two pastry cutters in, or make a special Ross shaped pastry cutter. To treat it you need a diagnosis. That's something that pissed Ross off at the time – labelling.

Ross: Yes, the whole labelling psychotic, schizophrenic, didn't sit very well with me. It was my hatred of the whole system.

Peter: One of the things that has impressed me about Ross more recently is that you don't seem bothered by the label. 'I was ill so of course I did really crap things, and I don't mind telling people about it'. What's the difference between that and having a bad back or measles or something?

Ross: Hopefully I'm not weird anymore

I think we're all a little bit weird in some ways...

REFLECTION

Peter and Ross tell a very moving story of victory of parental love over a harsh and overstretched mental health service. They have been helped to overcome through Ross and his brother Owen's musical skills which you can hear on their website www.huggingbarbedwire.com. The same site became the main vehicle for promoting our show by the same name in 2011.

What experience do you have of parents seeking psychological help for their children, and what words of encouragement would you offer?

JENNY: Helping your child is hopefully a natural desire - you want to take their pain away. It's so, so hard for parents just being there consistently and supporting and letting others help where appropriate, but also parents looking after themselves. The strain is enormous and it's very hard to be aware of the need to look after themselves, but very necessary. It can divide parents having a problem with a child, or make them closer.

Try to maintain a closeness with each other, however difficult, because we all experience things differently, and persist in finding out. Try not to pretend to yourselves. Try not to be hurt by cruel, unreasonable and ill-founded accusations from the sufferer – and that is indeed difficult to do. Seek any help from organisations connected to mental health. Above all, get strength and consolation from each other.

Psychological help can stretch from counselling through to psychiatry with children. I feel if children can be kept out of the psychiatric circle it's a good thing, very often something very simple can put them to rights.

I'm thinking of the difficulty they had getting Ross sectioned

JENNY: That's appalling. I think the medical world is scared now of getting it wrong and of being sued. I think the American culture is fast coming over here. But I do think if the young person is really showing psychotic signs, it's appalling that they can't be taken to a place of safety for themselves.

I'd like to think that the mental health system is trying to improve itself, but it does make big mistakes sometimes.

It is a very serious thing, sectioning people, because in the past people were committed or sectioned, often for life, they were put away and forgotten, because other people found them difficult to manage, or they had become pregnant out of wedlock, or they were just an embarrassment.

Now they do seem to have to be really very sure before they section anyone. But it must have been dreadful for his parents. And if he'd been on cannabis, that can set someone off into psychosis, even after 9 years. It can also topple someone into schizophrenia, if they have a propensity to be that way. Childbirth can also cause a transient psychotic episode (puerperal psychosis) or bring on a possible latent schizophrenia – infrequently, I must stress.

It is difficult for those sectioning when someone is articulate while being interviewed and appears perfectly OK effectively pulling the wool over their eyes. In many cases, I feel there needs to be good communication with those constantly caring. Then of course, the professionals have to determine whether or not those carers just want the sufferer to be out of the way to benefit themselves. It's a tricky situation but needs to be handled sensitively with the time allowed to assess correctly.

Water running in rivulets through her hair...

TRANSITION:

Edinburgh Day 7, Friday 14th August, 2009

Day 7, lucky for some - an easy, slow morning, reluctantly preparing for Liz to leave, waiting with her for the train, while it was spitting with rain. In the crowds, almost panic stricken on the train, helping her with her bag, petrified that I wouldn't get off in time before the doors closed - and then what would happen to the show!?

Picking up a paper, ecstatic to discover a four star review in the Evening News from the reviewer who was there on Wednesday night - fantastic!!

The Edinburgh Evening News

4****

The prospect of spending 90 minutes listening to a former environmental health officer describe in detail his very personal descent into madness is the stuff of Fringe Theatre.

This production promises to carry the story arc beyond Steve Walter's experience of locked wards, through to his recovery, but the fact that he's out there on the stage with his medical notes begs the question of how complete that recovery might be.

In fact, the audience is drawn into a powerful, emotional journey executed with passion and surety of purpose. Walter soars beyond the pitfalls of the self obsessed misery memoir describing instead a small but important history of a human triumph. The blend of poetry, self-confessional prose and performance is hugely enhanced by the music and song of Steve Antoni, whose contribution effortlessly switches the pace and tone of the performance without ever losing the theme.

Walter's motivation in all this is "the vision of mental ill health being discussed freely in every part of the country, over coffee, over a pint, without stigma, judgement or gossip."

The number of the occasions that the audience spontaneously identifies with his experiences suggests with this production we may be a step closer to realizing his vision.

Jim Ferguson

An old acquaintance, from Environmental Health days, turns up with his wife. I'm chuffed they made it and they really enjoyed the show - very complimentary. Later, the BBC cab is due to collect us at 7.30. It is still pouring with rain.

Steve Antoni's friend Ryk arrives from London just before the cab. He joins us in the studio, part of a new building, lots of glass, empty, only a security guy on the door. I'm interviewed by Stephen Nolan, an easy, if odd, chat via headphones & Steve Antoni singing Lifeline which for me has become our signature song. We celebrate afterwards in another pub in Rose Street - Dirty Dicks!

Day 8, Saturday 15th

Downstairs at Mad Dogs on George Street: three comedians; Jew, Christian, Muslim a dose of comedy before the show, and afterwards at 7 ish, back at the Assembly for Dixie's Tupperware party, riotous fun; like a wild, American Fanny Craddock but a six foot transvestite! And of course the Iris restaurant for dinner, in Liz's memory; with thanks for her finding the place through recommendations. At 10.30 we get to see Ali McGregor's Late-Nite Variety-Nite Night. I had been teased by the flyers; her wink, the hint of burlesque, but sadly far from titillating, we found it all rather ennui.

How many have never, not even for a fleeting moment, envied the ability of a dog to lick its own genitals…?

16 - GOING DOWN – (LEFT)

Stretch out, first with your left leg then, with your left hand reach all the way down to your foot, to the ground, then follow through with your right leg, dipping from the base of your spine, bringing your right knee up and your right hand, standing upright like a cockerel on your left leg.

The move is also referred to as Push Down and Stand on One Leg, Left Style and Right Style; or more inspirationally called Snake Creeps Down (left) and Golden Cockerel Stands on left leg, then Snake Creeps Down (right) and Golden Cockerel Stands on right leg.

This move involves the greatest stretch as if toppling an opponent over you, then standing like a victorious cockerel on one leg close to a natural pause in the flow.

Now I shouldn't be rude here, but every time my Tai Chi teacher introduced this move I raised a wry smile.

Sam said she'd go down on me…well, not in so many words - it was the look she gave, the glance…the twinkle in her eye...

Steve Anthony

What a hero! This guy was the main man in Brighton and Edinburgh. He made it possible by holding the show together with his singing, his guitar playing, his covers and his own songs. Winner of the Eric Gregory Award for poetry in 1987 his lyrics and music have inspired hundreds over the years.

'Let's get down to the mad stuff' he says, introducing his story.

"That way madness lies", *King Lear, Act 3, Scene 4.*

What has been your experience of mental ill health?

I can think of a number of people who've been quite close to me, whom I've been close to, and also myself to some extent. I don't tend to think of mental health as being mad people and sane people. In a way, we all act in more of a continuum: we all act in slightly mad ways at some point, under different stresses and circumstances. But nevertheless there are ways in which what's called psychotic states are quite different. There have been two or three people who have later been diagnosed as being bipolar, or manic depressive, whom I've known quite well, and other people who are clinically depressed or have been clinically depressed. And yes, suicide, successful or unsuccessful. And my own experience of depression, I suppose.

PAUL

I think of my friend Paul, who's dead now. He had to go through a lot of very difficult experiences - in the dark really, before he was diagnosed, years later, as being bipolar.

Before then, we just thought of him as being a bit "out there". His whole life, from the age of 11 at school when I met him, he was a creature of extremes. He did extremely well at school exams and used to argue whether he'd got an extra half a per cent – it was really 97% in Chemistry instead of 96.5%. He later went to the same university as I did. He was reading Theology. He'd first gone to Manchester to study Physics, because he'd done so well at school. And then I suppose the combination of being at university on his own and being away from his family, he just started to lose it a bit. He'd always had quite a Christian background, quite a religious background, and he became more involved with the CU, Christian Union, and all that sort of stuff. Anyway, he ended up dropping out; he moved back to London and did a few nothing jobs. And then he went to Hull and read Theology, I think partly, or mostly, because I was there. I was reading Philosophy there.

He was settling in well, doing okay, but then again, as happens with the illness, he started to have his highs. He thought he was John the Baptist or some sort of prophet, and he'd be just doing mad things, going around Hull overturning altars in churches. He went to this talk in the Theology Department, when they had a Rabbi there, and he asked: "Does the Rabbi believe in Hitler?" — which was actually quite a good question — but that didn't go down well. It was quite a provocative question. But it's a good question, about the problem of evil and about someone who just doesn't believe in you, doesn't want your lifestyle, your values, your way of life.

Then he started to get focused on me, because I was a good friend of his from school. And he started to get even madder. Because my initials were SA, I became Satan, and because Satan or Lucifer was the brightest angel, who fell from God's grace, I was then the friend who was now Satan. So that was a bit scary. He was a big guy! He stalked me around the university, followed me about. And I remember that he used to come round to my house, because he was living in central Hull and I was living in Cottingham, a village suburb. If anyone told me they had seen him, I would have to take evasive action and scarper. I didn't know how to deal with it; I was 19 or 20. I remember this time when he came round and I was in my room and I'd locked the door and he was coming up into the house and along the corridor and trying my door, and I was the other side of the door in bed, quivering. It was pretty scary, actually. Another time he came round and he came into my room and he said: "You may kiss the Pope's ring!" So I ran away! I just didn't know how to deal with it at all. He was obviously on a high, and there were other subsequent episodes that I wasn't so much a part of but he told me about.

Later, when he was at work (he worked as an accountant), there were various mad episodes then as well, which meant he lost those jobs. In what we called the Interregnum, there was a time, I think during the 80s, where I got a bit fed up with it really and he was coming round hassling me. So I wrote him this letter that I've always regretted, saying goodbye kind of thing, and we didn't see each other for about seven or eight years. And then I got back to see him again through my mum, because my mum was still running a furniture shop in Ealing, and he knew she was there, and went in to see her. We got back to see each other and had a few drinks, and went on from there.

He had a few more episodes that got more serious. He was eventually sectioned a couple of times. He had this thing about public schools, a la *Brideshead Revisited*, and posh lifestyles, but he took it further. He used to go down to Eton or Winchester and pretend he was an Old Boy and wander around the colleges, the schools. And then he'd go into restaurants and order loads of champagne, on his own presumably, quite sad really, but then attempt to drive back, and get into brushes with the law. Or he'd just go and stay at the Dorchester for weeks on end, running up his credit cards, and order champagne and speak to everybody. One of the times the medical authorities picked him up, he was wandering along Kensington High Street in a Dorchester bathrobe and bare feet.

When he was with the psychiatrist and he was being questioned about his suitability for being admitted to St Bernard's psychiatric unit in Ealing Hospital, they asked him three questions. They asked him: "What have you been doing today?" and some other question, and he said he'd been meeting some prostitutes; and then they asked: "What are you going to do tomorrow?" and he said: "I'm going to change the world!" That was answering "Yes" to the questions they had in mind! He got to see his notes, and that was in his notes, three questions, assessing his case. And he'd do things like ring up MI5, or phone and pester Peter Mandelsohn's office. He thought that he had a direct effect on things, that he could actually change the course of history.

Through these last experiences he was sectioned. The first time he was sectioned he went to St Bernard's in Ealing and had ECT and all that. This was the first time it was realised that he was bipolar, and he went for his assessment with the doctors and said to them: "I want the strongest drugs you've got and continuous ECT." They said they didn't think that would be necessary! So he got out of there after a few weeks. Then about ten years after that, when he had his second breakdown, he went into Hillingdon Hospital. There were a couple of times when he escaped (*like you did*). I remember once he told me, he got out and hailed a cab and said: "Take me to the Blind Beggar!" It's in Whitechapel; it's where the Krays killed one of the people who snitched on them; there's a bullet hole in the wall. So he went AWOL for a bit. I suppose he was in his late 30s then.

After that he came out of hospital and he was on Lithium, pretty heavy-duty drugs. I remember when he first came out. It was difficult, he was really, really depressed and low. He'd say things like, "there's no point to anything". It was very hard to deal with. What do you say to someone in that situation? I mean, that's how life is, if you feel that's how life is. But the drugs helped him quite a bit. He was okay; he was living on his own, had quite a reasonable lifestyle. I don't think he was working then; no he didn't work. So that kept him level for quite a few years. I used to meet him round here, at what he called "Cappuccino Corner": Old Compton Street and Frith Street, where Bar Italia is. He lived in Greenford, West London. I saw him every few weeks. Then I didn't see him for a while and I got a call from his sister saying that he'd passed away, which was a shock. He was 41. He'd had some sort of blood clot or something. He was pretty overweight; he was very big, about six-foot four or five and about 24 stone or something. A big bloke. That was also scary when he was mad. A colossus being mad was quite scary. I miss him though; he was a very good friend. So he was one of the more vivid memories of mad friends.

BROTHER-IN-LAW

I remember you describing the circumstances of finding your brother-in-law. What happened in his life that led him to suicide?

I don't know with things like suicides, and attempted suicides. I did write something about this once, as part of my counselling training. I don't know how much is to do with madness, if you want to call it that, or mental illness. I suppose it is temporary mental illness.

Given that the norm is to live your life until you die it implies that something has gone wrong.

I don't know a huge amount about his background, but he could be extreme in his reactions to things. He'd clash with my mum quite a lot; then he'd just walk out and go home. But home wasn't round the corner; home was a few miles away. So he'd just walk six miles or something. Two hours to get home. I didn't know him that well, but he was an all-or-nothing person. He was thrown out by his Dad when he was 16. His dad was a sailor and wasn't there very much. He was from Hull too. The family didn't work together very well. Almost the whole family has disappeared now – the only one left is his sister – because a couple of years after he died his dad had a heart attack, coming back from getting his pension, and his mum walked out in front of a bus. She was on a crossing and a bus went into her. All of them were extreme; if somebody slighted them they would just cut them off and would never speak to them again. So I think his background wasn't ideal. It was one where it's all or nothing, and my sister's a bit like that too.

The fact that he was from Hull was one of those chance things. I went to Hull University. Then when I met Sue, the people upstairs came from Hull, it was like a house share, and he was one of their friends. He came down and stayed and then he shared the flat with Sue. He was renting the other room and that was how my sister met him, because I was helping Sue to paint the flat and he was helping because he lived there too, then my sister came round and that was how they met.

They got married. But later their marriage was breaking down. There had been about a month or two when he was trying to win her back. He worked at Heathrow on the planes, for El Al, the Israeli airline, as a fitter. He'd be working, then he'd just go home and upstairs and read his fishing book, then go the whole weekend fishing. He was making an effort for a month or two but I think my sister had lost it by then, that's what I mean by her also being quite an extreme person. Because she'd sort of shut off and thought this is not what I want.

Also she'd fallen in love with someone before, which was the love of her life I suppose, a young guy, who was the brother of her best friend. They were really in love with each other in a very young love sort of way, all over each other. It got to the point when they were going to have a kid...so she was pregnant but she had an abortion because he was only 18, he wasn't up for being a father, he didn't want to take responsibility. But she really wanted to have kids, although she had the abortion anyway and then they broke up. About a month after that she got together with David, my brother-in-law; it was pretty much a rebound thing. There was a kid on the way, so they got married. Robert, my nephew, is now 20.

They were together a few years, then she met this guy again whom she'd known before and they sort of started to see each other again. Whether David knew about it, I don't know; we'll never know that really. My sister won't talk about it. Or whether he thought he was making an effort and nothing was happening, anyway they had this big row, he and my sister on the Saturday. They were supposed to have been going to see Guns n' Roses; he'd got tickets. They had this big row and she left, and went down to Cheltenham to see this other guy. David was left on his own. He rang on Sunday, because I was over at my mum's then and said things like: "Are the kids okay?" But no one heard any more. Then it was Monday morning and my sister came back and I was there and she said: "Will you come round with me to the house? I need to check everything's okay." Maybe she had some sort of presentiment, because he'd been on his own all that time.

So we went round there at midday on the Monday, 2nd September 1991. And we opened the door and immediately there was this horrible smell and some flies. My sister must have gone in first; she said: "Oh my God! Oh my God!" He was in the kitchen on the floor, with blood, the back door open, and a bottle of whiskey, Jack Daniel's I think it was. Anyway, I sort of took charge and got my sister out of it, because she had my niece Rhiannon in her arms who was only two at the time or one maybe, and she went to stay with a neighbour. I tried touching him; he was groaning a bit but nothing much was happening. I tried to get through to the local doctor and told him about it, I dialled 999 obviously and an air ambulance was coming from Whitechapel. He had this wound in his head, the centre of his forehead. The police came around, asked questions. The air ambulance came eventually. It was quite an old house in an original part of West Drayton, near Uxbridge, Middlesex, and the helicopter landed on the Green, which was about 50 yards away. There was a bit of a crowd outside then. They couldn't move him for four hours, because it was too difficult to move him, but eventually they did get him out and took him off to Whitechapel.

What was the wound caused by?

He was a fitter, an engineer at the airport, so he had access, as any person like that does, like my nephew has (he's a carpenter) to various kinds of equipment including a Hilti Gun. It's a nail gun; it shoots nails into masonry. So he'd basically put one of these things against his forehead, pulled the trigger and shot a nail into the middle of his brain. Surprisingly perhaps, it hadn't killed him. But he was groaning and there was a pool of blood on the kitchen floor.

I think it had happened that morning, I don't know how much before we got there, maybe an hour or so. I think he'd got out of bed and it was Monday and it had got to him, he'd drunk the bottle of whiskey, had a few cigarettes, and done it. So he was taken away and I had to deal with the clearing up, which wasn't very nice. He was in Whitechapel, in the Trauma Room at the Royal London Hospital for a week. The doctors couldn't really do anything, because he had this old rusty nail in the middle of his brain. They could try and remove it, but the likelihood was that he'd be a vegetable. So after seven days, they switched off the life-support machine. That was 9th September 1991.

It's my mum's birthday on 11th September, which with 9/11 is a big date now. When it gets to that time of year, around about late August, I always find myself thinking about these things. I don't know really what drove him to it. There was an inquest. I had to go and give evidence to the coroner. They said it was death by misadventure, but they tend to say that anyway. They rarely say suicide, because of the taboo. The door was open at the back, as the police said; someone might have come in, there might have been an intruder. But I don't think so. He'd also not left a note. But then, he wasn't a very vocal or articulate person; he wasn't very good with words really.

Do you remember in 1991 that Robin Hood theme song from Bryan Adams "Everything I Do, I Do It For You" was number one for the whole summer? He left a copy of that single with his wedding ring and a dead rose, which is pretty much tantamount to a note. In the song it says: "I'd die for you". That became a very hard song to hear afterwards. So I don't know. We'll never know what was going through his mind. That's one of the things suicide does to you, to the people left behind, all these questions. We'll never actually get closure. You don't have the full story; you've never been given the chance to have a row with someone, have a talk with somebody, or shout at them. There's all that unresolved stuff. You can never say "You bastard" or shake somebody; you can't do anything. You're left with this fait accompli; there's nothing you can do about it. It's a bit like having the last word and prancing out of the room – take that!

It really affected everybody afterwards, the whole family, in different ways. I'm sure it's really affected my sister but she's never talked about it. My family's never really talked about emotions anyway. They made up some story to tell the kids. I think probably they know now. I'm not sure whether they still know the whole thing, because there are little ironies. Like now, Robert's 20 and he's into carpentry, he's a carpenter, that's his thing, and he wants to have a nail gun, and he's bought himself a nail gun, and all the gear. He obviously doesn't know about that…so much his father's son in that way, always into tools. But, no, it becomes a very difficult thing, all that unsayable stuff.

When they were growing up, the kids, single parent, dead father, it wasn't really gone into. It's difficult enough if a parent's died anyway, but if a parent's died from suicide…there's still quite a taboo about it, I think. I still think about it quite a lot after all this time. 1991, that's quite a long time ago. I can't get rid of those images, you know, of finding him, the wound and all that kind of thing, you just don't get rid of that stuff really, it's just sort of in there. That's life I suppose. I've written about it, that helps, I've written a song about it and I've played that quite a bit recently but it is very hard to play. People say: "You should arrange that song, or do that song" and they don't really have any idea that it's not just material, it's cathartic every time I perform it. It's not just like, let's play this old tune, turn to page 56 kind of thing (The song 'In Your Dying' was to become a centrepiece of the Edinburgh show in 2009). I wrote a sequence of poems about it as well. "A Broken Song", using different song lyrics, seven poems in all, but I haven't read that for a while either.

MUM

My mum tried to commit suicide as well. In 1981, when my parents had broken up, she sort of disappeared for a while, she went through a period when I took a year off university and she was really in a state. She lost so much weight she was more or less anorexic – in a real state. There was a whole year when my dad hadn't really decided what he was going to do. It was crap: maybe I should stay, maybe I shouldn't stay. He left and then he came back and then he left again. My mum was very affected. She had an overactive thyroid through the shock of it and lost four stone; became "like a matchstick with the wood scraped off", as a neighbour said. She wasn't really aware of what she was doing, walking in front of buses and all that kind of stuff; we had to keep an eye on her. And then she disappeared one day. I saw this note saying she was going to visit a friend, an old school friend. My sister and I thought this was a bit odd, so we rang up the person and found that she wasn't there. Sure enough, she'd driven over to see my dad, who was staying in Hounslow then with this other woman (as he told us afterwards), and confronted them. Then she'd closed up the windows and driven off, taken some pills that she had with her, sleeping tablets, and gone to her father's grave in Northolt. Then kept driving along, the pills starting to take effect. She was quite lucky, really. She crashed the car in traffic. No one was terribly hurt, fortunately. She ended up in hospital, where she had her stomach pumped, and the police got in touch with us, so I went over there.

With suicide attempts, there are different levels of trying aren't there? There's taking the tablets and driving a car, and you may get unlucky, you might die. You may easily just take too many, or go onto a motorway and run into somebody, a full head-on collision. You are certainly throwing the balls into the air. But firing a nail into the middle of your brain is something else, there's no way back from that situation. So there must be something different going on there. I don't know what that is, whether it's madness, depression if you want to call it that, more like despair I think. There's a belief or feeling that this is it, there really isn't anything afterwards. Because certain things are done, like maybe my mum's attempt, when although you may not acknowledge it, at some level you're aware of the effect that you're having. You know that this attempt might have an effect, and when you come back some people might be nicer to you, or whatever it is, being crude about it. But there are other times when people take their own lives, or try to, and they don't care about that stuff; they're depressed, they don't care whether anybody meets them again, whether there's any more life. It's just: "This is it, I'm finished". And maybe that was it with him, although it's very hard to be black and white. There's obviously something directed at my sister, in order to punish her in some way. And the whole thing with the song and the dead rose and the wedding ring given back – that was primarily to get at her, wasn't it? For me it was indirect; he didn't know it was going to have an effect on me.

Then, years later, she came across the tickets for Guns n' Roses that they were supposed to be going to see when they had the big bust-up. She found them on the exact date that was on the ticket ten years from then. So it would have been end of August 2001, exactly ten years afterwards. She was just having a tidy up and she came across these tickets by chance. She's never talked about it very much. It's a hard subject to broach. It must have really affected her; she's never been out with anyone since. She's 45 now. She would have been 29 or something. She's not seen anyone, as far as I know; she's just completely shut down that side of herself, as if there's just too much pain in that direction. Maybe that is a common reaction, I don't know. Her mum's been quite like that, too. Since my dad left, there have been various people who have been kind of companions, but no full emotional involvement really.

RYK

Then there's my friend Ryk, whom I met when we worked for the *Pink Paper*.

He's on anti-depressants, quite long-term. He'll send me texts several times during the day... He'll want to meet for coffee so I can provide some impetus for him getting up or doing something with the day. Otherwise he might just stay in bed all day, and the next day. So if we meet for coffee at 11 or something it means he has to get up. But you can't really do that when you're working, when you've got a full-time job. Other people's lives are their own responsibility. But sometimes I haven't heard from him for a couple of days and he'll say he's been in bed or something, not dealing with things, not getting up. He'll send me texts or he'll phone me when he knows that I'm not there. It's a bit like call dumping, or like counselling, phone counselling, he'll just dump his problems on my answering machine. It can go on for quite a while, and you start to think, hmm why am I hearing this? It's a different kind of madness really. It's not like suicide or anything like that, more everyday in a way, but it's still not quite dealing with life in the normal way. Whatever that is.

He has quite a strange life, he's on Sickness Benefit, I guess because of the depression, or Incapacity Benefit, whatever it's called, and he's very, very careful. He doesn't really have to find his way out of it. He's got a lot of friends or acquaintances, so he's always seeing someone every night. He doesn't spend that much time on his own, and he has various back-up or contingency plans so that if he's not seeing a particular person one night he'll be seeing somebody else instead. He's always very, very busy doing lots of things, like courses, this that and the other. It's kind of a mad life, certainly different to other people's lives. You'd think, like other people of his age, mid-late forties, that he'd be stuck into a job or starting to get managerial or quite serious by that stage, yet he's still sort of living like a student.

It's not as spectacular as I mentioned with Paul; it's a different kind of thing, more like neurosis than psychosis. It's more of an everyday thing that he can manage now, with the drugs, the anti-depressants. With depression, if you're really feeling down you withdraw. So you stay in, you don't see anyone, you stay in bed, at home. Whereas psychotic states are much more about making things happen, or believing you can make things happen. Or they can be, and tend to get you more noticed.

ME

I have a tendency to depression myself. I've had various times when I've thought, what's the point of anything, and you just don't do anything, you can't cope with seeing anybody, and it has its own momentum. You don't want to see anyone, or do anything social, so you think you're not worth seeing, so it goes on... There are things you can do in this state, like some ten years ago when I was living with my mum. I wasn't getting out, I wasn't happy; there were various issues that I hadn't resolved. I was arrested by the police and got a criminal record. I was working for Virgin at the time, and I can remember I took some CDs from the returns box where people bring things back, they're usually ok, they just don't play on their CD player or whatever. And I was caught. But the thing that stands out in my mind is that it was not like being in the supermarket and not being charged for something and thinking you got away with it, like lots of people do; or doing some photocopying and no one knows about it, all that middle class stealing that goes on. I took a couple of things and I can remember feeling maybe this wasn't a good idea, and I was putting them back and then taking them again.

It was almost like I wanted something to happen, I wanted to be found out, at some level. Anyway, of course people had noticed this and I had that awful time when I was interviewed and the police got involved. Anyway, I spent a few hours in a cell, which wasn't very nice, but I got away with it, well I just paid a fine. It's always something I have to explain when I go for teaching jobs. It's not something I can quite understand. The only way I try to understand it is that part of me was trying to push…my unconscious was trying to make something happen…was trying to push me out of the situation I was in. In the same way that George Michael got caught in a toilet in Los Angeles, or wherever it was, with a policeman before he'd come out really, to everybody. And there's a way that sometimes things need to come out, or things need to happen, and if you don't actually do it consciously it has a way of happening anyway. It's human behaviour. That's my theory anyway. Yes, I'm a certified villain!

(You must be too, You must have a record, for your brushes with the police. No? I bet there's some record somewhere of your mental misdemeanours.)

In what way would you go about reducing the stigma associated with mental illness?

Well, I think one of the ways is this understanding, or intuition maybe, that it isn't an "us and them" thing – that some people are mad and everybody else is normal, but that there is more of a continuum. There are gradations, there are stages and there are places where you definitely step over a line but nevertheless there are other times when we're all acting more or less oddly, in unhinged ways. Or there are times in our lives when we're under different kinds of stress, difficult circumstances when we all act in slightly unusual ways. It's not actually to do with different kinds of people...it's not that some people are mad and other people are not. Although, it's difficult, isn't it; there are certain kinds of congenital conditions. The other day I was passing the town hall and there was this woman with her son and he was wildly waving his hands around in the air, uncontrollably. There are certain congenital conditions, things you just do involuntarily. They're different, things I wouldn't be doing no matter how mad I got, probably. There can be other ways of being a bit unhinged that we all can be involved in. So I think the recognition of that can help reduce stigma: it's not us and them, we're all involved in it to some extent.

Do you think there's any link between mental ill health and creativity?

That's the divine madness idea isn't it?[6] I'm not sure of the answer to that one. I mean I'm a creative person and I get depressed, but other people get depressed and they're not creative or they haven't got the same outlet. If you're creative you have some sort of outlet, which helps.

An outlet for what?

---

[6] *(Much Madness is Divinest Sense - / to a discerning Eye - / Much Sense - the starkest Madness – by Emily Dickinson, Much Madness).*

Difficult emotions I suppose, feelings that you can express, or issues you can't really resolve, like my song about suicide. It's very sad and it's trying to talk about it using words, using poetry, whatever. But the other half of the song, which probably affects me more, is just this sort of thrash where I try and lose myself in the guitar. It's very cathartic, and that almost has more of an effect on me because it's more…it's not so intellectual…it's just trying to deal with the anger, I suppose, the unresolved feelings. I think art can do that, or any kind of creativity can do that. It's an outlet in that way. Talking about it is an outlet. I don't know, I don't know about that one, it's one of those unsolved romantic notions, creative people being a bit unhinged, divine madness, I don't know. I'm not convinced, I don't think it's as romantic a picture as that. It could be anybody.

Apparently the chances of poets having mental ill health are higher than any other group or occupation.

What's the lowest then? Accountants? I would have thought poets would be the least susceptible because they've got a way of expressing it. Being out there, saying things you can't normally say. Connecting A to K or whatever. It's using a different part of our mind isn't it?

Have you found any strategies or techniques that bring relief during periods of mental strain?

I think there were some researchers in America who'd discovered that there were elements of cognitive behavioural therapy and meditation that helped people. And I did this eight-week course - meetings with other people who'd experienced depression. It was interesting, useful, giving you some structures, I suppose, for dealing with it or trying to get some sort of handle on it. Some were more to do with meditation, like having a three-minute breathing space at different points in your day and just trying to relax a little. And another part was to do with cognitive therapy in terms of questioning thought patterns and how true they were – the validity of certain ways of seeing things. A lot of it was to do with being aware of that moment where you have a thought, and it's not even really a thought, where you become just second nature unconscious. "Oh I'm always like this; this always happens to me", that kind of thing you get when you're depressed, you sort of spiral down. And it's about catching it before you get too far down. Saying, no it isn't actually, sometime that happens sometimes this happens, and other things happen.

Negative internal dialogue.

Yes, the way you interpret things that happen to you. You don't have to interpret them that way but when you're getting into a depressed frame of mind you tend to see it, you know, that kind of black-and-white thinking. So that was quite useful, as a combination with practical things like yoga, meditation, just sitting and not actually trying to have a dialogue with yourself. Sometimes that can make things worse thinking you can always come up with an answer, that you have to somehow resolve the issue by finding the right answer. "If I could just think hard enough about this then I'd get to the bottom of it and it wouldn't be bothering me any more". That's usually counter-productive, because then all you're doing is increasing the power of the thoughts, which then go on and on and on in a spiral.

So, actually, by countering them with thought you're fighting like with like, you're not really making any headway. You think you are because our upbringing in the West (certainly mine) is academic – questions and answers – if you just apply yourself enough you can do it, you can resolve this matter and that's it, it's done and dusted and you can get on with things. But things of the mind are often not like that. The more you try and battle against these things, the more power you give them. So the meditation is more like a Buddhist thing, more to do with cutting off. Letting it go, disengaging. If things on your mind are bothering you, you don't try and engage in a dialogue, or try and resolve them, you don't try to argue, you don't try and find out what's happening, you just let it go. If you can; it's quite hard. But it seems to help more than trying to battle. So the combination of the two was actually quite good.

It's hard when you're out of these courses to try and do it everyday. But I do the three-minute thing because that's something you can put into your day. If I'm having a stressful time at work, instead of having a fag or whatever, I just go outside to find a few minutes. It's easier than full meditation where you may be counting your breaths, which is fine if you have a full day to do it, or a week of a retreat. But during everyday life it's more achievable, more of an everyday salve that you can use. It's also like gathering things around you, so you open out and become more aware of sounds without necessarily labelling them. It's very hard, because when you normally hear a sound you immediately think: "plane", "car", etc. It's about trying not to do that, which is very difficult. It's about becoming more aware of sounds or even thoughts; you allow your thoughts in and kind of accept them, not having an argument with them or a dialogue with them, you're just becoming aware that they're there, like clouds going by. A few times in a day that really helps. It's the sort of thing you can do on the tube; you don't have to be in meditation posture, in the optimum conditions. I think it's finding things like that, which you can do in everyday life.

It was called 'Meditation for Depression' but it's really cognitive therapy and meditation. That's because in the last couple of years there's been some research on that. I think it started with some cognitive behavioural psychologists who sat in on some meditation sessions and found there was something useful going on and they started to build this whole approach around it, called Mindfulness Based Cognitive Therapy (MBCT). Cognitive therapy is to do with challenging your behaviour and doing something practical, and meditation is not about judging, it's about accepting what we have here and now, wherever you are, wherever your body is, wherever your mind is when you come and sit down. It's about acknowledging that and then trying to work with it rather than trying to change things. It can be quite a useful technique; it's definitely helped me.

REFLECTION

Steve Antoni (as his stage name is spelt) has become a close friend through our poetry and other creative performances over the years, not least at the Brighton and Edinburgh fringes. His story brings together close friends and relations and their traumatic experiences. The backdrop is his own experience of depression which still gets him on occasions, in spite of all the good music.

To what extent do you think depression is overlooked as a common mental health problem?

JENNY: Far less than it used to be. But again care has to be taken not to diagnose it too quickly. You can't be happy all the time. it's normal to have bad and uncomfortable times. I think GPs are far more tuned into it now.

Is it any less serious than other mental health problems?

JENNY: No. Depression can be fatal. Admittedly people will say, 'Oh I'm depressed!' when they're not really clinically depressed, they're just feeling a bit down. But real depression, clinical depression can turn to suicide as this tragic example shows. And it's insidious too. Especially if you're living with someone who's being a bit miserable and gradually it develops into more. Because you're living with them, you don't really notice it. It creeps up and then it overtakes. But not always.

It is a serious illness. And people can have a propensity for depression, perhaps through what they've experienced as children. And what is the norm? Think of a mother and baby. Imagine the mother looking down at the baby. If everything's fine you look down and say ooh you're wonderful, you're beautiful, you're fantastic. And the baby waves its little arms and smiles back. It's happy, it doesn't know why but it's mirroring what it's seeing. Then if a mother is perhaps depressed herself, or has problems, financial, social, whatever, she might be looking down at baby with a totally disinterested look. The child is looking up at her and all it sees is a disinterested, nothingness really, so that's what the baby feels. Whatever the baby sees, it mirrors and if it sees anger or frustration it will become fearful. This is where I feel that early nurturing and experience has a huge effect on a person's life...

Even after she'd taken off all her clothes he was still undressing her with his eyes, removing veil after transparent veil...

TRANSITION:

Edinburgh Day 9, Sunday, 16th August 2009

The finale. I'm possibly even more nervous than usual; Steve Antoni's two friends Ryk & Ant are coming to see the show. But they enjoyed it! For the week, we've had a total of 128 through the door! We celebrate with dinner at my favourite restaurant - Maxies. Then there's a Fringe Party at C SOCO on Cowgate. We meet up with Beccy, Helen, Luke & Chelsea from Paradise Green. Glenlivet after chips, and more chips.

Day 10, Monday 17th

On the train heading home. A pentacle on my little finger. My heart in Edinburgh.

But we had no photographs! What evidence did we have that it had happened? At least, the most precious words from the audience in their own hand in the notebook Liz had bought me (entitled 'Notes from the Couch'). So after two years of planning, no one else would see this. No one else would realize the story, identify with the protagonist, come to know what it felt like to be insane in this way, for a fragment of time.

Guess I was expecting something more, something to come of this, without a photo or video only these fine words from the audience keep it from vanishing into thin air…

Here are just a few of the many kind words from the audience, so supportive, not just to boost my ego but so that you have a feel of how other people experienced the performance and empathized with its content. It reaffirmed to me that this is a universal story of overcoming and growing through all the unexpected things that life can throw at us.

"Beautiful

Wow. Fantastic, thought provoking and moving. Thanks

Refreshingly honest, thank you.

Good to hear a sufferers view and fight with an illness.

Beautiful piece. The train incident was so much like my own.

Thank you for your honesty.

Excellent performance.

Well done for making it through your own personal hell. I know how terribly difficult and painful that journey is. Thanks for everything.

I thought it was great. Well done. V brave.

Moving and illuminating.

Thanks for such an honest and giving performance – I am an editor of www.disabilityartsonline.org - I will write a piece about the show in my blog…

(See opening pages)

Wai kika moo kau for early tea - cappuccino with halloumi…

The perfect, curved swell of hips, something to hold onto, to push into…

17 - PUSH DOWN AND STAND ON ONE LEG
(RIGHT)

From pushing down on the left side move from the cockerel position, sweep down your outstretched right leg then stand 'like a cockerel' on the same leg. Alert and upright, poised before the next move of her friend, Susan, a fellow writer, a fellow American, surveying the moment.

Joyce and I were married for 21 years, from April 1987 to October 2008 (the last seven years living apart). She moved over to the UK from Florida in 1985 (with Amy my daughter to be), following a visit earlier that summer through her law school programme.

Joyce

In the garden of the Hotel du Vin, Tunbridge Wells

I know it seems strange, since we've known each other so long as husband and wife, but I normally kick off by asking 'What's your experience of mental ill health?'

Well, I suppose it's always been an interest. I've had personal traumas as a result of breaking down of mental health in my life, including both of my husbands. The first one tragically ended when he killed himself and the second husband, his state of mental health, or lack of it at times, caused huge traumas and potentially also fractures in our relationship. So, deeply personal experiences of mental health not always being sound and the impact it has on relationships, on my relationships, I guess.

Do you want to say any more about those or reflect on what you've learnt?

My role, my chosen career now in life, and this is no accident, is to help other people through therapy pick up the pieces when relationships break down. Looking back at what happened in my own personal history, I'm incredulous at how little support was offered to me. I don't know quite why I never asked for it, but I didn't. I don't think I could see that far to ask, I was always having to be the strong one the supposedly "sane one" so it wasn't me who needed the doctors, according to the norms of society anyway. But when I look back on it now, and I know through my experience of being a therapist, it's not just the mental health of the individual that breaks down, it's the health of the relationship of the whole constellation that's around the individual. When that's not attended to as well I think the ripple effect is much bigger and harsher than if one would be able to contain and attend to some of the ruptures and hurt and trauma that's sustained by the close family members.

I suppose it's a bit of a hobby horse for me now that you don't just treat the person with mental health problems you treat the system, you treat the whole family,. It's important for the person with mental health issues to be treated but it's also just as important to look at the system that person's in. It's no good treating just the person if the system is ignored because they have to re enter that system and they're entering a system that is potentially very fractured, and hurt and traumatised and those sort of wounds need to be addressed. This needs to be addressed as a priority in the mental health arena. I don't think that's being done from my experience of what I've heard of people being affected by this, and I don't really understand that at all.

I would have thrived, truly I think and had a much less difficult time, if I'd been offered a support group for example, to be with other people who have been through similar experiences as myself.

It's pretty ironic to me that when you go to Ticehurst Priory, that I visited many a time to visit you, that the schedule is all with different groups for the people who are patients and yet, at least to my knowledge back then, there was no group for the families or partners or parents or children of this person. So that's what I'd like to see, is more of an awareness I think...

Pause

When you were in the hospital, particularly, I was labelled with the role of 'carer' that's how they referred to me when I met with them, as your carer. I really resented that label! Yes I was there as your partner, and you were having an illness, but putting a label of carer felt like they took away the role of wife, of lover, of partner because suddenly I was in this other place and I didn't understand that. Why because I'm your wife am I suddenly labelled as carer? I still haven't quite got my head around that. I think that's quite destructive to a relationship, when you talk about someone being dependent or unable, and someone being a carer, as opposed to being partners in something together, that is a trauma. I know when it's the mental side of things that breaks down that it's different than if someone has a broken limb, but I still never saw you as incapable, as someone who couldn't care for themselves. Maybe that was just my warped way of seeing it, I don't know, but I found that very unhelpful, and I guess there should be a willingness on the part of the person to call themselves what they want to be called and not be labelled by the particular hospital or professional nursing staff as something other than you see yourself. I know it seems a small point, it's only a word, a label but I found it really quite a big thing and it's something I think needs to be rethought...

Caring doesn't necessarily have to imply that someone's incapable

As a wife you care for your partner, it doesn't matter whether they're healthy or not healthy, but when they put the label of carer on it implies a power differential somehow to me. As though you're the one in charge somehow, the one who knows best and I think that can really create havoc when it comes to relationship dynamics. I'd like to see it more as a team effort, between you and your partner...

Like when given a rehabilitation plan on leaving hospital?

Yes, but not just for the two of you - for a family. It's looking at the whole system that you are part of. We all assume certain roles in a family but I want it to be a mutually chosen role I don't want to be assigned a role just because someone's health has had an issue. It's about having respect for the integrity of the person who's not healthy, rather than putting them in a position of needing a carer. Maybe the reality is that they do need a different way of being in this relationship while they're ill but I would have loved to have had the opportunity to talk about that dynamic with someone who knew about these things, rather than trying to work it through totally on our own.

Somebody like a facilitator?

Yes someone who looks at the relationship as the "client", which is what I do with couples now. This has become my life's work, each one of the people sitting in front of me is not so much the client as the relationship they create together. That was never done, that was never considered. I look back and I wonder with incredulity why. I just don't get why I didn't recognise the need for this kind of help and ask for it. Surely I was an aware and intelligent person (and I thought emotionally reasonably healthy) and I don't get why I didn't ask or explore the options for that kind of help. And if I didn't then I imagine most people don't. It must take an awful lot for someone to ask for help. I would have welcomed with open arms an offering of help to look at the relationship and what's going on it and how is this mental health issue impacting on that relationship.

It wasn't until you were very much in a place of recovery, and that was I think a few years down the line, that we decided to go to Relate. But if we were to get that sort of help from someone who was experienced in dealing with mental health issues and relationships and how it impacts them, in a more timely way, I think there would have been a possibility of shifting the outcome of the relationship...that's a very potent message I feel needs to get out there.

Do you think that would have changed things?

I think the foundation of the relationship had a major crack in it, and you can't paper over the cracks. A few years down the road at Relate those foundations need to be attended to - the people in the relationship need to be nurtured by each other when the trauma is still fresh. I think the years that go by after that, it becomes harder and harder to put it right. So, I would certainly say sooner rather than later...give both people a voice for the relationship, don't revolve the relationship around the ill one, attend to the needs of both people in it. Otherwise you become, as the partner of someone with mental health problems, you run the risk of becoming, if you use the metaphor of a vessel, one that keeps giving out all the time and nothing coming back in again, so that you run on empty and then there's nothing left to give. So how can you fill that vessel during the times of great stress and trauma to keep going? The answer is with more resources, and more support.

Do you think that if it hadn't happened to me then that we would still be together?

It's hard to have a crystal ball isn't it.

Do you think that that period of illness is what broke us apart?

Yes, I do think that that was a very significant contributor to the dynamics of the relationship shifting, without a doubt. I think there were issues there before this that probably would have had more success at being attended to in a normal couple way but once the seismic fractures occurred as a result of mental health problems it became harder and harder I think to put the normal sort of issues into perspective. I don't think we ever really fell out we never really had the kind of situation where we ever stopped loving each other but it was just a situation where we couldn't continue a romantic loving relationship together because all that felt like it was behind us, it had died, the energy wasn't there any more...

Seismic is certainly a word I've used in poems about the experience, because it's like that...I think the reality is that some of the things I found difficult to express about the relationship and how I was and who I was, are reasons that contributed towards the breakdown. It wasn't as if it just happened and then it all went wrong, it wasn't quite right before...

No it wasn't, if I had to put it in a nutshell from my perspective it was quite a lot of years of not feeling an emotional connection and that's the sort of thing that can potentially be attended to and sometimes resurrected if you get help, but not always. I remember thinking about your notebook, where you wrote all your deepest thoughts, most personal intimate thoughts, I remember thinking of your notebook as the other woman in the relationship. And that was before, it was during a lot of the time when we were together, the deepest and most intimate feelings were not being expressed to me but were being expressed to the notebook. And it's crazy to feel you could be jealous of a notebook!

But there was a part of you being a writer and poet and the sensitive side of you that was something I was very attracted to, certainly in the early days and yet it didn't come to me, that side didn't turn to me or have an outlet to me so I guess I felt somewhat frozen out. And if that was the issue and we were a couple seeing a relationship counsellor I'd be looking at how we could take some steps towards creating a bridge[7] of intimacy from that part of yourself that sensitive, emotional, poetic part of yourself, to include your partner in that, to include each other. And that's the work that could be really fruitful potentially, if we could have been helped and guided in that way, but we didn't do that and it broke down.

[7] reminds me of Mindbridge Over a Rainy Day, a joint poem written together in 1985

At least that's my hindsight view, somewhat detached view now of how I see it.

The notebook was ideas and things, deepest personal thoughts makes it sound a lot more profound than it was

It's not that it's profound necessarily but it's you and wanting a window into who you were, into what was going on for you. It didn't have to be the deep stuff but almost the everyday stuff, the stuff going on in you was mostly, it felt, inaccessible to me. I know you read your poems to me but that was the fully formed poems that you'd share with the rest of the world, it wasn't the churnings of what was going on for you in the immediate day, or the immediate moment, that's what creates intimacy between two people. I'm not saying it was your fault, because where was I with all of this? I can remember very clearly sitting on a train with you coming up from London to Kent and wanting very much to talk to you about a play we'd seen and I remember not feeling there was any way of getting to that with you because you were so deeply engrossed with writing in your notebook on the trip back home. Any time I tentatively interrupted I got a sense of cut off. Now that's just one memory but it symbolises to me what it was like, it was quite lonely, it was not the opening to who you really were on a day to day basis on an emotional level, it wasn't there. It was locked away in a drawer.

I think that was a big symptom for us of a lack of connecting on that level together and I think that spells trouble for a marriage. You want a glimpse into each other's psyche's, each other's souls if it's going to be a closely connected relationship...I know there was probably something about that in you that attracted me, not having that accessibility. I know that through the stuff I've worked through in my therapies, that having an emotionally unavailable man is a pattern for me, something I'm attracted to, something I create in my life, in one way or another. So this worked in my pattern of fit with you in a way, but it wasn't functional. It goes way back to childhood for me, I'm sure, of someone who really wasn't there for me on an emotional level, in a way that would be really healthy and intimate.

It's just as much my doing as yours in a sense because you create what you create in a relationship, it takes two people to do that. So what did I do when you were not sharing with me what was going on for you, when you were not relating to me, what did I do with that? I shut off. I got distant perhaps. Either that or I pursued you then I gave up for a while. I can't even remember, can you? It takes two...Anyway it's probably a bit off tangent.

Not really, it's quite profound about relationships and expectations, and it's an important part of mental health - communication...What did I do? I was just into writing really, very happy writing in my notebook, and was unaware that you felt that way. I thought the 'other woman' was really only a joke.

I see that as where I failed in communication to you. If I have a client sitting in front of me and I say 'so when you feel like he's shutting you out what do you do?' What would my answer be? If you weren't aware of it we wound up shutting each other out I suppose...If you could turn the clock back and create bridges of connection[8] between each other at a much earlier stage then who knows, would it have potentially stopped the mental health issue? I don't know. It may have stopped the breakdown in the relationship, which, if you're feeling fed emotionally in a healthy way perhaps you have

---

[8] a second coincidental Mindbridge reference

Steve Walter

less risk of mental health issues. Having a close emotional bond can be a real prophylactic when it comes to having good mental health....Chicken or egg, I don't know...

In terms of stress, clearly relationships are a big factor in mental well being

It's the biggest stress there is...especially feeling you don't have the emotional closeness. And the 'baby', the 'child' inside ourselves perceive that as panic, as being almost as bad as dying. It can become that extreme in a subconscious place in you, that little child who isn't being given the nurturing or the love or the attention that it needs to survive. And there's that part of us as adults, that part of our brain that makes us almost believe that's the case as adults. So I believe that making strong, robust, emotional bonds as partners is the biggest boost to good mental health you can have, because it replicates the close parent baby, parent child bond, that as human beings we need all of our lives, to feel fully content.

In general terms, it is my belief that the best remedy for mental health problems is a close loving, secure attachment to a special someone in your life, and that starts from babyhood and goes on to the day you die. And when that isn't in your life you have to compensate in all sorts of ways. I don't want to minimise that there's genuine, chemical reasons why people go off the rails and there's mental health issues that may have nothing to do with their lack of close emotional bond. But I do think that if you have to have one magic bullet for most mental health issues, my vote would be that to have a close, secure, loving attachment to a special someone in your life, someone you can trust, and respect and who values you that would take a lot of people a long way towards good mental health. If it isn't with an individual it's getting that within your community, within your constellation of close people around you. It's not being cut off from that in your life, because it's not just babies, or children that need that, it's all of us...

And I think that it's the childhood wounds, the core wounds for most of us, that get in the way of us accessing that in many relationships. And I'm sure in my case that was the case and in your case too. It's the stuff of therapy, and of self-development and growth, that gets you to bypass those issues in order to allow the love to be received and to be exchanged...

People have coping mechanisms as a result of childhood wounds that serve them, that make a lot of sense in childhood, but they don't serve them when they get to be adults. You don't willingly accept close intimacy because of hurt from childhood, always at a subconscious level. Those coping mechanisms that served you at some point in your life, as a teenager or in childhood, can get in the way of receiving loving contact as an adult. I think that's the stuff of growth and therapy and I believe that's what needs to be overcome for good mental health.

Yes, I can certainly understand that through my own therapy. I always remember when I was in hospital and you visited, having this sense that you were really damaged on one side of your brain, I saw this physically in your face, and that I was damaged on the opposite side, so we had some bond being in a way mutually beneficial. But that was also a cause of problems because there was a disconnect.

That's interesting you had that insight because there's a lot of research... I don't know if you've heard of imago work, but it's about how the wounds from childhood reflect the partner fit. The couple fit is trying to address the needs that you didn't get in childhood and it means that you fit quite perfectly with people you pick from a subconscious level. It's really interesting work, Harville Hendrix calls it the imago fit. It's quite profound, potent stuff and they actually do workshops on this for couples to bypass the blocks that get in the way. It's no accident that we pick the partners that we do.

I hadn't appreciated how much had been going on for you in terms of the rediscovering of things about your own childhood and your development.

Yes. It's been a massive growth process, and really empowering rather than getting stuck and trapped in it, it's enabled me to really do good work with other people because I've had insight into my own blocks, into myself.

I think that's enough for today...

REFLECTION

It is with some regret that I reflect on Joyce's words. Clearly she found aspects of our relationship and our divorce somewhat traumatic. And she makes her case powerfully for attention to be paid to those who are partners, family, or other relations of those who are, or have been, mentally ill. She emphasises the impact of childhood on the psyche but leaves us with a more optimistic outlook.

How do you think 'carers', to use that almost medical phrase, are treated now?

JENNY: Hopefully with a lot more understanding and with recognition of how difficult and alarming it can be when someone becomes ill, or becomes different from how they are usually, or have been. Joyce says that "it's not just the mental health of the individual that breaks down, it's the health of the whole constellation around that individual" and this confirms my feelings that everyone connected needs care. Sadly this rarely happens.

Joyce's feelings about being labelled a 'carer' are understandable. However, often the sufferer with severe psychological difficulties is invariably incapable of joining in a "team effort". I agree wholeheartedly with Joyce when she talks about "one magic bullet for most mental health issues" being to have "loving attachment to a special someone". With early loving attachment, I believe this strengthens the person's inner core and their ability to survive many of life's ups and downs.

When working in psychiatry I always used to try and involve those nearest. I think it's important. One of my catch phrases for students was always 'Who cares for the carers?' Don't forget them. Don't be judgmental.

Did you teach a lot?

JENNY: Yes, for several years in psychiatry on the acute wards. Staff in psychiatry can become very flippant because they feel quite powerful and in charge of the person who's not well. They can forget that the carers have perhaps had 24hrs a day with them and don't go off duty, and they care and are worried about the person who's ill. They need help and support through that.

The wheels of her suitcase running over cross-hatched steel…

TRANSITION: More from the Fringe

Closing comments from the Edinburgh Festival Fringe audiences:

A great show, it was very informative. For once I could understand how it is on the other side – to have a mental disorder.

Great experience being part of a brave entering of art into the world of painful experiences.

Enthralling, entertaining and very moving. Thank you and well done Steve.

Appreciated the humour related to the medical profession – having written many nursing notes it made me think how ludicrous they are!

Great show with a great humorous slant! Thanks

Very unique and very entertaining. Well done Steve!

Steve & Steve fantastic show, very thought provoking and life affirming. Excellent show!

Healing from the inside and educating the outside.

You gave me hope – that dark times can bring productive creativity – from a newly diagnosed patient.

It's good to see others are trying to take the stigma away from the illnesses and that life doesn't have to stop.

I read your article in the Kent and Sussex Courier which interested me – we visit the Fringe regularly. By coincidence, I worked at Ticehurst House (2000-2007) as a teacher of young patients! Have also visited White Lodge in Speldhurst."

I experienced a breakdown myself & found your performance very enjoyable and comforting. Liked the Lord's prayer bit.

It was always consistently and tremendously rewarding, reassuring and motivating to have such delightful, voluntary feedback from the audience.

18 - LADY'S SHUTTLE

Step from the Cockerel to Holding Ball then push your left hand (which will be on top of the ball) out to the right then turn and step Holding Ball again and push out with your right hand to the left. With each push the opposite hand defends your head and upper body. This is also known as Fair Lady Weaves the Shuttle (right and left).

It's appropriately named, as if a feminine move, one which is both positive, assertive yet also powerfully defensive. Susan weaves her own story reflecting on past and present.

Susan Kerr

Susan is a poet and writer a teacher of creative writing and a fine sculptor of extraordinary papier mache creations. I first met her through my ex-wife, Joyce - they were both members of the Women Writers' Network which met in London, and both are American. Her husband Michael also shares his story with us, of his experience as a carer, as one on the outside, trying to help. Here Susan describes the path of her breakdowns, which now are well behind her.

Susan was born in America. She came to live in England in September 1977 to be with Michael who was to become her husband.

What has been your experience of mental ill health?

There were a wide variety of factors which affected the experience: one was changing country and having a new relationship, a very happy relationship, but still one of those adjustment factors, those stress factors and also definitely the change of culture. And the third thing was that I had a miscarriage on Boxing Day only a few months after arriving in England. It was a total shock.

It was March 1978. We'd known each other for a year and we were in love. I was working at Revlon, but I wasn't very happy there. I didn't have a clear job definition (yet another factor). Once I was sitting, after hours in the graveyard slot, at the desk of somebody whose seat I really should have had permanently. The phone rang and I picked it up and they said, 'The white cab is here'. This was it...the white cab had come for *me*.

I remember I'd been going about the place with a glass of water, I was continually thirsty, which seems to be one of the signs. The glass was a tumbler, it had black and white spots on it, a sort of mystical thing, as if I were a Seeker climbing the stairs. It was an old building in central London with little rooms in garrets up winding staircases.

We had been working on a promotion to do with the movie the Turning Point. I was excited about the possibility of having posters of ballet shoes displayed in Selfridges. I remember I had to go to talk to a distributor in Soho to get tickets for buyers to go to a preview. He had very liquid, brown eyes - he was Asian, British Asian. I was offered a cup of tea. In those days people offered you tea and coffee in china cups and saucers, and he asked, did I want 'one lump or two?' His eyes were so dark and guru-like and making this decision about whether I had sugar or not felt really profound, it told me something!

These events happened within a couple of weeks. At the same time there was a BBC dinner for Michael's department (Outside Broadcast) at the Hurlingham Club. Now I know it's quite famous I'd never heard of the club before. There was so much in England I'd never heard of: 'One lump or two...?' So I had to get a dress to go to this fancy company dinner party. I remember shopping only to find that suddenly all the store names had meanings: Selfridges to find my Self; I went to Liberty's to get free, and I got a wonderful pair of gold sandals - everything had this heightened significance and meaning...the little evening bag I bought had three little fishes in satin and I remember coming in to the lobby area and one of Michael's colleagues who was there said 'Ah three little fishes!'...And I thought 'Oh wow I've done the right thing', it meant something again...

I also experienced what so many people speak of - hearing meaning in the television - the news broadcast and the radio talking directly to me, I can't remember exactly what, but it held extra meaning...

And I remember having to choose - an atom bomb was involved and it was either going to fall on London or Birmingham, I had to choose which it was to be, of course I didn't want to choose Birmingham, and I didn't want to choose London! It was a horrible dilemma.

Ah a magpie...three of them...! ...in the garden...

Then it was either the night of, or the night after, the dinner party and I wanted Michael to have a bath with me. I was very insistent. He was a bit perplexed but went along with it. I was behaving very strangely and didn't know what was going on...He made dinner - soft boiled egg and toast - and I remember sitting at the dining table and saying 'Into thy hands I commend my spirit' as a prayer. That night I kept waking up from sleep terrified, beating on the bed, very afraid. The next morning Michael called the GP, a private GP.

I can still remember trying to prevent Michael phoning, and I remember cowering, sitting at the bottom of the stairs where the phone was and looking up and seeing the toes of Dr HC's shoes and thinking he was the devil and had come to get me. I was absolutely terrified, terrified out of my mind.

Dr HC arranged for an ambulance. But it was a police ambulance - I was sectioned. I remember being carried out of the house still wearing my lovely nightgown and robe set which Michael had given me for Christmas, and I remember the grip of the policewoman. Michael went with me in the van and they were holding my arms and legs. I was terrified, I thought I was dying or being killed... It must have been about sunset when we arrived. There were big gates at the entrance to the hospital, a stone wall, and the sky was a pale pink, a sunset colour. And I thought, 'This is the pearly gates of heaven!'

I was put in the Bluebell ward in Tooting hospital (NHS) for observation. There were two words I kept hearing - Tooting and Boopa - and they seemed really weird words...

So, it all happened over a couple of weeks in March, 1978. I remember, as it were, waking up in hospital, coming to myself. I think I was there about 7-10 days. I can vividly remember sitting at one end of the ward by a white window sill and looking out at the grass which was green, bright green and trees which were bare and I thought 'Where am I?' I had no idea. But I was aware that I had no idea. You see, if this was America and the East coast it wouldn't make sense...in America when the grass is green the trees have leaves and when trees are bare the grass is brown...it's the way things are...

I was on medication for quite some time...it wasn't a bad place (I'm all for asylums). It was an observation ward - there was a dormitory with about 20 beds in it, chenille bedspreads and a pink ward – the women's ward. I remember Frieda who was catatonic, she would just sit there, rigid. There was a fireplace, a hearth, high ceilings...You had to make your bed in the morning and you weren't allowed to stay in the dormitory during the day. We each had a locker, a cabinet. I was still acting bizarrely, looking in other people's bags and things...And there was a bird in bird cage - Percy a parakeet - I remember reaching in to try to free him...

On the first night I was put into a small room with an examination table, and I found a little doctor's examination kit for looking in the eyes, ears and nose and it was just like being a child discovering this. I remember looking through the eyepiece and towards the door and seeing this nice nurse looking in, with liquid brown eyes. I was filled with wonder, and with terror...I remember being put in the bathtub a few days later. I probably needed a bath by then!

That was like a wake up because there were these Jamaican and West Indian nurses and they were laughing at me but laughing nicely and that woke me up – because it was a real experience not a weird experience...

I saw Frieda ...or heard other patients say she's gone off to ECT and when she came back she was a human being again. I've said to Michael, if I'm ever in a state again and one of the suggestions is ECT I'm not against it...

Michael was able to take me home on some kind of a release but they mis-prescribed the medicine. He tried to sort it out but the doctor was on holiday and the nurses couldn't do anything because they can't change what a doctor has said and has written. That was really nightmarish for him.

We went down to visit his mother at some point but, because of the medication (Mellaril), I got really sick and threw up on the bedroom floor. Again, probably because of the medication, time took on this really peculiar quality, the click of clocks or light switches... I remember mum came to visit me and, as I was talking to her, I'd turn my head away and it would seem like a century had passed when I turned my head back to her.

Susan describes herself as foggy and unhappy for the rest of that spring and summer, even into September when gradually the fog turned into a really bad depression.

I'd been diagnosed as a chronic depressive before back in the States but this was not like that, this was a teeth gritting depression which I feel was a chemical thing as opposed to a neurotic type of depression. We went to the Lake District, my first time there, and it was beautifully sunny. Michael said 'this is really great but this isn't the way the Lake District usually is'. But all I felt was utter bleak, black depression, despite the sunshine.

I went back to seeing Dr HC, the private GP that helped us through this. I said that I wanted to talk to someone but that the psychiatrist had said it was too soon. This was still in the Spring. I was full of energy. I said 'I'm going to do crafts' - I needed to make things, I needed to create. But Dr HC said 'No you're not going to do crafts, the best way to get well is to be really ill, be sick'. I was very taken aback but I heeded it. They were very wise words from a very wise doctor. That may have been the beginning of the depression, but it was also the beginning of the healing. At around the same time my medicine changed to Stelazine, which seemed to suit me better, (but this was before my depression).

We went to the US for my sister's wedding, and toured National Trust houses and visited Michael's mother. It helped to let me down from a high. I needed to be down in order to rest. I just was depressed but I really wanted to talk to someone. I'd had talking therapy in New York a year or so after the death of my first husband. I'd learned to talk to my therapist. I just wanted to know what was this about? What was going on? So, in the autumn I was sent to a private psychiatrist in Harley Street. But he was just arrogant, condescending and patronising.

So, later Dr HC referred me to Dr C (may she rest in peace). She was based in Hampstead, and was a psychiatrist as well as a therapist - a leading figure in her field, a teacher and associate at Tavistock. She was the right person for me.

The second breakdown

Our daughter Katie was born in September 1981. Well before I got pregnant with her, in the Spring of 1980, I had another breakdown. But this breakdown took Dr C completely by surprise, she had no idea I was vulnerable. That again was in March - always a fragile time for me.

So it was a similar thing, I was working again part time, at first just twice a week. This time I was reasonably happy in my job. I'd gone shopping in Oxford Street, I wanted a picture for my office but it was to become a mystical search with a mystical meaning for the picture.

I remember I must have been behaving strangely, because after work I went with my secretary, Marie, for a whisky (which I guess she felt would be good for me) and we sat in Berkeley Square on a bench and I was crying. She brought me home to Michael (she was the only person I was really friends with at work) When I got home I said to Michael 'I think I've killed someone.'

This time at least Michael knew who to call and what to do. They probably upped the medication. I went to Greenways nursing home in North London. I had a private room and a nurse and Dr C came to visit me. I remember an Irish nurse at the home saying all will be well when you've had children. Michael and doctors arranged for a nurse to stay with me at home for a bit. I had some time off work but I don't remember much about recovering. I think I had a horrible depression again, but I did manage to continue with my job.

Maybe twice since I've had thoughts that things were moving too fast, making connections, as *you* say - everything connects up. When I was back at home after the first one and still not well, I remember looking at Michael's bookcase and reading the titles and the names of the authors on the spines and I could make each one relate to the others in the row, I'd find some connection between every single one of them, whether a letter of the alphabet, some word, they all connected... Which is like being a creative person. When we write poetry we make things that don't always make sense, make some kind of sense...

What have you learned from that experience? What does it tell you about imagination and creativity?

I think that making connections between things is - certainly with poetry, using metaphors - making sense of things. Seeing sense in things, if your interest is visual you would paint those things. And I could definitely see. I'm thinking of William Blake, where it could be a kind of visionary thing, where the connections join up to make sense and perhaps it's a kind of gift gone too far, connections going too fast. So maybe it's a question of being able to contain this or, some people have more of it, some less, and sometimes it goes awry beyond the world of making sense into the realm of terror.

I think of two of my favourite artists, Picasso and Matisse. When you see what Picasso painted, he'd such prodigious energy, prodigious talent, and prodigious bravery, entering the realm of terror. How did he contain that? I think it takes a rare, a very rare combination of connections. I'm trying to make a distinction between wilfully making connections and the ability to make or see connections that come unbidden. Like haiku, I write haiku. They just drop like manna from heaven. It's about awareness on several levels, seeing connections between things and wanting to communicate so that in a successful haiku, a good haiku, the reader gets the connection too.

Great artists must have that ability to go where others dare not tread.

What have you learned?

Well an awful lot of people do have breakdowns, and a lot don't talk about it until somebody owns up to having one, or says their brother or sister did. I've been taking a counselling class recently, and having had two breakdowns makes me cautious and wary within myself, not all the time but I'll always be aware, am I getting weird or scared? And I guess that's happened about twice. I definitely would take Stelazine if I felt unsteady. I went to a therapist about a year ago. I was in a 'stuck' place and needed to talk through it. My mother had died, my writing had got stuck, my teaching writing therefore had got stuck, I was turning 60, my husband's that much older. I could see the dark at the end of the tunnel. And I just needed to talk that through. I wanted somebody to hold my hand as I worked through these things, because I don't want to go insane, if I go too far. I'm scared! If I probe too much I might set that off.

I've also become really interested in Jung. I took a course on the meaning of fairy tales and I'm totally smitten. In a way, I wanted to rummage around in myself with Jung in mind. I took a one term introduction to counselling class last year and in one of the early sessions I shared my fear of bringing on a breakdown. Later in the course I realised that I'd laid it to rest. I'm not worried about it any more, it's a fact, it's there. I'm just aware.

What has it told you of the human condition?

One thing that Dr C told me that made me angry, and I'm still annoyed at it, was 'Susan you can visit that land and return.' Well I don't know if I argued with her or not, but it makes me angry because when you're in 'that land' it isn't a visit it's a capture, a kidnap, an assault, an attack. And if you do return (some don't I guess) you don't want to go back there again. I don't want to be reassured that this could happen again and return. It makes it sound like it's a romantic thing that I might wish to do. No, I don't want to do it again.

So back to the planet, the human condition - things are fragile. You just never know. All we see around us, the reality that we all live in and take for granted, it's a blessing, but it's a predicament, we have to take it for granted, we have to regard normality as normal. And those who haven't been touched by death or serious illness or mental breakdown, just take it for granted and they don't know how fragile it is. And yet we have to live and have our little worries about stylish shoes and all that...

How do you think you can break down the stigma associated with mental ill health? And what message would you give to people concerned about mental illness?

You can visit that land and return! People who have had a breakdown can and do become themselves again.

How about at work?

When I went to work for Richmond Adult College, twice I had established posts and each time I had to go for a health check and fill out a health form and both times I had to say about breakdowns, miscarriages, operations etc. The doctor asked 'Did you have suicidal thoughts?' and I didn't really want to answer that. I didn't particularly, actually, even in deep depression. It was only a consideration of suicide, but not suicidal thoughts. She could see I was taken aback, she said it's all right you can say it, so I said it was sort of in a philosophical way. It felt very threatening and intrusive to be asked something, but also reassuring - she said it was confidential.

I think one of the things more broadly about mental health, as you read in the newspapers, particularly about young schizophrenics or those who turn out to be schizophrenics, is an appalling lack of joined up care and lack of intervention. They say you can't section somebody until they've done something, well that's horrible, that can mean the death of someone. I personally know someone whose sister in law was murdered by her nineteen old son. If the child is over 18 the doctors will not tell the parents what the diagnosis is, or what it means, even when the individual's clearly not well. In this case, the parents didn't know he'd been diagnosed as schizophrenic, they didn't know what medication their son was supposed to be on. I think they need to know, when they're the carer, about medication, prognosis and the warning signals and whether they're a danger to others (obviously) or to themselves.

Is there anything you'd like to add

I do wonder about other cultures, older cultures about the whole shamanistic thing and spiritual practices: are some of those practices, those dimensions, the same as what we call breakdown?

Is it possible to - I don't think it is, I think it's too romantic an idea – to regard and treat people in this condition gently, to find a sense of comfort and respect for people having breakdowns, as opposed to them entering a state of terror? It's about not treating it as a terrifying illness but still treating it. It's about the way society regards ill people, such as the risk of stabbing somebody on a subway. Many people don't know what breakdown is. We probably need more definitions, more warning signals - how do you know when your beloved family member is breaking down? Is there an answer? How can you recognise it? If someone wears a silly hat 'Oh my God they're having a breakdown!' I don't know the answer to that. We need to know more, there need to be more definitions. 'Mental illness' is a big phrase that can mean anything from chronic, mild depression to serious depression (they called mine a psychotic episode) to schizophrenia, and there's probably lots of others in between that I haven't even thought of...

REFLECTION

Susan has flowered into a great teacher of creative writing and a fine sculptor. Her experiences of delusion and mania are well behind her although it seems she is always prepared in case she senses the edge of a relapse. Her story is in some ways similar to mine; the disconnected thoughts, and conversely the connections, the delusions and the slow return to sanity, whatever that may mean.

How do you think mental health problems may be related to creativity?

JENNY: I think creativity often equates with sensitivity, and sensitivity can heighten perception. I think we touched on this with your aunt Jenny.

This lady had several very distressing situations including the miscarriage, which obviously affected her deeply, and for which there was little understanding in those days. I don't think it's a romantic idea to 'regard and treat people' who are experiencing serious mental problems gently. I have always found that combining gentleness with firmness and conveying a feeling that they are safe – contained -.is the very best way to regard and treat those struggling with such difficulties.

What matters is to feel that we are not alone…

(Sally Brampton, Shoot the Damn Dog)

TRANSITION: 2010 to 2011

 Some time in October 2010 Peter Wilson rang and asked whether I'd like to join him in a show at the Brighton Festival Fringe. I hadn't been planning on another performance, I'd hoped to finish this book. But the show would combine An Acute Psychotic Episode with some of the work he'd done with mental health trusts and schools with his son Ross (see Peter and Ross Wilson). He said we'd need to think of a title and mentioned his website Hugging Barbed Wire, named after the title of a song by his son Owen about his brother Ross and his experience of schizophrenia. *Hugging Barbed Wire* seemed like a perfect title for a show to me.

It was Christmas 2010, Boxing day Monday when we were called to the hospital because Caroline had taken a turn for the worse. She died later that same day.

We had only been to her wedding a few months earlier. Often a tear is shed at a wedding, but her beautiful wedding was especially poignant for a very different reason.

Caroline

I could have said, it should not ever

have to end like this, and that would be true

but what is also true is how much

you held our hearts - even though

I hardly knew you, you'd won me over.

And when you said, with pain
and jaundice, that your fiance hadn't reckoned
on marrying Marge Simpson
we cried with laughter, and hugged you.

Waiting with you, as grains of sand tumble
towards their resting place, as if
through the eye of some universal clock,
we remember the oh-so-happy times
and one by one bid you sweet farewell.

…

Caroline was only 38 when she died. We were with her almost to the last, surrounding her hospital bed, family, friends. She was deeply jaundiced and dosed up with morphine, which inevitably signals the end. Her grandmother was beside her, holding out hope that she would recover. But her granddaughter left the planet before her, and how we cried.

19 - NEEDLE IN THE SEA

From the last stance, bring both hands round together and dive deep, reaching and pointing down to the ground, as if to the bottom of the sea, bending low, then look up and forwards, before rising to the closing moves...

I like the way this move brings the expansive open feel of the form down to a tiny point searching in the great sea. Diving deep, Michael searches, to begin to discover, to understand what was happening to his wife.

Michael Kerr

I first met Michael through Susan, who in turn was first a friend of my ex, Joyce. I've always found him to be friendly and engagingly articulate. He was a BBC TV Director, and as well as many well known shows such as One Man and His Dog, and Favourite Things, he's written four books[9], including a novel (Benjamin Seven) and a biography of the international pianist, John Ogdon, who himself suffered from bipolar disorder. However, it was Susan who experienced breakdowns (diagnosed as acute psychotic episodes). Here Michael describes his experience of caring for Susan and coming to terms with her illness.

What has been your experience of mental ill health?

---

[9] Also the Kutzov Haul and a children's book, The Lazy Princess

My experience of mental health of course has been through Susan, before which I had very little awareness. I didn't really know anyone who'd had a breakdown – hers was the first one. This eventually lead me on to do the biography of the world renowned pianist John Ogdon, because I thought I'd learned certain things that were perhaps important to say, which wouldn't otherwise get any public attention. I only did it because he seemed to have come through the other side - his fame meant you could write about things that would otherwise have been ignored.

At first, as is the way with so many people, Susan was behaving a bit oddly and I supposed it was through overwork. I never really thought it was anything serious because, like most people, you never feel that somebody you know and are close to and are familiar with, you might think them a bit odd, but you never really think that they are actually going crazy. And I think very often the people who are living with someone are the last ones to actually admit that something is seriously wrong.

Well, it all came to a head one night when Susan was obviously upset. She was cooking dinner, I think it was scrambled eggs or something and she just did such a tiny, little portion. Then she was frightened to walk through the door because it would have so many repercussions – like the famous pebble in the pond. She was terrified of just doing simple things. I said that I'd have to call for help. Suddenly she turned into somebody else entirely and tried to pull the phone out of the wall and was hysterical. So, I had to go upstairs to the neighbours to say my wife's gone out of her mind, can I use your phone. I phoned a doctor we'd been to several times and he came round at once and said that she had to be committed.

She was absolutely terrified of him because she thought he was the Devil. She had to be carried out on the street, yelling and fighting. We had to go to the police station. She had to be sectioned. Then she was taken to Springfield hospital, Tooting I think, and I had to leave her there. Again she was frightened about going through doors into the ward because for her it meant either going into heaven, or into hell. I was absolutely stymied, really almost in a state of shock, it never occurred to me then that (and thank goodness it turned out not to be) it was something that could go on and on.

I would go and see her each day. She wasn't in there for very long, she was actually quite calm and rational, she seemed to have returned to herself. The doctors also believed that she'd had this episode and had seemed to have come through it, and let her out again. She seemed all right. By this time I was very cautious and I was very lucky because I was working for the BBC and for once I hadn't anything immediately pressing to do. They were good at giving me time to look after her. But she seemed rational enough and we went and saw some relatives of hers from Australia. We all had a very good time, only later did Susan tell me that she was having all sorts of fantasies and connections. But again I didn't realise that she was relapsing, or maybe had never really recovered, until we were walking along and we saw some black cats sitting on a doorstep and I said 'Oh look at those cats' and she said 'I wouldn't want to live there' and I said 'Why' and she said 'Well it's obvious isn't it, it would be dangerous to live there.'

I took her back to the hospital the next day. It turned out that they hadn't given her the right dose of medication, and the nurse wouldn't change it because she said the doctors had prescribed it. But it was wrong, she was in an awful state, she was quite sure that the doctor she'd seen had raped her. But they didn't keep her in because her psychiatrist was away (I think he was on holiday). He was responsible for her, nobody else was willing to sign her in. So I had to take her home, which was terrifying. She just lay on the floor in the foetal position and I didn't know what to do. It's hard to remember how it takes over your whole life. If you are looking after someone in those circumstances, you just have to do it. I was frightened. My mother was very supportive, but friends tended to keep a distance.

I was quite upset by Susan's family who are lovely, warm people but something like this isn't mentioned. They are American, and I wrote to Susan's mother and told her what had happened and I got absolutely no support from any of them. And when we went to America later nobody even mentioned it, although she was still clearly ill. I remember her father saying to me 'Michael if you'll excuse me saying so, Susan doesn't look very well', which was one of the few times I've really wanted to throttle someone, because of course I assumed he knew about the severity of her breakdown. Recently, though, I've learned that his wife, Susan's mother, from whom he was amicably separated, had never told him how ill she'd been, in which case his comment was not after all insensitive, but well meant, being based as it was on ignorance. Which just underlines again how vital open communication is. So I did feel very isolated

Back in London, Susan did seem to be getting better - she was quite lively. I remember when she first came out of this, we were sitting at a table and she'd been miles away from me mentally, and she suddenly turned to me and said 'Its not true about Rory is it?' and I said 'No' and she said 'Yes, it's all right I'm here at home aren't I?' It was like seeing somebody coming back, entering the world again. I took her to see that marvellous doctor, who'd seen her the first time when she'd been committed, to show him her progress. She was all made up and she said afterwards we're going to go to John Lewis and do some shopping. So she'd been in to see the doctor, he spent some time with her and she was looking very smart. And then he called me in and I said 'She's a lot better isn't she?'; he said 'No she's not, you're not to go shopping, you're to take her home, she's got to realise she's ill.'

And she did, she actually took that message to heart. But she just went into a completely closed state after that, very white, very pale, ill. She was not responding; she went into a depression which, in a way, I found almost harder to cope with than the wild sort of thing she'd been, because she showed no interest in anything; she lost all sense of humour, all sense of irony, things that I meant to be funny she would take absolutely literally, it was like living with a potato! So we had quite a difficult time, over several months, then she seemed to have recovered.

But one day, about two years after her original breakdown, she came back with somebody from work, (she was working for Elizabeth Arden) who said I'm very worried about her because she' thinks she's killed somebody. I think this may have been tied up with the fact that she very much wanted a child and thought that I didn't. I think there was some sort of a connection there. Anyhow I phoned up her psychotherapist who was totally taken by surprise and said 'I saw nothing like this coming, she's an intelligent woman and gave me not a clue that this was going to happen.' She wasn't sectioned this time but went to a private home.

She went through an awful period then when she used the wrong words for things. She would talk nonsense as though she was actually trying to say something but her vocabulary had gone. Which, even in her condition, the psychiatrist afterwards said he thought was very funny. She's never quite forgiven him I think. Again she got over that, but it was altogether about two years of relapses. And then she got pregnant.

By the way, it took a long time to find the right medication, but eventually they did find something that worked for her. The original doctor was very, very optimistic. He said 'She's very intelligent, she can recognise the signs, I'm sure she's going to be all right. I'm sure she'll be able to step in before things go too far, if they do, which I'm sure they will not'. And I think something that helped Susan is that she got pregnant and ever since then there has been nothing - no problem, not for thirty years now.

Except just once, when she went to a writing weekend with D M Thomas, the White Hotel author, who had very sexual agenda, and she found that a bit disturbing and she suddenly felt, for the only time, some sort of warning system. She took the medication which she used to carry with her always, and this was a few years after her breakdowns. And that was fine. It was just a shadow. But, for someone like me who'd read about mental illness yet had no idea how to cope with it, it took over your life, it was very frightening.

One of the things that I found was that it was amazing how many people, when they hear this story, say 'I know someone who...' or 'I, went through it'. Mental illness is so much more common than people realise...

She didn't trust people. She trusted me but she trusted almost nobody else. But it's the not knowing – you don't know where her life is going, you don't know where your own life is going, you don't know. The other thing is the temptation for the carer, the husband, the wife, or whatever, to try and make sense of it, to say this has caused it, or that's the reason, or what is he or she trying to say and can't they pull themselves out of it? You need to accept that you can't explain it, you can't deal with it logically. I think that's very hard for people.

My mother was wonderful, totally supportive and I think, because she wasn't living with it all the time, she probably went through more than I did, in the sense that you may not understand it, you may be totally thrown but you are living with it from moment to moment. You don't have time just to sit by yourself and think how awful it is, unless she was in hospital of course.

Also sometimes it was quite hard not to get irritated, particularly where she lost all sense of humour, or irony, of the ridiculous. I mean, what am I talking to, a stone wall? We know she couldn't help it but - and the other thing is, which is why it's so hard - they are still essentially the same person. The mind may be doing strange things but they look like the person that you know and love, and sometimes it's hard to believe that that person is the same person, but is different too...

What has the experience told you of the human condition?

I'm not sure how it applies to humanity generally. There have been civilisations where people with mental problems have been looked on as holy, for that reason - a connection with underlying spirit.

I'm sure that Susan does not connect omens but she will never forget what it meant to her and how vivid and real it was. And not something that you'll look back on and dismiss.

People are living their reality. It's a reality at the time. It's real for the person.

What does it tell you of imagination and creativity?

Well you can't be totally ordinary if you have that drive, that creative thing. But I think it would be a mistake to equate mental illness with creativity, with creative people, in the sense that anyone could become ill - the accountant, the bank manager, the intelligent, the foolish. Perhaps it is that lots of creative people don't live ordinary 9-5 lives because, if you're writing a symphony or a novel, or a poem, it's not quite the same as going out and working 9 to 5. To be creative, why shouldn't a physicist be creative – they are – it's something that will take you over, so very often creative people are put down as being dreamy and impractical, but it's because you don't switch it off.

How do you think you can break down the stigma associated with mental ill health?

I don't think it's something that you deliberately bring up in a conversation, but if it comes to it - just do not be ashamed. So many people have said they'd had experience either first hand or second hand of something like this but wouldn't talk about it, and the relief they felt when they could talk with someone who'd been through it. In the same way you'd say I had a bad case of flu last week, not to hide it, not to be ashamed of it. I think that's something to try and persuade people that it's not to be ashamed of, and not something that has to be covered at all costs.

Thankfully, Susan's been fine for many years now. I often wonder because people open up to me and sort of say, oh yes, they've been through this, or we've been through that, or we know someone or other or our best friend, or our sister, but even now most people don't talk about it. Or they only talk about it given an excuse. But otherwise it still tends to be hidden, as something people are ashamed of, perhaps because it's threatening, because it is so illogical and can happen to anyone.

Is there anything else you'd like to add?

I'm sure there will be, but only after you've gone.

REFLECTION

Michael is one of the few 'carers' in this book. His sense of utter helplessness is clear from his early experiences with Susan. All too often nobody knows what to do because we so rarely talk openly about these things, about breakdown and recovery. With Michael we also share his insight into the life of John Ogdon and John's disorder.

How can we find a way to talk more often about mental health problems without judgement or gossip, to learn how to cope?

JENNY: Probably fear is the thing that blocks out understanding. I think the only way is to help people overcome their fear. That's a fear of difference and a fear of possibly becoming ill themselves. Again it boils down to education wherever possible.

I think the things you're doing just show how brilliant it is really. If something comes up on TV or in conversation and people laugh it's important to put another point of view, to highlight how serious it can be for those affected. And there but for fortune go I, which reminds me of a Joan Baez song (There But for Fortune, written by Phil Ochs).

Poor man he must have felt helpless about Susan, terribly helpless.

Windows that won't open…

TRANSITION: The funeral

 Caroline had planned her funeral meticulously as she had planned her wedding only 8 months earlier, knowing how close she might be to the end of her life. Here is an extract from the Order of Service.

Farewell my friends

It was beautiful as long as it lasted,

the journey of my life.

I have no regrets whatsoever,

save the pain I'll leave behind.

Those dear hearts who love and care,

and the heavy with sleep ever moist eyes.

The smile in spite of a lump in the throat

and the strings pulling at the heart and soul.

The strong arms that held me up,

when my own strength let me down.

Each morsel that I was fed with was full of love.

At every turning of my life I came across good friends,

friends who stood by me,

even when the time raced me by.

Farewell, farewell my friends,

I smile and bid you goodbye.

No, shed no tears for I need them not.

All I need is your smile.

If you do feel sad do think of me,

for that's what I'll like.

When you live in the hearts of those you love,

remember then… you never die.

Attributed to Rabindranath Tagore

And she also added what seemed a sparkle of humour, playing the Foo Fighters *Everlong* after the Committal. At least, the brash, metallic sound raised a smile, but if only I had known the lyrics then…

.

20 - FLASH THE ARM FAN THROUGH BACK

Rising from your focus deep in the sea, push your left arm out straight, your right arm raised as if protecting your head, then turn…

This move is both offensive and defensive and preludes the closing form. It represents an ending, there is no further movement to the left, here we pause before beginning the turn, and the final close and reflect on the biography of the famous pianist, John Ogdon, which Michael Kerr wrote with Brenda Ogdon.

John Ogdon, Virtuoso

Written by Michael Kerr and Brenda Ogdon

John Andrew Howard Ogdon (1937-1989) had an internationally famous career. He made his London debut in 1958 playing the Busoni Piano Concerto at the Proms. He first came to international attention when he won the Liszt prize in Budapest in 1961 and the first prize in the 1962 Moscow Tchaikovsky Competition jointly with Vladimir Ashkenazy. He leaves an invaluable legacy of recordings made over a span of 30 years (John Ogdon Foundation).

One of the reasons Michael and Brenda wrote the book was that it was a 'secret' within the music community that John Ogdon had had a nervous breakdown and might never go on the platform again. It was never admitted publicly, and outside the music world it wasn't generally known, but he wasn't getting concert engagements anymore. As Michael says, part of the reason for the book was just to say 'Look he's been through this and he's come through the other side, he's better and he can play again.'

Michael on John

His wife Brenda, who is also a concert pianist, had stood by him through thick and thin, but for a long time, she was unable in her heart to accept that John couldn't help himself. She felt that if he could make a supreme effort then he could pull himself together and get out of it. With John people were saying again and again, 'Oh he's got to be sheltered and looked after'. The thing with him was that what disturbed him and worried him and frightened him was simple things like going to a bank or going shopping. Give him an interview or put him under a spotlight and he was perfectly happy, He felt much safer there, or playing of course. Not because he was egotistical, because I don't think he was, not in the usual, the sort of me, me, me sense. He was just in many ways very self-absorbed as well as being very generous. But he felt safer removed from the minutiae of ordinary life.

I wrote the Ogdon book with Brenda and it was an interesting exercise because obviously she'd lived the life. She was very loyal and brave, much more so than people realise. Unfortunately many people tended to blame her for John's breakdown. and still do, but it's not fair. They were oil and water in a way, but couldn't do without each other.

What was John Ogdon diagnosed with? Was it bipolar?

John went through all sorts of things. They said it was schizoaffective, then, in the end, manic-depressive. It was Lithium, that was not used that much then, that put him back on the path. He had an extreme breakdown, but the disastrous thing with him was that (a) he was spending money like water, before he actually had the breakdown. He had such a great arrogance and confidence in the months before he crashed and (b) he was being horrible to his wife.

It first of all started showing because he imagined he was getting messages in newspapers – amongst them one that he shouldn't premier a particular concerto. And then one day he came back from Ireland with crosses cut into his forehead, which he'd been told to do by a charity organiser – or that's what he believed. Then, from having a house on Regents Park, one of those Nash houses, and a house in Spain, they were left with nothing…he couldn't play. He was advised by some doctors that he could but of course he couldn't. The music world was appalled and, almost no one would employ him any more.

Brenda left him temporarily. I was working on the book, and she'd come over to England. Then John was due to come back to England and Susan said to me 'I think Brenda may ask if John can come and stay with us'. Katie, our daughter, was very young at the time, just a baby. Susan said 'I can't have John in the house because he drops everything all over the floor, he smokes, leaves ash all over the place, cigarettes just put out anywhere, he needs looking after' and, she said, 'I just wouldn't be able to cope.'

And sure enough Brenda did ask us and I had to say, 'I'm really sorry, but no'. But then, two or three years later, when John was much better, we went to hear his 50th birthday concert at the Festival Hall where he played both his own piano concerto and the Rachmaninov Paganini variations. It was a really thrilling concert. It was sort of tightrope playing - you thought he might fall off, but he never did. It was absolutely dazzling, and I remember that Susan was so moved. She said 'It was one of the few exhibitions I've seen of something approaching genius. If Brenda were to ask me now, I would say 'Yes. I couldn't say no in the face of that talent'.

John was the sweetest, gentlest giant of a man but in his illness he was also capable of violence. Many people didn't believe it, but I remember once when Brenda was going to give a concert and she was practicing. John had just flown over from America and turned up to give Brenda advice on what she was playing. Then we decided to go to a restaurant next door and have dinner. And Brenda got a bit picky and said 'Oh John why are you ordering that?' and John just suddenly stood up, picked up his chair in the restaurant and hurled it across room, with a look of such savagery! Of course we were asked to leave immediately, which we did...then he was very calm and sweet again.

I wanted to co-author the book for various reasons: I've known a lot of musicians in my life – soloists - and even shared an apartment with one; it is such an extraordinary life, I don't think many people realise, this constant touring, constant changing, changing of languages, changing of people, and hotels, changing pianos, changing of orchestras and conductors. It's a life that I just wanted to highlight in some way and also as I say, the breakdown side of it and getting through, both for him and for her. Some people thought that one shouldn't write about the mental illness of a living person. But people write about other illnesses, look how much they wrote about Jacqueline du Pre or Clara Haskil. Clara had a brain tumour and curvature of the spine. She was a fabulous pianist. People talk about how great she was, with no shame attached to her illnesses.

I think one of the things that went against his treatment was that people said 'he's behaving so oddly', but he never was your ordinary boy next door. He always was distracted and off in his world a lot of the time, and he never had much small talk. He was always brilliant with music, about that he could talk up a storm, and write. But he couldn't teach very well. He had this absolutely extraordinary, phenomenal technique which just seemed to come to him naturally. So he could play Liszt and he could play really difficult, technical pieces like a storm, and beautifully, but he was never happy with Mozart, because that demands...well, I remember another pianist telling me that Mozart was superficially the easiest to play but actually it was like walking on eggshells. To get the most out of it, it's the opposite of the easy that it seems.

Extracts from Virtuoso

> *p173 (Quoting Brenda)...I did not dare to insist; his rages, which were sudden and frightening, could be triggered by the least show of will on my part...*

> *p193...First of all what is a nervous breakdown? Most people think of it as a kind of opting out – as a time when things become too much to bear and one goes to bed and refuses to get up again. Probably that is the most common kind – but of course, there are many variations included in the overall heading of a "breakdown". For example, far from opting out, the patient can be so convinced that humanity's fate rests squarely on his shoulders that he becomes afraid to make the smallest of movements for fear of the consequences world-wide...*

Work or a passion can be so important. Because, alas, when ill John couldn't play very well, he played without expression (he played the notes but he didn't play the music) for some years. But when he was better (although he never practiced enough) he just had this extraordinary facility. Playing the piano, going out there in front of an audience and playing was very important to his balance. It was the same with Vivien Leigh, who was also bipolar - even when she was quite ill she could go on and act. In fact she hardly ever missed a performance. As she herself would admit, it kept her grounded like nothing else did.

The whole idea of the book was to show that he'd come through it. In fact, he did still have the occasional episode, but those moments were rare, thank goodness. He was on Lithium and had to have blood checks because it can be toxic. Then they discovered too late, and in spite of all the blood checks, that he had diabetes. Which is what he died from...

At the close of the book, the authors wrote:

If John's story is exceptional, it is because he is an exceptional man: his illness (or variants of it) is not exceptional at all...The truth is that mental troubles can attack anyone...

Almost every family in the country has been affected, if only indirectly, by mental illness of some kind or other. Since John's breakdown, and more particularly since his recovery, I have been amazed how many people have confided in me, as if to a comrade in arms, that a spouse, a relative, or a friend – even, on occasion, they themselves – had undergone a comparable ordeal (if not often so extreme a one). But why have they hidden that experience from the world? Why, when most of them admit to having been deplorably ignorant when they were first forced to cope, do they not give advice and warnings to others? What is it that they are ashamed of...?

From Virtuoso.

REFLECTION

Clearly John was a creative genius, someone who stepped beyond the limelight of fame and into a place of magic and even greater insight. But he was dogged by demons too, as Brenda and Michael share in their commentary. There can be a lot of positive energy in a manic episode and yet it can also destroy.

Another, and on this occasion famous, link to creativity...

JENNY: But possibly also another sort of problem underlying that. Incredibly creative on one level but seeming completely unable to deal with ordinary everyday things, which is like a milder form of autism or Asperger's syndrome isn't it...? Maybe a lot of people who are really brilliant in one particular direction but are retiring and loathe to be part of the world outside that particular direction, are struggling with an underlying problem.

I'm seeing a lad at the moment, he's fourteen but looks about 9. When he talks to you he's very precise and doesn't like to be taken off his track. One thing he said to me one day was 'I'm different to everybody else.' I asked him why... and he said 'think of it like a motorway, all the traffic's going by and that's everybody else and I'm in the slow lane, quite often on the hard shoulder, and I'm not going along in the same way.

Quite an insight for him

JENNY: Yes, yes it is... It was clear to me after reading Virtuoso that John had early difficulties. His amazing gift was also obvious from an early age and fostered by his mother by her pandering to his every whim. Perhaps this enabled John's incredible gift to blossom and flourish, while his behavioural oddities and complete lack of life-skills were glossed over? Perhaps if his mother had not done this, John would not have become the brilliant concert pianist that he did? Who knows, but Brenda unwittingly at first and knowingly later, continued this process in order to keep John amiable and able to perform – often, it should be acknowledged, to the detriment of her own brilliant career. If she crossed him in any way, or if he thought she did, then John could not tolerate it. He ceased being the easy-going, brilliant man-child and changed into a very large and fearsome man.

As the grandiose life the Ogdons had grown due to John's fame began to crumble because of financial difficulties, John began to crumble as well. Brenda had no knowledge of psychiatric problems and was used to John's unusual ways, so she continued trying to 'carry' everything - managing John, the finances, the children and John's concert performances. She sought explanations from doctors with little success, possibly because they themselves were perplexed at that time. Incredibly, he continued performing with varying degrees of brilliance until he became extremely ill with what was eventually diagnosed as bi-polar illness. Once he was prescribed the newly discovered leveller of moods, Lithium, John gradually returned to his amiable self and to performing wonderfully with fewer big ups or big depressions.

It is so hard for people nearest to those struggling with mental ill-health, and especially for Brenda as she received some condemnation from various others who saw only the affable John who responded so well to affirmations. They didn't see the dark, desperate and difficult John that Brenda saw and remained remarkably faithful to. One is made aware of how awful it is to be the sufferer and how hard to be the carer and this book demonstrates how difficult it can be when there are less obvious psychiatric problems because of brilliance or of creativity. Equally, it could be so helpful for many to recognise that they are not alone either as the sufferer - brilliant or ordinary - or as those watching the sufferer and trying to make some sense of it all.

TRANSITION: Time to change

 I fervently believe in the drive to eliminate the stigma associated with mental health problems. The same stigma that was very real for John Ogdon it seems, among his peers. Yet, even as I write, I have not yet openly discussed the issue at my new job where I've been for over a year, although occupational health know, and so do HR. However, I feel I can't discuss it because people may doubt me, dismiss me...

But when a colleague shares with me his wife's experience of anxiety and depression and openly admits to taking a daily tablet of Seroxat, I disclose my breakdown for the first time, and he takes it in his stride.

Ironic then that I should be so open in some environments, yet so reserved at work. But stigma is insidious, belying prejudice, ignorance, bullying, pervading society.

In spite of it all, in the face of death and adversity, sex keeps you going...the hope that something of you, someone will continue beyond your own horizon and do great things, even just to be, my child, my children...

Or even if not a child, still the connection with love, with how it could be...

21 - TURN, DEFLECT DOWNWARD & PARRY PUNCH

As you turn from facing left to facing right bring your left arm to your body and sweep your right hand underneath, masking a fist... Push forward with your left hand palm up and slowly punch through the space between your thumb and forefinger with your fist...

I like the way the hand comes around in a shielded closed fist (not tightly clenched) prepared for any attack, and overcoming.

Amy

Amy is my daughter by Joyce's first marriage. Amy chose to be adopted by me when she was 17, and I was very proud and delighted that she did. Here she shares some of her own story, coming to terms with the death of her father when she was very young, and then coming to an understanding of my breakdown as she became an adult.

Amy's place, Primrose Hill

What's been your experience of mental ill health?

Well, my father committed suicide when I was little and I didn't really know him. He committed suicide when I was four and he was mentally ill, so right there I was born into drama around mental illness. So that was number one. And I think that even though I was never aware of the actual circumstances until I was twenty one, I'm sure it had an effect on my childhood in lots of ways. And the next time, I guess I ever really thought about it was... Well, I'm Jewish and my family come from New York originally and there's a lot of humour around mental illness, around mental instability, anxiety and neuroses within that Jewish New York culture. So I feel I've always been pretty comfortable talking about all of that stuff. And I feel that New York Jews are always self-diagnosing themselves, very comfortably, with all kinds of symptoms.

Twenty-one was a really monumental year in my life. I came home from a summer of being a camp counsellor in the USA and I think you told me when you were picking me up from the plane in the car. I think you said to me 'Oh I have something to tell you - its been a rough summer...' I think you told me that you had been mentally ill but that you were doing ok. And then I got home and Mum told me about it...I don't remember the timing exactly but I think I had one more year of university left and I think you had a breakdown when I was in college in my last year. I would come home to stay and I'd be aware of what was going on. And we went to that facility in Sussex, what's it called, that posh mental health retreat place....

Ticehurst

I remember going there a few times with mom and I remember talking to Ted about it as well. I remember him being incredibly articulate and helpful when it was all happening

I think when I was living at home after university, because I don't know the timings of your breakdowns, but I think that one was when I was living at home after college. I just remember the night, I remember you not being there because you just disappeared. And I remember Ted coming over, Mum called Ted, or you called Ted and he looked after you. It didn't really affect David very much, because I think that he just heard murmurs that you were in the hospital or something. Someone said that you'd gone off on your motorbike…

I didn't have a motorbike then…that was the fourth time

Oh. Ok. I think I was only living around the house for one time when it happened. Maybe it wasn't a motorbike, maybe you drove away.

I remember you would collect things and you collected bottles, you had them all over your little study. You just had lots of little objects, and I remember Mom commenting on it as being something that she found strange because it was peculiar and she wondered about it. And I remember …as you were starting to get more into Nature and the environment, protecting things, I remember her saying she wondered about all this passion …it was just very intense and I think sometimes with mental illness you direct your energy in a certain way…it's like a coping mechanism. I'm not saying that's what happened but…

My impression is that this was all sort of around the same time as when the marriage was breaking down, there were things going on with the mental illness and that was having an effect. So when the illness happened…Yes I just remember Mum saying it's OK Ted is with Steve. You were somewhere and they found you and took you to the hospital. Ted was just so articulate in explaining to us, or explaining to me, what was going on. He was a beacon of calm and strength, I felt that he was like your primary care giver. That was my memory if it.

I moved back home in 1998 and stayed there 'til 2001.

In 1999 Mum was in Italy and I left David to go up to my Mum and Dad's and David actually called Mum by getting the number off the fridge and ringing her when she was in Italy. But what I'm not sure of is where you were at the time. I think you had to take him to school or something…. my Mum said you both were on the phone to them.

Actually, yes, I vaguely remember being alone, but I do remember talking to Ted about it at home in Arundel Road.

I don't think when we were in Ticehurst that there was much talking going on in depth about what had happened, about what this meant and all that. I don't remember much dialogue about it, with Mom or with anyone really. I'm not quite sure why that is.

It's an odd thing, you can't really explain when it's happening to you

I was in therapy for many years in New York and off and on here. I think I'm a lot more self-aware than I was when I was 21. If this had happened now I would've been much more able to articulate it all - what was going on - and I think I would have paid much more attention. I think as a 21 year old I had no clue at all of what were the signs. Now I know a lot more about it, about mental illness, through people I've met along the way, including my therapists. It was just that David and I were young.

I remember lithium being a big deal. I remember at first that they put you on lithium which was way too strong, or that was the perception, and I felt like your personality changed and that was difficult. Then finally they had the right dose for you... I'm not sure when this was but I remember Mom explaining what lithium was and what it does and why it was necessary, and how it took a while to get the right dose. And I researched it on my own...

I'm fairly sure I didn't go onto lithium until about 2002

By then I was living in the US but I still saw you. My perception now is that your personality has not been affected, you seem normal to me... you have a great sense of humour, you're still coming out with wisecracks. When you were on the lithium that was too heavy, I felt those characteristics were mostly gone...it's like you were, what's the word? Doesn't lithium just even you out?

Yes it evens out the highs and lows

But it was a bit... boring ...it wasn't like the jazzy Steve that I know... I think Americans are more comfortable talking about these things than the Brits.

Americans generally or New Yorkers?

I tend to hang out with quite a lot of New Yorkers. But I do think Americans in general tend to be a lot more open. I think in England there's still this stiff upper lip culture where things don't always get talked about. I think in the US there's a longer tradition of all of this being out in public...

For example, I want to do one of those charity walks for suicide prevention. There's a US charity which organises at least one walk in New York city every single month of the year, and people can sponsor you to walk. I only found out about it recently and I thought this is great - there must be one of these in England. But there's not an organisation like that here that does walks. There's a couple of websites on suicide, one is just for teenagers one is just for families but not as big as they are in the US where there are big charities that raise lots of money and do lots of fundraising. I would like to be involved with something like that, but I haven't seen the opportunity for it here...

I find it interesting as an individual that my two father figures in my life have both been mentally ill in very similar ways. Obviously it will have an effect on me in the sense that I am interested in learning about it... it's always been something that's interesting to me in my adult life.

When you think of being mentally ill what does that mean to you?

I mostly think of men! *(Good natured laughter)* Because that's been my experience...

I think it's neurological often and although obviously environmental factors play a part. But for people who are mentally ill it's important that it's recognised early so that they can be offered help... I've known quite a few friends who've suffered from depression and I have a couple of friends who suffer from anxiety and they take drugs for it. This is again a very New York thing 'Oh you're anxious - I'll give you some klonopin' (clonazepam). But I think it's a different culture in the US.

And with two of my best friends, both of their husbands have suffered from clinical depression. So I've counselled them, listened to their stories, watched their boyfriends try different drugs, come off them and go back on them again. Maybe this is why I keep thinking it mainly affects men because I don't know many women.

I've always thought that problems with mental health are probably more common in women than they are in men. I'm not sure how it's broken down by type, maybe more cases of anxiety in women.

I've learned about clinical depression through my friends, so I think it must be very common. I know it is.

1 in 4

I didn't talk about anger...I remember lots of fights when I was a teenager, like in the car, or in the kitchen, between you and Mom. I also remember lots of happy times as well, it's not like the fights dominate. But I remember you being very, very angry, you'd explode and slam doors and then you would apologise afterwards, and you'd be very remorseful. You were always very sad that you'd lost your temper. Now you strike me as someone who is not angry; you seem very calm and very peaceful. I really can't imagine you getting very angry, the way you used to...

I must confess that I have been, but rarely...

You used to go ride your bike as therapy ... so I think that's connected to mental well-being and how you manage stress...

I'm sorry that you remember so many times...

Don't worry, that's life...As I say I remember you being very apologetic for it. You were never, ever angry at me...

I do remember one time when I was upset at you not eating and I threw your food away and stormed off down the canal

I don't remember that at all...and yet I remember things when I was a lot younger...

I don't know whether to share this, but I only found out in that summer of 1997 how my dad had died, my grandma told me. That was a huge thing. When I got back, I spoke to Mom about it and it was upsetting for us both. I now realise that was around the same sort of time as this was going on. That summer literally changed my life. Basically I was becoming an adult, the summer it all went down, in a good way...

I spoke to some of my close friends about you at college, I confided in them. I think it was really nice having distance, being in college and not having to be at home. But I was clearly keen to be at home because in 1998 I moved back into the house and I was excited to do that. So there wasn't any tension around that. It feels like a lifetime ago...

Does consideration of mental health enter your life as a teacher? Do you find you recognise children with potential problems?

Yes, it is part of what I need to do and I think having had this life experience with parents and having lived in New York (which has to be number one in terms of world ranking of places where mental illness is talked about and out in the open). In the schools where I taught, we worked really closely with the educational psychologist. We met with them every week and talked about individual children and were always diagnosing things. Now I work in an American school, so yes it's a big deal, and there are sometimes kids who are mentally unstable.

There's an educational psychologist at my school, on site all the time. She does individual case studies of children, she interviews them, she does tests on them and then she creates a report. So I refer children to her. In New York I just remember one particular girl who would throw chairs across the room. She was completely wild; she ended up having to leave the school in the middle of the year to go to a special school. Apparently the walls of that school were padded because kids would throw things all the time. They put her on pills to regulate her behaviour. She was 9.

What do you think about the stigma associated with mental illness?

I don't often think of a stigma, I'm quite open telling people about it. But I probably would censor myself, depending on the situation generally. I feel very confident in my beliefs about the causes of mental illness. It's nothing to be ashamed of. Just like everything else I think people should be given time off work when they need it. For instance there's somebody I work with who clearly needs to take some time off but if he told people it was because he was mentally unwell that would not go down well. He'd have to make up some other reason, so yes I'm sure there is a stigma, which is a shame.

Anything else you'd like to add?

I'm very interested in the link between creativity and mental illness. Just because a lot of my favourite poets and writers killed themselves: Sylvia Plath...Anne Sexton...Virginia Woolfe, and a lot of people that I really admire and respect creatively I know have suffered from depression. And I know a lot of research has been done about it already...they actually call it the Sylvia Plath Effect when female writers kill themselves.

Maybe that falls more heavily on the poets than other writers...

REFLECTION

Amy's is a powerful and traumatic story having lost her father when, like Jenny Parkes, she too was so young. Through psychotherapy she has greater insight into her experience and is both creative and reflective herself. She hints at mental illness amongst many well-known writers and poets, as if one were connected to the other.

I wish I could have done more to help Amy through the pain of her experience. What advice do you have for parents?

JENNY: It's just so hard for parents. As I said for Peter and Ross, just being there consistently and supporting is important, as is looking after themselves, their own well-being and their relationship. I can understand your feelings of helplessness but don't think you caused her any grief.

If anything you have enabled her to have a deeper, more accepting understanding of how mental ill-health can happen to anyone. She knows the value of seeing 'shrinks' which is more accepted in America and holds little stigma there. She is both pragmatic and confident in her appreciation of the frailty of the human condition.

...a cafe full of men, with women cooking and serving...

TRANSITION: Brighton Fringe 2011

 We had two slots on consecutive Sundays in May. We'd not had a complete run through although we had rehearsed our pieces individually. And we did map out the stage in Peter's garden and took a walk through the positions, a kind of pre- technical rehearsal. Then the real technical took place on the morning of the first show. This gave it an edge which I believe helped our performance. It was fresh, stimulating and we had great feedback.

Preparations for both of the shows were set against the tragic backdrop of Liz's sister, Sue, (Caroline's Mum) deteriorating mentally and eventually, just before the second show, being taken into hospital with what seemed at the time a bizarre diagnosis of cognitive dementia.

We believed all she needed were a few of my anti-psychotic tablets and she would be fine. But apparently these held an increased risk of stroke, especially as she is paraplegic and also on warfarin.

It was with some trepidation that I visited her in hospital one evening during the week after the show on my motorbike. I arrived in the psychiatric ward for the over 65s squeaking in my leathers to a slight frisson amongst the nursing staff and held a conversation of sorts, an hour or so passing the time of day.

And yet her balance and recovery were compromised because it was a mixed sex ward and deranged men were shouting, intimidating or directly pestering her.

Hugging Barbed Wire - Comments

As with Edinburgh, I do not include these comments just because they say good things about the show, but to record that the experience meant something real to the audience, they identified, they understood and they shared the pain, and the joy of recovery.

Sunday 8th May 2011

Extraordinary – brilliant x

Everybody knows 'somebody' thank you for insight and honesty

This production touched the inner most sense – truly heart searching backed up with great musicality and true stories

An excellent event. This was a very moving and thoughtful tribute to both those experiencing psychosis and their families. Remarkable insight, touched my heartstrings, very honest and thought-provoking

I appreciate the glimpse of what a mental health condition can be like from the inside and for the family. For my own taste rather less music and rather more talk would be better (!) ☺.

To anyone brought up on classical music the volume of the guitar music was extremely unwelcome (!) ☺

Thank you for sharing your stories. Good luck for the future!! Brilliant!!!

Very moving and utterly brilliant!

Sunday 15th May

Thank you all for your honesty. I hope it inspires others as much as me to acknowledge the elephant in the room xxx

Disturbingly accurate

Powerful and thought-provoking

Heartfelt stories. Very moving songs and gripping. Really enjoyed it – if that's the right word!

Hi, we have just got home from Komedia having seen Hugging Barbed Wire. I came to see it with my daughter who has had a similar experience to Ross and has spent almost 3 years in hospital, been sectioned etc and we too had the inevitable struggles with funding and battles with the Trust.. I wanted to thank you for the honesty of the evening and we both related to aspects of it very closely. It was refreshing to have an honest account and I feel full of hope. The devastating effect of mental illness on the whole family and friends came across so clearly. Thank you

From my perspective (daughter) I just wanted to say thank you because since coming out of hospital I have felt so alone in terms of being a "mental health' patient, sufferer, in recovery- or whatever the technical term is. I just wanted to say that after seeing your show I feel much less alone so thank you for bravely sharing.

For extracts from the show visit:
www.huggingbarbedwire.com

Out like a light, no longer of this world. The fear is in the waiting…

What does it mean? What does it mean Mummy…?

22 - WITHDRAW and PUSH

After the punch unclench the light grip of your fist and, with both hands palms upward, break away as if breaking an opponent's grip, then after coming to your centre roll your hands forward, pushing away from you, as if rolling a huge ball.

This move is like that which repeats after Stroking the Peacock's Tail, another point of focus, of stabilising.

David

My son, David, was born in February 1989. Here he takes a step back from his experience of his father's breakdown and recovery, and reflects on our (lack of) understanding of the mind and normality.

David's perspective

If there's one thing I learned from three years studying Psychology, it's how little we know about the mind. We're comfortable with the physiology of the peripheral nervous system in that we understand simple reflex pathways and the biology of neurons. We've even started to scratch the surface of how the complicated bit at the top works; we can localise certain broad brain functions, read brainwaves and are making headway into computer-modelling a brain. But I was surprised to find out at the end of my degree in the 'study of the mind' that we don't even know what 'the mind' *is*. What is the relationship between that physical lump of neurons – the yolk in the eggshell – and our sense of self, or our consciousness? This is still the realm of Philosophy.

How, then, can we begin to study Abnormal Psychology? What is an 'abnormal' version of something we don't understand? The answer lies in statistics – the *normal* distribution. Everyone is unique, but taking a large enough sample of almost any characteristic (be it height, IQ or the results of a psychological mental health questionnaire) will result in a lovely neat 'bell curve' distribution. If you happen to lie far enough away from the centre of this distribution, in its thin tails, you may be labelled 'abnormal'.

I watched Stephen Hawking's *Universe* the other day, and it brought home the fact that absolutely everything is at the mercy of chance. Here's why. After the Big Bang, it was chance imperfections that allowed gravity to collapse the otherwise evenly distributed gas into stars. These burned and exploded to create the elements that solar systems are made of, one of which is ours. The chemicals on one of these planets, travelling at exactly the right speed to orbit the Sun, spontaneously combined under the Sun's energy to form DNA and RNA such that they could replicate themselves – life. Natural selection, a process governed by chance, then produced new species, sperm and egg repeatedly coinciding, generation after generation, until the current animal and plant population of the world existed. The chance of any one of these organisms existing is almost infinitesimally small, having been multiplied through every generation of its prehistoric ancestors, and even in the stardust before our Sun was born.

One of the most spectacular chance creations is the human brain, which grows at the rate of over 4,000 neurons per second in early pregnancy, after which it sheds about a neuron per second and restructures its 500 trillion synapses as it learns. This organ, spontaneous organisation of chemicals from the stars, allows logic and Science, the Arts and Culture, self and consciousness. It also allows hypothetical decision – decision based on things that don't exist. It is these sort of decisions that help us make choices about the future, like whether to bring an umbrella to work, whether to go on that second date and whether to have children. And of course, the outcome of such a decision is influenced (or determined) by the prior reshaping of the brain through its unique interaction with its coincidental environment.

Talking about this sort of stuff always makes people feel uncomfortable. It makes us feel small, insignificant and as though we are not in control of our own lives. I think that this last niggle – that we are not in control – accounts for other things too. Think of times when you were really frustrated, angry or even scared. Perhaps you were frustrated in a 5-mile traffic jam on the M25, angry at a telephone call centre, or scared when walking alone at night. All of these seem to me to be because you were powerless to do anything about them and were at the mercy of other forces.

Perhaps this also contributes to the stigma of mental health. The stigma goes hand-in-hand with the attitude that a mental health problem makes someone a 'mental patient', not simply a person who developed a mental disorder; they are a 'schizophrenic', not 'a person with schizophrenia'. That is, you categorise them as different to yourself. After all, you would be able to stop yourself developing such a ghastly thing, right? In other words, you reduce the perceived risk that you, too, as a perfectly 'normal' person, could develop schizophrenia, and convince yourself that you would be able to control it if it did happen. Your brain is always pulling tricks like this to make you happy, most of the time without you noticing.

An all too common illustration of this innate wool-over-the-eyes treatment is the phrase, "I never thought it would happen to me." That is, it was less likely to happen to me than to you. Our brains even try to maintain an air of control in the face of overwhelming evidence. Denial – "I can't believe that just happened" – acts as a defence mechanism by withholding an event from consciousness. Stock traders convince themselves that they knew all along where that stock would head, despite being outperformed at their own game by a parrot[1]. Gamblers reassure themselves that they were unlucky if they lose, yet attribute a win to their own ability[2]. I am still unable to recall any memories of my dad's mental illness, but reading a mundane detail in this book, where I retrieved my mum's phone number from the fridge during an episode, triggered a flood of emotions and images of me doing so. That simple fragment of information struck a chord with the structure of my brain such that I remembered walking into the kitchen, looking for the note that mum left, thinking about whether it would work as she was in Italy, worrying that I was overreacting, not being sure what was going on and being relieved when mum seemed to know what to do. I did not intend to suddenly be able to recall such things, nor did I know it was going to happen until it did. My brain made it happen.

The above are examples of our brains influencing (or dictating) how we perceive the external world. Like a simple reflex is built into a neural circuit, such responses are genetically predisposed in the immeasurable complexity of our brains. Just as we cannot understand or control external events, nor can we understand or control internal events, be they the mundane evolutionary artefacts described above or mental illness. Perhaps it is this assault on the last bastion of control – ourselves – that inspires the fear and stigma towards mental illness.

However, I think that realising this, and accepting that we all fall somewhere along the continuum from insane to sane and out the other side again, will help reduce the stigma of mental illness. Just as we can learn ways to overcome a reflex (think of intentionally preventing the knee-jerk reflex), we can, and should, learn to overcome our tendency to underestimate risk and overestimate control. In doing so, we can recognise firstly that each one of us could develop mental illness, and secondly that those who suffer from it are no more at the mercy of their brains than the rest of us.

1: http://tinyurl.com/n5t7gt

2: Fine, C. (2006). *A mind of its own: how your brain distorts and deceives.* NY: Norton & Company.

REFLECTION

David has few clear memories of my breakdown. Here he shares a tender, yet logical, insight into our understanding of the human mind and where it leaves us when we consider what is 'normal'.

How did you react to David's perspective on mental health?

JENNY: I felt it was very sensitive and I liked the fact that he was really saying 'there but for good fortune go everyone one of us' which is something I have always said. I felt he was able to air his knowledge which was good, it was a platform for him to do that. But I also felt he was carefully sidestepping anything that was too personal which is perhaps his own protection. It might also be that he just got on with life which kids sometimes do. But it was very sensitive and he's obviously very interested in what goes on in the brain, which is great!

Yes I was delighted he came over to Brighton last weekend from Bath… I think he's pretty confident in himself about it.

She arrives home at half-past midnight carrying other voices into the hallway and up the stairs…

TRANSITION: Spirit

 Mostly we do not even think about it. There's rarely any sense of anything other than what is seen or heard or felt, tasted or smelt. Nothing other. Few attempts to answer the big questions - in fact often no questions at all except perhaps: which channel, what price and where to buy?

Our lives mapped by ignorance by the obscure, by the edge of dreams - the not knowing...

What is left, other than the body, when we become detached, disconnected from our DNA? Some speak of subtle energies, which influence our lives and our becoming. Visit Knights Rose[10] to learn of my brother Tim's experience as we move into his story.

The silences, the silences are too, too long and yet they precede moments of such brilliance and delight…

---

[10] www.*KnightsRose.com*

23 - CROSS HANDS

Sweep your right hand out to the right and bring back both hands to your chest, crossed, gathering yourself to your centre, as you bring your feet together, first flicking your right foot surreptitiously, as if to trip an opponent.

Approaching the closing move: the voice of my dear brother and, as well as his view of my madness, his own disturbing experience. The penultimate move coming to a resting place, complete.

Tim's story

I can't remember when or how I heard that Steve was in Ticehurst hospital. It seems strange, it seems like the sort of thing that you should remember like where you were when you heard Kennedy or Lennon were dead.

I do remember going to visit him in the hospital for the first time. I sat on the edge of the bed on which he was huddled under the blankets motionless and I thought he was dying. He was basically so drugged up by the doctors that he was virtually unconscious. I sat with him for maybe twenty minutes before something shifted in my mind and I thought "bugger this, he's not dying. Why do I think he's dying?!" And around that time Steve started to stir as well. I can't help but feel that it wasn't a great decision to let close family and friends into Steve's room when he was so freshly into care like that. Or maybe it would have been handy if somebody had had the time to explain the condition my brother was in before they let me in the room. It's disturbing enough going into these hospitals when you are not used to them with their unfamiliar sporadic and somehow haunting, arbitrary yells from other patients a long way off. So a little briefing could have helped. We did have on the way out – we bumped into a doctor who explained Steve was so heavily medicated. That was handy! This is not a criticism of the hospital, just an observation.

Why did I jump to the rather illogical conclusion that he was dying? It seemed like the end of the world at the time. I wasn't clear exactly what had happened to him. "Nervous breakdown" had been talked about, but what does that mean exactly? Manic-depression, bi-polar disorder, acute psychotic episode these were words that were yet to come to mean something to me.

Steve and I don't see each other very often. Even when we lived in the same town we weren't that much in each other's lives. But you know, if anybody were to ask, I would always say, "Yes, we're close" as brothers. I guess that comes from the closeness that we had as children. I couldn't have ever wanted for a better big brother. Got no idea why or what it was that made us close, but it seemed to happen. And even though we don't see each other very often these days as middle-aged, pot bellied (one more than the other) balding (again, one of us more than the other) blokes we're still "close".

So, seeing Steve lying in that hot shabby room... how did it affect me?

When Steve did come to, a bit, he mumbled something like "What have I done? Oh god, what have I done?" That set my mind racing and all sorts of possibilities flooded into my far from innocent mind.

Peculiarly one of Steve's old school friends turned up while I was still with him and, as Steve was so medicated and out of it, we popped off for a drink at the local. Turns out later that this friend also had a breakdown a few years later, but he had the sort of character that almost made one expect it to happen. As far as I was concerned there had been nothing in Steve that would indicate he might be ripe for this sort of illness. Let's call it an illness.

Looking back to before the breakdown, yes he did show signs of doing some peculiar things. He collected bottles. So what? I collect some pretty bizarre stuff now and again. He booked the Albert Hall for a big end of millennium "do". I was just surprised that the Albert Hall was bookable. Good for him, that's something I'd like to do, not for the end of millennium I didn't think that was anything special - it was just a man made date clicking over, no relevance to reality. Ah... and I was off on my own hobby horse and looking at the world through my eyes and not seeing what my brother was going through.

He showed me his plans, his to do lists, his ideas written down for the big event. Loads of ideas. Loads of them...loads and loads. He carried them to the pub one evening in a plastic bag rather like a homeless person walking the streets carrying their possessions with them in a torn white plastic bag. Nothing unusual in that either 'cause I had carried plastic bags with me for years – it was my security blanket, I just didn't know it. Steve had his security blanket, but his life was unravelling despite it. When he rang one Sunday afternoon and berated me for not using the contacts of the family to further my business I thought this is odd. But it hit some personal buttons within me and made me mad and for the first and last time in my life I hung up on him. When he rang back I apologised and we carried on the conversation.

When his wife rang to say she was worried about Steve and she thought he was having a nervous breakdowns I sad "No, surely not – it's just Steve he's like that." It brings to mind now a famous saying by Homer, the cartoon character not philosopher: "DOH!"

How wrong was I? But you see it does demonstrate how blind we can be to these changes in people we think we know.

Steve's illness has made me more aware of manic tendencies in both myself and others. I can see, most of the time, when the manic genes kick in and I hit those (admittedly) rare highs of hyper productivity and then there are the days when the blackness creeps from the Id to shut off the world's beauty.

We are lucky enough to live in an absolutely beautiful part of England. The Forest of Dean is a heart shaped ancient woodland and past-industrialised community sitting between the rivers Wye and Severn. It's a magical place.

Steve used to pop over to the West of the country from Tunbridge Wells to see us, and one day he arrived on his motorbike (July 2004). It was great to see him. He looked well, he had been out of hospital for some years. We sat at the kitchen table to eat our evening meal. He had some red wine and the conversation flowed. Or rather the conversation started and then Steve kind of flowed.

Ever since the first breakdown I was so conscious to be aware of any tiny signs in conversation or in his manner that would give away the first indications of a relapse. It was difficult on the phone as I would be listening for the inflection that meant he was heading off the rails. Any expressions or conversation where he would get hung up on detail and add too much weight to coincidence. Tell tale signs. And now sitting at the kitchen table with my wife and him was an odd experience. It hadn't struck me straight away that the signs I had been watching for over the past years were all there for me to see that evening. He was "hyper" but I put it down to the wine. He was ebullient and he was more candid and risqué in his language and topics of conversation than perhaps the "well" Steve would be. As my wife later described it, "He was Steve, but more so". Only when there was a lull and Steve put his head in his hands resting his elbows on the table and said, "Lately, I haven't been feeling very well" did that immortal quote later sum up my instant feeling: "Houston, we have a problem."

Poor guy. He sat at the table, now quiet and was confused. He was subdued as though somebody had just removed the "Joi de vivre" chip from the matrix life support.

We decided he would be best leaving his motorbike at our house and I would drive him to the hospital the next day. 200 miles with a potential loon in the car! But he wasn't so off the rails that it looked like being a problem. In fact he was very "together" considering. Steve rang his psychologist doctor and I had a few words with him. "Steve sounds confused" said the doc. "Yup. I'd agree with that" said I sounding confused myself. "I think it's best if he does pop back in where we can keep an eye on him" so that was it. We popped Steve in the car in a fragile state and set off. Not long into the journey he mentioned his new lady friend who I had yet to meet, and I said, "She sounds nice." And Steve burst into tears. Everything seemed to hit home to him. He seemed raw at that time as though the wounds of life were all at the surface and all open waiting for a prod. And as we know, there's no greater wound than those of the heart.

I delivered Steve to the hospital and it wasn't long before the prescriptions had been rebalanced and he was a 'right as rain' again. And the fact that Steve's new lady friend is indeed very nice has helped tremendously.

This second minor relapse seemed to be caused by him wanting to cut back on the medication (he hates that word) and it was Springtime so the Universal energies were at their most productive. Say what you will, those energies played their part. The best cure for Steve is that he has learned to be grounded: to be in his body, to understand when his mental concentration is drifting away from our carbon based reality into the whispy excitement of the ether, of the boundary-less mind. There's nothing wrong with going off with the fairies, as long as you know how to get back again.

***

One thing you can say about somebody who's gone through what Steve did is they are certainly not themselves for quite a long time afterwards... and to continue with the crass, corny statements, that's putting it mildly!

Around the time Steve was breaking down things became not so hot in my life either. For some years I had suffered from what can only be described as anxiety attacks. When I started having them I hadn't heard of the phrase so I called them panic attacks. Not a big deal, but a darnn nuisance and a very unsettling experience.

You'd think it's just a matter of calming the person down and they will be OK, rather like a child that has woken terrified out of a bad dream in the darkness of the night. But anxiety attacks are somewhat different. I mention it here because they affect the way the person sees the world. I would imagine they might be rather like a minor version of a breakdown. Don't get me wrong, I am not suggesting my little anxiety issues were anything like Steve's catastrophic breakdowns, but there are some interesting parallels.

The fear, the irrational thoughts that spiral and feed one greater than the next until you disappear into their belly to be regurgitated and spat out to be frightened when the only place to escape the terrible whirlwind of speeding thoughts is to hide and ...fall... to ...sleep.

Sleep: it's always been a great healer for me. Never had problems going to sleep. When an anxiety attack gripped me I would retreat to the bed, if I could and sleep it off.

I remember one of the last attacks I had was here in our Georgian house which has its own very distinct history which sometimes comes back to let us know through the subtle energies of our existence, but that's another story and another book. But it was here one evening when my brain was slipping into anxiety and the reality I experienced around me shifted into ghastly non-presence and my actions and awareness of self became so overblown and over emphasised and the interrupted thinking led to alarming thoughts of irrational behaviour and ultimately all led toward death and dying and ...paranoia.

So, climbing the stairs in this beloved house towards the bedroom where I knew I could hide in a state of sleep if only I could get there I glanced out the window to see the gently swaying empty seat of a child's swing in the garden next door. This completely innocent motion gripped me, held tight on the landing, and forced my attention on it as if somebody had just leapt from the swing and left it hanging on its chains back and forth back and forth and they'd run away. They couldn't let me see them as I passed the window because they would be undone, they would be scuppered in their murderous plans. This person who had leapt from the swing moments before I saw it was a threat, in my mind it was a devil, a demon come to cause whatever dreadful fate it could upon my soul and steal my life in a swift and final gasp. It was…

…It was but the wind blowing gently across the fields and into the well kept garden and tugging playfully at the Summer branches of the trees and the long hair of carefree young beautiful people out in the evening sunshine smiling and laughing…

…It was the devil himself. I had to find comfort in my bed. I moved. I opened the heavy, wooden white-painted door to the room in which to sleep but fear pounced and grabbed me and tore at my neck and my mind and shook awake my memories of… of something… something so awful that even here as I sat now on the soft, clean, crisp quilt and looked at my feet in socks that were wearing through and thought I must get some more maybe for my birthday… but the terror of a person coming into the room to … get me… was … absolute.

Absolute and irrational. I buried myself deep into the pillow I couldn't hear anything but my fast heart beating and my fast breathing shallow, shallow, shallow… and that was the problem…. Shallow….

We're a delicate system us humans, relying on deep breaths of new air provided most often by a regular usually automated process. Nervous anxiety will as we all know create shallow breathing. Ask anyone who is stressed and suffers from sleep apnoea: its amazing how long a person can hold their breath.

Shallow breathing tells the body to up the adrenaline: the fight or flight mechanism kicks in, the body says it's ready and the brain says for what? The body says I'm ready - I'm ready to do what ever I have to do to get away or to fight, the brain says fight what? The body says I'm ready I'm bloody ready bring it on I'll fucking fight it the bastard! Bring what on... oh I see, bring that on - bring on that great threat you've always wanted to run away from, bring on that stuff from childhood that you want to fight and scream about and have buried for decades and bring on the fear and tension and devilment from our daily lives that we simply can't cope with and so sweep aside until the day when oh bring it on here and now and you can run or you can fly away. Do it. Now.

And on it comes tearing in at you from the depths of your psyche the depths of the generations not just your problems, and your inadequacies on a daily level your insecurities and all your emotional baggage arrive in one go that shifts the perspective of your reality into a terrifying place when to just sit and think is more than scary ...but don't think and now see how the colours have changed how they look different now but how do they look different oh my god what's happening to me and listen can you hear that? Our house doesn't make those noises. What's that out in the hall? How can I hear things in the hall when I'm sitting here in the living room watching television which is sounding like a distant cinema screen of artificial noise? But I can hear beyond it behind it and oh my god what's happening to me and sit quietly and breathe slowly breathe slowly the breath of life remember to breathe its only the breath but what if it's not, what if I've got a disease that's killing me and this is the symptom of breathing slowly and deeply and go and lie down before the humming the artificial humming electrical humming like the soundtrack of a disturbing David Lynch film gets too loud inside my head and I speak and it sounds calm but it sounds strange and she's worried about me but there's nothing to worry about as the darkness creeps in to the edge of my vision and I make it through the door and I can see the stairs and I can breathe and breathe I can feel the stairs under my feet it's all normal all normal, all normal all normal Christ! What *is* that outside?! ....

And that's just an anxiety attack, so Lord knows what a breakdown is like!

REFLECTION

Tim has been my rock and dearest friend for all of his life and I welcome his contribution here, which is both candid and salutary. His experience of anxiety, bordering on the psychotic, is represented powerfully and in a tangible way. May the universe heal us!

How would you interpret Tim's experience?

JENNY: Tim was a surprise wasn't he? He was to me anyway. Very much your friend and brother; knowing you as I do I think it's reciprocated, 100%.

There does seem to be some sort of thing that goes through the family. I don't know if it's because there's such sensitivity in the family, or because you're an artistic family -

does being sensitive and artistic have any bearing on it? I still don't know the answer to that one.

It seems to me he had quite a serious panic attack. It was clearly terrifying for him! He said it was the devil himself. His description of it, 'fear, pounced and grabbed me, and tore at my neck and my mind and shook awake my memories of... of something..' is very powerful, something so awful.

It sounded like a psychotic episode to me

JENNY: Yes it did...'In my mind it was a devil.' Yes, beautifully, eloquently described. I found it very interesting. But very horrible for him!

I was so moved by his care about you. He is very sensitive. I'd like to meet him.

A parallel community of Spirit...

TRANSITION: We can cry, oh yes, we can cry...

And we will. And we do.

24 - CLOSING FORM

Push forwards with both hands and let your arms settle slowly, and sink your body slightly then bring your legs close together as you bring your hands back to the tops of your thighs and stand once again as you began - still, silent. Still.

Bringing the story to a close, the end with the seed of the beginning (yin and yang), standing as if ready to repeat the dance again

Although coming to a close this is only a beginning. This is a summing up of the positive change and healing, brought about from those very first words with Jenny, formerly my counsellor and psychotherapist.

Jenny Bloomer

I first met Jenny when I went for counselling, for psychotherapy, after my second breakdown in the summer of 1999. I began seeing her on 28th June, right up until 6th June 2005, but with a couple of sessions, with long intervals in between, after that. It was the beginning of a relationship that has lasted well past the end of my treatment, to the present.

I didn't know what to expect when I was standing on her doorstep that summer's evening, listening to the birdsong, the peace, a little way out in the country. She led me to her study, a small, cosy room, that would have been a fourth bedroom, and I chose the comfortable armchair in the corner, facing the window. That first evening I cried, and cried again after barely introducing myself. And those tears were such release.

Of course we exchanged pleasantries, I asked how she was but, impeccably professional, she kept her private life to herself and only focused on me. How selfish do I feel now, having discovered what she'd been through, as she reveals in this interview.

What led you into psychotherapy?

The brief answer to that question is that from a very early age I have been extremely compassionate about the helpless, the hurting and those who have to contend with 'difference'. An early example of that is being asked at the age of 5 to look after another little 5 year old with hydrocephalus who had joined the class. I would have defended her to the end!!

As my life took shape different experiences and situations happened to me – some had a profound effect on me. I became aware of the fragility of humans, but also of their great inner strength if it can be accessed and developed. These experiences and situations, whilst unbearable at times, have in fact helped me in the work where I eventually found my niche – psychotherapy.

For instance, the experience of my sister dying when I was 12 made me painfully aware of the fragility of life – that it can stop suddenly and at any time. Life became precious and the threat of death was real. There were many lasting effects that only emerged eventually when I had my own therapy but the positive gain is that I could empathise fully with bereaved adults or children.

The experience, when still very young, of believing someone who threatened to kill himself if I didn't marry him, led to 25 years of confusion, pain, and of being trapped until I eventually decided to cease being a 'victim' and made my own way.

In those 25 years, I had 3 children and experienced 3 miscarriages. The youngest child developed leukaemia in 1970 when he was 2 & a half. We were told he'd die within 6 months, but thankfully he didn't. However, there were 6 or 7 years of living on the brink, the threat of death never far away with the constant stream of Great Ormond Street visits and in-patient times plus the cruelty of the treatment which, had it not been in a hospital, would have been considered torture. Wonderfully, he survived and is now a father himself.

During those unbelievably difficult years, my beloved mother died without any warning and I was shattered. Not only was she a wise, kind, gentle and intelligent woman, she was my mother and loved me unconditionally. Fortunately, my father also loved me dearly and lived until he was 90, but it was not the same as having my mother.

In that time I went back to work to keep strong for my 3 boys, because by then, I knew my first husband was having affair after affair and I had (to all intents & purposes) a terminally ill child. Keeping strong was hard and I felt very alone but wanted to keep my children in a family situation. Apart from which, I had absolutely nothing; everything was in my husband's name. Therefore, I just accepted all that was going on. It was terribly tough and I felt very badly about myself. I really believed I was rubbish and a failure.

At 18, my oldest son had a dreadful accident that changed his life forever and caused me tremendous sadness. His legs were smashed in an accident where a car slid on black ice into his bike and into him. Although the initial decision was to amputate, the skilful young surgeon spent a year putting my son's legs together again with many, many operations – bone-grafts, skin-grafts and hospitalisation. A few weeks later, his younger brother, my middle son, was beside him in the Bristol Royal Infirmary having been dragged along by a tractor resulting in a very badly damaged knee!

Because of my state of dependency and my increasing feelings of wanting to get out of what was a travesty of a marriage, I decided to train and qualify in psychiatric nursing. This choice was mainly because the hospital was close to my home in Somerset and I had already qualified as a nurse in the early 60's. My rationale was that I'd now had many knocks in life and was mature and I could therefore understand those problems that people had, more so. That didn't prepare me for what I actually found!

I trained and qualified and became very interested in the fact that people who, if they had had intervention earlier, may not have needed to be there. Of course, it was a place of safety and comfort for many who **did** need to be there, but for those others and for some who simply were admitted for temporary psychiatric problems, I felt strongly that there was more that could be done. My interest and ability were fostered by a psychiatrist who believed strongly in psychotherapy. He said my skills were being wasted and suggested I should go on further and train, which I eventually did. I counselled in a CMHT (Community Mental

Health Team) and worked as a CPN (Community Psychiatric Nurse) both in this country and in Australia. This way I worked with the ill in the community and with those who needed psychotherapy which would lead to healing.

During this period I had gained some self-esteem and divorced my first husband – the best thing I had ever done. I started to get my life together. I had at one stage wanted to end my life but the thought of my sons stopped me and I was determined to get out of the 'victim' place. I took control of my life as is obvious from what I've already said. The wonderful thing that happened after that was meeting my 2nd husband whom I've been with for nearly 20 years.

So, all these experiences of life and its knocks have been of valuable help in the work I chose to do. The psychiatry has been invaluable. It has meant that I am not phased by 'difference' or by strange behaviour and has also enabled me to decide when people actually need psychiatric care rather than psychotherapy. That doesn't mean the two can't work together, often they go hand in hand.

People sitting opposite me in therapy might think my life has been trouble-free and "what can she know" but often some of my experience has helped people to realise that there is a way through. I never feel 'in power'. I sit with another human being who is as unique and valuable as I am and who is not enjoying feeling vulnerable or a disaster. Through having my own therapy and ongoing supervision, I am able to contain anything that might trigger off a memory for me and keep the other person safe. I care very much that people feel OK again and feel able to live their lives as they wish to.

What message would you like to share with others?

The first thing that comes to mind is that... it's never hopeless. It might feel it, but it never is. When one is in a state of hopelessness it's very hard to see outside of it. That is where someone who is able to get through is invaluable in convincing the other person that there is hope. It's important to talk about these things... It very often feels as though you're the only person who's in this sort of state, therefore it's always a comfort to know that you're not and that there is a way through. I'm thinking of depression, of mental illness, of bereavement, in fact any, or all, of life's conditions.

What would you like written on your Tombstone?

I'd probably find a quote but the first thing that comes to mind is' She did her best!' I know what I'd put, well one of the things: 'She thought everybody mattered' ...and also she loved life and was interested.

What would *you* put on my tombstone?

What would *I, Steve,* put on *your* tombstone? She loved life, yes, and 'She cared for everyone!'

What did you discover about me?

I've said quite a bit of that in my 'blurb' haven't I, in the book? I discovered that you were very intelligent, very sensitive, that you had a tremendously creative spirit, that you hated imperfection, and that you hated the thought that you had a psychological problem. I discovered you to be warm, extremely human, and with me you were incredibly honest – I think that comes out in the book as well.

Yes, that's interesting I was thinking that you might say some psychological profile kind of stuff...

No, I don't think like that, that's for psychiatrists to do, I think in human terms. I think of the person. I deal with individuals. Letting them be their own way of being, rather than trying to inflict on to them what I might think. Putting people into boxes doesn't work, For psychiatric diagnosis this has to be done in order to have some way of communication, but actually people don't go into boxes.

How big a factor do you think sex is in influencing people's psychological condition? Or is it just one of many factors that varies with the individual?

I think you've answered it there. It does vary with the individual. It's one of many important factors. People may become very uninhibited when having a psychological disturbance, but this can also happen when people have been drinking and, although in certain situations people do become uninhibited, people can also become sexually uninhibited when they've been drinking. Sex is a very important part of life and of our physical make-up. People are often very restricted in ordinary life with their sexual tendencies, because of culture, because of what is 'nice' or not 'nice' and when people become uninhibited either through illness or drugs or alcohol or whatever, often these very repressed feelings emerge, they come out.

I guess I'm wondering how big a factor it is. I mean your parents play the largest part in shaping your psychological development. But how much is influenced by that innate part of you, the sexual drive. Because as you say you're not always able to express

yourself in normal everyday life the way you might wish to.

Even in relationships it's not always easy to express what we want to express about our sexual feelings and fantasies. Sex is a drive and not only for men; of course women have the drive as well, although perhaps differently - it is part of our whole animal condition. Animals do it without thinking and humans do it thinking. It's a drive and it's what keeps the human race going. That of course has changed. It used to be a requirement for survival. We had no control of the results. It is no longer survival because we don't rely on children and grandchildren so much - our lives have become different, but that's our culture, it's not the same in all cultures. Am I going in the direction you're asking?

No direction really. I mean, I suppose I discovered certain things about myself sexually, over the ten years. But I guess in a way I was still looking for some kind of revelation, a greater understanding about that side of me.

What were you wanting?

Some kind of realisation, some understanding or recognition of a link between my feelings, connected to instinct, or experience in the past which has affected or shaped the way that I express that experience. I never quite made that link. I remembered the time most powerfully, in response to a visualisation, I'm pretty sure it was real, the sense of being alone in the house, and cold and isolated. That came through as a real kind of bolt of lightning...so that's how it was for some of the time...I guess I would like to shape my own understanding of how my sexuality has developed, how

it's been shaped. Apart from the obvious things after puberty and in relationships, what was it earlier?

Well the first sexual relationship we have is with our mother isn't it. And then that is either abruptly, or gently cut off. Then I suppose, if one follows the Freudian way, the next sexual thing is the father. The Oedipal stage and so forth. These are only theories, The more I meet with people and talk with people and explore these things with people, the more I realise that theories may be helpful but actually it's the person's own experience.

For instance, if a mother were depressed, then the child might feel cut off, even when feeding. One of my theories is that you have been looking to women to get that mother love back, as well as a sensual adult love.

Do you remember the person who drew his mother as a witch? Well his mother had tried to potty train him from the day he was born. To be dragged off the breast and popped onto the potty – well, it's unbelievable! This had a huge effect on him. One needs to combine the emotional content with the sexual.

I also think about how many people have worried about their gender because of a parent they were absolutely terrified of, or hated, or disliked, and caused them to seek the opposite. They then thought their gender was in question where in actual fact they were looking for relief and difference because they didn't want to be the same as that parent. There's an awful lot of sexual stuff in psychotherapy because of its importance in our lives.

I'd like to come on to talking about stigma. I think a lot of that is about sexual repression, people not wanting to be open about the tensions of things which are always under the surface, and are capped because of society's culture. And they never get opened up, never get talked about openly - people react in exaggerated ways.

Yes they do, and particularly our parent's generation. I was lucky I suppose, I was brought up on a farm. And from a pretty early stage I'd be seeing animals playing piggy backs and when I wanted to know why, my mother very sensibly told me. It was just a natural sort of thing and very helpful to grow up with that. My parents own relationship was very warm, comfortable. My father would be a hundred now so he was well in advance of his time. For instance, he used to pull my mother down on his lap and give her a cuddle as well as being openly loving towards my sister and myself. Men of that generation didn't do that.

Is there anything else that you'd like to add?

I think I've said – yes - I've said that I've learned from everybody I've seen professionally as well as from people generally. From a very early age I'd been extremely compassionate about the helpless, the hurting and those who have to contend with 'difference'. As I mentioned earlier, at the age of five I was asked to look after another little five year old girl with hydrocephalus. I didn't understand why she was different. This would have been 1947, when there was no help for hydrocephalus. All I knew was that I felt she needed protecting. I would have defended her to the end!

I've also said that as my life took shape and different experiences and situations happened to me, some had a profound effect. I became aware of the fragility of humans but also of their great inner strength. I do believe that humans are very strong - humans are very fragile but also very strong. And I'm constantly surprised and delighted at the strength of human beings when they discover this.

Resilience.

Yes, absolutely. We are very fragile, all of us are, fragility can be brought to the fore very easily, it just needs a particular thing, someone or something, to make us so. An innate resilience may continue to be present but the strength needs to be teased out in order to create determination to change if necessary, but importantly, to move on.

I also like to think there are 'reasons' - probably a parallel to your 'connections'. I like to think of reasons and with reasons there can come understanding and understanding can lead to greater depth, greater insight and change if we want to. I'm thinking of these when I'm with people - when I'm working with people and taking notes, I'm continually thinking ahead about various possibilities or causes as to why situations have arisen.

For instance, reasons how we've learnt to survive. We've all learnt to survive from birth and our ways of survival might no longer be helpful to us. They might have helped us at one time but they might no longer be helpful, therefore we need to make changes with how we approach and deal with things. Nothing stays the same. Nothing is ever the same - things are changing all the time. In order to survive we need to make changes where necessary.

Another thing that might be interesting...I like to think of us as we're travelling through our lives as having little bits chipped off, things that happen that either hurt or change us or alter our perspective on life. We become 'fragmented'. I like to think of psychotherapy as putting all those fragments together - putting the person together. The thing to remember is that all the cracks in the person put together are valid because they are the life experiences of that person.

I'd liken that to an ancient vase, where it is shattered and all the fragments have gone everywhere. We've then put them back together into that analogous vase. I heard a professional person who puts damaged items of great value together something she does for royalty and for museums. This item was on Woman's Hour. She was saying how she put all these bits carefully together. The interviewer said 'I suppose you do it so they don't show, so that it looks like new?' She replied 'No the cracks add to its value'. This tallied completely with my Grecian vase idea[11] - the fragments of the human being put back together again. The cracks matter - that life experience that we're made up of.

Like the 'Living Human Document' in a different form

Yes, and another analogy I use is that when people are struggling, they put themselves into a sort of cocoon – they shut themselves off into this silken cocoon that's very safe and comfortable to be in. But the sad thing is no one can get in and the person can't get out. So they're actually trapped in this silken cocoon. One of the things I like to think of with psychotherapy, is of enough trust being generated for the person to allow the psychotherapist in. This will gradually breakdown the cocoon and then the person emerges as a

---

[11] Hints of Keats: Ode on a Grecian Urn

beautiful butterfly – they're freed, they can grow and develop. Life can hold more meaning as well as being an exciting process. I'm not foolish enough to believe that everything will be wonderful from thereon-in because life is full of ups and downs, but it becomes possible to recognise just that – that life IS full of ups and downs and that the downs CAN be weathered.

***

CREATIVE VISUALISATION

Jenny led me through a series of creative visualisations. This one, a couple of years into the treatment, takes me through woods to a cottage in a clearing, a place I'd visited with her in previous visualisations in 1999. Like a dream, visualisations are packed with symbols, references, associations. Through them I explored the experience of healing, of understanding childhood and the transition to adulthood. This example is based on memory and Jenny's notes at the time...

Cottage in the woods

15th October 2001

I am in a forest at night-time. In a clearing there is a bright light shining from a little cottage. There are two doors adjacent to each other at the nearest corner of the cottage. Old fashioned, flaking yellow paint on one door opening into a ramshackle derelict utility room then off that into (PRESENT) a splendid hallway with a white, wooden, moulded door leading into a drawing room. A classic spacious study, rich carpet, lots of old books, panelling around the walls, with old furniture.

There is a mischievous little rubbery gremlin type creature telling him to close the door to the upstairs brighter future. (PAST) He didn't want to go to his past at all. Steps down into an empty wreck of a place under the building. Damp, dark rotten wood. He propped up a precarious corner with a good bit of timber. He wanted to get rid of rancid wine. His Dad was saying, 'Come back!'

(FUTURE) He went up the carpeted stairs. On the first floor there were three bedrooms; bright and sunny. Up further into the attic, he found it decked out in pine and an artist's studio with a writing desk and sunlight. There was a turquoise figurine, which he remembered from his Nan's. Beautiful. Dancing.

▪▪▪

EPILOGUE

'Nothing is the answer to everything...'

Liz's words as we headed into town on a shopping trip, meaning: there is no one, single answer to all the world's problems. But then it sounded even more profound. As if the answer to everything were its antithesis: complete and total annihilation, absolute zero, zilch, nothing. And if it were possible to be in this state of sublime nothingness, it would be nirvana, a whole, unified state of being, perfection - the infinite in nothing.

An infinite number of connections, which in the end bring us back to the beginning, never ending...

'Nothing' can seem an attractive prospect in the rush of a hectic pace of life and of conflicting demands at work, at home and competitive play. *Nothing is the answer to everything* - a defiant statement in the face of scientists' search for the Unified Theory of Everything...

In contrast to nothing, life is everything, and everything is connected. So, what of these connections? The connections between the nerve cells in our brains form our reality, and between us form the human race. I hope you have found and made connections through these stories, as they interlink and interweave different worlds, and perhaps have even made some friends here.

Sudden in a shaft of sunlight there rises the laughter of children...

The words sculpted in a massive round, stone table in Tim's garden

(T S Eliot's No 1 of Four Quartets, Burnt Norton)

As I said at the beginning, mental health goes to the core of our being, it touches the very reason, or lack of it, for our existence. As beings (our outward appearance so very much less than the sum total of what we are), like animals, plants and trees, we share a similar spiritual substance - life, interconnecting – and realise our interdependence with all of life on planet Earth.

The unique nature of the individual is perhaps the most remarkable thing about life, the sense of personal identity, what makes you, you, and me, me...

Here's an update on a few of our friends since the original interviews, and where they find themselves now (Spring 2012)

Jenny Parkes - 'Where am I now?'

> "Older and calmer I hope, but still fascinated by the workings of the mind. My art work continues to run as a metaphor, a means of exploring thoughts and feelings – the latest piece is called 'Thinking in boxes'.

> Since our first interview I have undertaken a course in energy field therapy and now enjoy helping friends through tough times whenever I can.

The learning continues but from a stronger base, a still point within me. Recently I have enjoyed working with Tim Walter on a 'Focused Thinking Project' which is bringing people together to focus positive energy to the planet at this time of growing crisis.

It feels good to be doing something positive and less self orientated.

I am deeply grateful for all the years of therapy since 'knowing thyself' is all important if we are to love and be-loved which is surely why we are here."

Jenny Parkes

Don't kill the dragon…!

Janet

"It's been approximately 2 years since I decided to pour my soul out on paper for 'Treading On Eggshells' (as the book was then known). I was seeking closure. I am thankful for the opportunity - my life has improved immensely. Two years on and I'm no longer crying alone. I'm still standing, and feel stronger than ever. I've never once, in the past 2 years, had to fall back on my medication, even though my doctor allows me to have a box in my medicine cabinet on stand by. It really is just a safety net now. I even found a diet I could stick to and have now lost over 3 stone, and go to Zumba twice a week. I am a totally new person, full of confidence. I am closer than ever with my partner. Having a relationship is something I thought would never happen to me, but it just gets better. My partner is extremely supportive.

I hope that anyone reading this, who may have encountered mental illness, whether that be through a loved one, or maybe the reader themselves, will gain hope from my recovery. Even when you have travelled to the darkest recesses of your mind, there is hope. There is always hope. I don't get complacent though, I am aware that I have to stay away from stressful situations when I can, and I am always vigilant in recognising signs of a relapse. This is the formulae I use to help me stay well, and its working.'

Release These Chains

The frightened child I used to be,
is exorcised and been set free.
Step after small step,
not leaps and bounds.
Finally I stand my ground.

Putting pen to paper, has for me,
broke my chains and set me free.
I've left behind, my broken past.
look to the future, here at last.

So '*Tread on Eggshells*',
with me no more.
To the highest peaks,
I will reach and soar.

Janet Hart

Abacus

"Things are going well thanks. Had a relapse a short time ago but I'm picking myself back up. I've had both CAT therapy and DBT and I've managed to move forward and live my life as best I can :-). I accept the relapses as just a small step back and things really do get better.

CAT therapy is cognitive analytical therapy. It lasts for a set amount of time (in my case 24 sessions) and its designed to make you see how a certain set of events or thoughts make you act in a certain way. So it showes you how behaviours, thoughts and emotions are all interlinked. It's really useful but I've not met many people that have ever had it. It's really good to know how long it lasts because it makes you get the most out of each session.

DBT is dialectical behavioural therapy. That's more commonly used for people with Borderline Personality Disorder and its designed to validate feelings and point out which ones are potentially harmful and helps to find ways to challenge and change them. It worked really well and it helped me see things from a much different perspective."

Abacus

A lifetime of kisses…

Dad

Early in 2012 Dad was diagnosed with cancer...on the 14th April 2012 he died having had a severe reaction to his chemotherapy. It was the chemo that killed him not the cancer. And we cried, and we knew him in spirit among us.

Flood Gate West 3...

As we have seen, our creative drive is also frequently affected by our upbringing, our formative years. Madness has been associated with creativity, and there are even links between psychosis and spirituality[12]. Plato said that creativity is a "divine madness...a gift from the gods". Seneca recorded Aristotle as having said, "No great genius was without a mixture of insanity." And sometimes that madness, that creativity, seems to come from spirit, from outside of the everyday. Or is it actually more common, more everyday, than we are prepared to acknowledge?

We've seen something of the strength and power of creativity through Jenny Parkes' work, as represented in one of her sculptures - the Kiln Door - a reflection of the raging emotional and creative forces within. Forces which are occasionally released from the right brain; a place of patterns, of connections, of fire, and of spirit.

See the girl standing in the shadow of the petrol station, concentrating on her phone, sending and receiving texts and crying. Alone...

---

[12] Isabel Clarke:
http://www.isabelclarke.org/psychosis_spirituality/

For most of us, our day to day experience of mental health amounts to ordinary fluctuations in mood and the stress we feel because of different pressures in our lives, from the situations in which we find ourselves.

Stress

A real, almost physical change to the body, a chemical rearranging of hormones, transmitters, biochemical connections…

Stress can be the driver behind psychic change. It can have an effect over time like being caught in a fractured relationship, or trapped in a high-pressured job you don't enjoy.

When I've spoken to managers and directors, in workshops on health and safety and stress, about carrying out organisation-wide stress surveys they've consistently said that they would never want to admit to 'stress'. Especially middle managers, those who are trying to rise to positions of greater responsibility. To admit to stress is taken as a sign of weakness, an inability to cope.

One of my friends, who became a senior director and is now retired, told me how he'd felt close to the edge when climbing the ranks of middle managers. At one stage he was promoted to a post where he felt out of his depth. He began to truly hate Sunday evenings. He had a constant inner sense of panic and anxiety. Thankfully for him he was moved to another area, which he felt more at home with and grew and adapted his skills more gradually.

I'm not where I really want to be... I feel I have more to say but I'm blinded by circumstance, ice-cold lager and red wine...

In many cases, those in charge seem more than willing simply to try and get rid of such 'weak' individuals. On one course, a director calculated that, based on his experience, 4% of his workforce might have mental health problems. When it was pointed out that the reality is closer to 25% (1 in 4) he was aghast. And neither could he believe the hoops he'd have to jump through to sack somebody whom he assumed, mistakenly, would not be up to the job.

And here is romance, the huge blown sky of it, lifting her skirts, dancing with the wide blue sun, her feet tingling with the lyrics of snow white surf, the hush and ruffle of cotton and lace, sounding out the sheltered bays and coves...

The still small voice

I remember being told as a kid to listen to the inner, still small voice of calm - there's even a hymn with the phrase, which I used to love to sing at church (Dear Lord and Father of Mankind[13]). I've since interpreted this small voice as way of finding an inner peace. Not an easy thing to do. Nevertheless, underlying it all, beneath the surface of the ordinary, and in the commonplace of the everyday, there is a source of the extraordinary, the magical. It can be found in many ways. It is about being open, sensitive to events that are happening around you. It can be found through the practice of mindfulness, of being aware of the moment, even when doing household chores, such as the washing up.

---

[13] John Greenleaf Whittier, 1807-1892, composed by Sir Hubert Parry

After writing a poem of the same name, I rediscovered this truth in a book by Thich Nhat Thanh, *The Art of Mindfulness.*

We sometimes find ourselves surprised by coincidences, these may be moments of synchronicity which connect deep roots within us, perhaps a vein of thinking which, apparently out of the blue, also profoundly connects with someone else's life, someone else's thoughts. We are never apart from the world, we are always influenced by events. Even seemingly distant world events pierce our psyche: cruelty, torture, the destruction of habitats, the extinction of species, climate change, everything that the so-called 'normal' human race is responsible for.

What does this have to do with mental health? For most of us, our lifestyles are having a direct effect on the wellbeing of the planet. Our home, the planet suspended in the universe - Mother Earth. A planet which deep down we care for, and for which we may feel guilt and sadness at its apparent demise at the hand of our greed and carelessness. Our health and wellbeing are tied to that of the planet. Even a simple walk through the woods on a Spring morning, in contact with nature, can be healing, restorative. Connect.

In spite of our passing, or because of it, we still want the planet to be a viable home for future generations, so it matters what we choose to do today, how we choose to live and how we influence change. It is important to understand the connections between our choices and their effects on others, and the planet.

I ask how she is, 'Like a pig in shit,' ☺ she says from her deck chair, happily sunning herself at the edge of the expanse of the ferry's steel helideck, facing the sun to the

South, and the retreating wake as it vanishes across the massive weight of sea…

We each have our own unique experience. We are both fragile and resilient in different ways. Sometimes we have to take a step back, to look at the whole person – to consider what makes us who and what we are.

Pink Floyd, 'Wish You Were Here', playing in a bar in the High Street, Logrono, Spain…

Our experience shapes the way we think, our inner feelings, our hopes and fears, how we respond to our environment and to changes; moments, sights, sounds, smells, touch - our senses help create associations, to remind us of those experiences – memories, many with roots deep in our subconscious.

Slowly, so very slowly the rapid motion of atoms in the whole room melts the ice left in his glass, traces of whisky…

Of course, underlying it all are the BIG questions; questions that we grow up with, that we may try to resolve: Who am I? Why am I here? What happens when I die? What is the purpose, the meaning of life? What makes us tick: spirit, soul, belief, religion? And if and when we feel stress, it's about the whole person not just our work.

I remember the BBC used to use this slogan: 'We all need space to think.' And we do: space to help make sense of our experience, our place on this planet, our relationships, the demands placed upon us. It is important that we have both space and time to connect with the roots of who we are on this Earth and to realise (in spite of everything!) how amazing it is to be alive! And yet...

Death, the final taboo

Death has wound a thread through the core of this book, the loss, the grief felt within these stories and the impact on those left living. Moments when the big, unanswered questions remain unanswered, often even for those with faith. Although death is inevitable, for most of our lives we sidestep the issue, refusing to accept our own mortality, the nature of impermanence, the constant shift and cycles of birth and death for all living things.

We avoid death. What do we do? We deny death. What would it be like if our lives were structured around death, acknowledging our final ending with positive, supportive rituals? If we could each share how we wish to pass, how we wish to be remembered, wouldn't that be a more respectful place to centre, more humble in the face of infinity?

However, in the West we have few rituals to help us through grief. The funeral is the final resting place, the only point of closure, before then we are helpless. And after? We can only imagine what, if anything, lies beyond...

It was said she used to go to bed with a piece of string tied to one of her toes, the other end of which hung out of the window. Each morning the gardener would pull the string to wake her up...

On Eve Fairfax's mother.

A Book of Secrets: Illegitimate Daughters, Absent Fathers.
by Michael Holroyd.

And of course, there would come a morning when, however strong the tugging from the garden, she never woke...

Set fire to the rain...
(Adele,21)

For Caroline and all who loved her...
For Ted and all who loved him...

The last word...

Of Influence
by Ted Walter, from Choosing Yellow & Blue Moon

Sometimes an early autumn light
seems to lift from silent earth
regret that knowledge comes too late.
Yet harvest on the heels of life

is not the end but simply change.
Wheat becomes the flour, the bread,
becomes the man, becomes his child;
seeds fall, the earth asleep not dead.

And when we die all we have been,
all we have ever done or said,
having made our shape, lives on,

whispers in a winnowing wind

and time ensures the earth is sown
with what we were. Ideas we held,
our grains of truth, our quick seeds thrown
at random, soon become a field.

APPENDIX ONE - WHAT YOU CAN DO

My personal tips

Which one day I may even achieve...

- Drink less
- Rise early
- Imagine
- Connect with nature
- Exercise
- Learn

Top Ten Tips

Here are my, more expansive, Top Ten Tips (based on good advice from the Foresight Project (1-5) and Rethink) for helping to prevent, identify, manage and overcome mental health problems...

1. **Connect...** With people, with family, friends, colleagues and neighbours. At home, work, school or in your local community. Think of these as the cornerstones of your life and invest time in developing them. Building these connections will support and enrich you every day.

2. **Be active...** Go for a walk or run. Step outside. Cycle. Play a game. Garden. Connect with nature. Dance.

Exercising makes you feel good. Most importantly, discover a physical activity you enjoy and that suits your level of mobility and fitness. Exercise is proven to reduce stress, so why not suggest a long walk after dinner or a game or two of Wii Sports (if you must!)... and more...Take notice...

3. **Be curious...** Catch sight of the beautiful. Remark on the unusual. Notice the changing seasons. Savour the moment, whether you are walking to work, eating lunch or talking to friends. Be aware of the world around you and what you are feeling. Reflecting on your experiences will help you appreciate what matters to you.

4. **Learn...** (& keep learning). Try something new. Rediscover an old interest. Sign up for that course. Take on a different responsibility at work. Fix a bike. Learn to play an instrument or how to cook your favourite food. Set a challenge you enjoy achieving. Learning new things will make you more confident as well

as being fun.

5. **Give ...** Do something nice for a friend, or a stranger. Thank someone. Smile.

Volunteer your time. Join a community group. Look out, as well as in. Seeing

yourself, and your happiness, as linked to the wider community can be

incredibly rewarding and creates connections with the people around you.

Foresight Mental Capital and Wellbeing Project (2008) Final Project Report. Government Office for Science.

Helping others – care givers...

6. Presence is the greatest gift. You don't need to be a mental health expert to support a vulnerable friend or family member. Just being there to listen and talk and also visiting people who may be vulnerable can make a big difference.

7. Talk to friends or family who need support about any worries or concerns they might be feeling. Talking about the things concerning them can help to bring focus and put things into perspective.

8. Try not to put pressure on loved ones if they are feeling stressed or upset. Leave them to take time out and have a few moments to themselves.

9. It's proven that gardening, growing things, having your hands in the soil or even just sitting in a lovely garden lifts the spirits, it's part of that connection with nature. For example, Monty Don (BBC Gardener's World) has a history of depression and he says that gardening is his salvation.

10. Live in the present moment, avoid dwelling on the past or anticipating and worrying about the future[14].

Plus

Finally, everyday doesn't have to be perfect. Some of the best times are had when things go wrong and you find yourself having to make things up as you go along instead!

---

[14] See mindfulness in the booklist

And ask for help: share the burden of caring for an estranged loved one…

APPENDIX TWO - SOURCES OF ADVICE AND INFORMATION

Psychotherapy and dream interpretation can help one understand oneself, as Jenny Parkes found. It can help to understand sources of worry and anxiety in your life. Here's a few useful and interesting contacts.

British Association for Behavioural and Cognitive Psychotherapies (BABCP) – www.babcp.com

Full directory of psychotherapists available online

British Association for Counselling and Psychotherapy

BACP – www.bacp.co.uk

Search the website for qualified and experienced practitioners in your area

Hospitals: many have supportive counselling groups like those found for Amisha

HSE's Stress website www.hse.gov.uk/stress

HSE Personal stress case studies
www.hse.gov.uk/stresss/mystress.htm

Hugging Barbed Wire www.huggingbarbedwire.com

Imagine Mental Health www.imaginementalhealth.org.uk

Knights Rose www.knightsrose.com

Making Connections Matter
www.makingconnectionsmatter.org

Mind www.mind.org.uk

Mental Health Foundation www.mentalhealth.org.uk

Rethink www.rethink.org

Sane www.sane.org.uk

Shaw Trust www.shaw-trust.org.uk

Stand to Reason www.standtoreason.org.uk

Time to Change www.timetochange.org.uk

Together www.together-uk.org

YoungMinds www.youngminds.org.uk

BOOKLIST

Fast Train Approaching... by Steve Walter, published by Chipmunkapublishing.com

Self-help books

Those I've read and found often both moving and helpful include:

- **An Unquiet Mind**, by Kay Redfield Jamison

- **Touched with fire: Manic-depressive Illness and the Artistic Temperament**, by Kay Redfield Jamison

- **A Beautiful Mind**, by Sylvia Nasar

- **Insiders:Outsiders**, by Steve Scott

- **The A to Z Guide to Good Mental Health**, Jeremy Thomas and Dr Tony Hughes ('You don't have to be famous to have manic depression').

- **Me, Myself, and Them: A Firsthand Account of One Young Person's Experience with Schizophrenia**, by Kurt Syder, Raquel E. Gur M.D., and Linda Wasmer Andrews (Adolescent Mental Health Project).

- **The Art of Mindfulness**, Thich Nhat Thanh

- **Mindfulness: a practical guide to finding peace in a frantic world,** Mark Williams and Danny Penman, Piatkus.

- **Shoot the Damn Dog**, by Sally Brampton

- **Stop Walking on Eggshells**: Taking Your Life Back When Someone You Care About Has Borderline Personality Disorder.

Poetry & creative writing

Some of these listed I found in a display of poetry and mental health at the Poetry Library at the Festival Hall on the South Bank, in November 2010.

Beyond Bedlam, poems written out of mental distress. Introduction, edited by Ken Smith and Matthew Sweeney (Anvil)

A Alvarez, **The Savage God**.

Selima Hill **Accumulation of Small Acts of Kindness** presents the strange diaries of a young girl, before during and after her treatment at a psychiatric hospital. In her collection, Bunny, (2001) she opens another door on madness, revisiting the haunted house of an adolescence cut short by breakdown.

Leanne O'Sullivan, **Waiting for my clothes** (2004) traces a deeply personal journey, from the traumas of eating disorder and low self-esteem to the saving powers of love and positive awareness.

Introduction to the Selected Poems of Anne Sexton, by Dianne Wood Middlebrook and Diana Hume George. 'Anne has experience of being hospitalized in mental institutions and treated with psychoactive drugs. She often claimed that poetry kept her alive.

A-Cute Anthology, Lynn Harle. (2000). This book began with one new friend and fellow patient at St George's hospital, Morpeth, asking her to write a poem. Consequently she wrote 90 in 2 days, at the time the doctors thought she was suffering from a mental illness (Manic Depression).

'**Poets on Prozac, Mental illness, treatment and the creative process**' edited by Richard M Berlin, M.D. (2008) This shatters the notion that madness fuels creativity by giving voice to contemporary poets who have battled myriad psychiatric disorders, including depression, schizophrenia, post-traumatic stress disorder, and substances abuse.

John Hemsley, **Placid Waters, Savage Waves** aims to encourage the reader to take a positive attitude towards mental illness, bearing in mind that there are people with difficulties who also possess creative talents from which we can all benefit.

A Knowable World (2009) (Bloodaxe) follows Sarah Wardle's detainment in a Central London psychiatric hospital for over a year for manic episodes of bipolar disorder. The poems chart the stresses of thirty-something city life through police arrests and hospitalisation under section orders to achieve a way out; then the threat and frustration involved in the fight for liberty and the patience needed to achieve recovery.

We Have Come Through, Edited by Peter Forbes (2003) (Bloodaxe). We Have Come Through brings together 100 poems celebrating individual courage in resisting the ravages of psychological trauma, induced by both external events and breakdown.

The Mind Has Mountains, (quoted from Gerard Manley Hopkins) poems by Elizabeth Jennings (1966). Many of the poems in this collection have grown up from her own experience of breakdown and the pain of recovery in hospital...These poems about sickness, love and art can only increase our appreciation of life and our understanding of human beings.

and to close…

10^{14}

We live in the middle distance

we experience the immediate past,

our now has already happened.

When I begin to smile

you have already laughed.

When I dream, you are only

playing with the neurons in my brain

the ten to the power of fourteen

connections which tell me this is good.

And you hold me, hold me close

as hard as I hold you

and our immediate futures

are scattered like raindrops

across the warm skin of universal skies.

Voices

Lightning Source UK Ltd.
Milton Keynes UK
UKOW031649051012

200096UK00001B/2/P